CREATING BONSAI FRO PLANT

1. Carefully transfer the starter to a 5 or 6 in. plastic training pot, using Plants for Pleasure Bonsai compost.
   DO NOT DISTURB THE ROOTS AT THIS STAGE.

2. Allow to grow on. Feed and water regularly.

3. When the seedling has reached the height of your choice remove the leader as shown in diagram 2.

4. To create the basic framework remove all unwanted branches. Refer to pages 8 and 9 of *A Guide to Indoor Bonsai*.

5. Allow to grow on. Continue to water and feed regularly.

6. To enhance the basic framework, the trunk and branches can be wired. Refer to pages 9–10 of *A Guide to Indoor Bonsai*. Use aluminium wire as recommended by Plants for Pleasure.

7. Continue to water and feed regularly. During the growing season prune back the new growth to produce smaller leaves and more compact growth. Refer to pages 11–12 of *A Guide to Indoor Bonsai*.

8. When the branches have set in position carefully remove the wire.

9. When the trunk and branches have thickened up and the tree has taken on a pleasing appearance, transfer to a ceramic Bonsai pot.

Note. The basic technique is a continual process of growing on and pruning back. Root pruning is required in the later stages when transferring to a shallow pot.

The time taken to produce Bonsai varies according to the growth rate of the plant and the conditions under which it is grown. Pleasing results can be achieved in three to five years, but valuable specimens can take twenty years or more.

CREATING BONSAI FROM A YOUNG PLANT

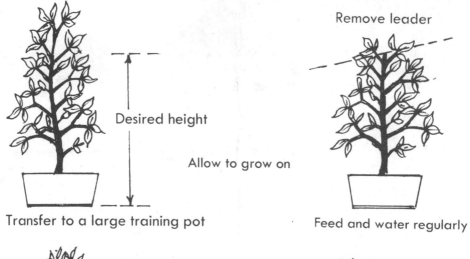

Desired height

Allow to grow on

Transfer to a large training pot

Remove leader

Feed and water regularly

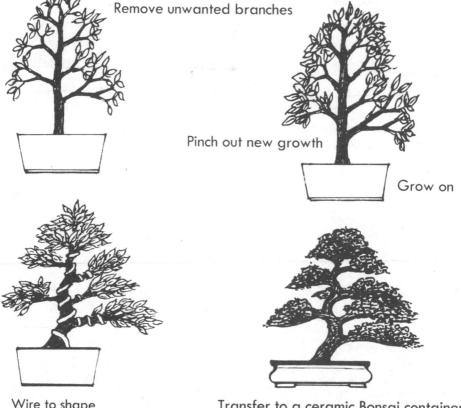

Remove unwanted branches

Pinch out new growth

Grow on

Wire to shape
Prune back new growth

Transfer to a ceramic Bonsai container
Remove wire when branches have set

Extract from *A Guide to Indoor Bonsai.*

DK
POCKET
ENCYCLOPEDIA

BONSAI

DK
POCKET
ENCYCLOPEDIA

BONSAI

Harry Tomlinson

DORLING KINDERSLEY
London · New York · Stuttgart

A DORLING KINDERSLEY BOOK

First published in Great Britain in 1994
by Dorling Kindersley Limited,
9 Henrietta Street, London WC2E 8PS

Text copyright © 1990, 1994 Harry Tomlinson and
Dorling Kindersley Limited, London
Copyright © 1990, 1994 Dorling Kindersley Limited, London
Reprinted 1995

Designed and edited by Kelly Flynn Design

A CIP catalogue record for this book is available
from the British Library

ISBN 0–7513–0139–6

Reproduced by
J. Film Process (S) Singapore Pte Ltd
Printed in Singapore by
Kyodo Printing (Co.) Pte Ltd

CONTENTS

Introduction 6

INTRODUCTION

No one browsing through this book or enjoying its illustrations could remain totally unaware of the nature of the word "bonsai", although other people do have some misconceptions of its meaning – some believe bonsai to be a form of martial arts; others, that it is a breed of long-haired dog.

The meaning of bonsai

Bonsai is a Japanese word, but is now used around the world to describe a tree or shrub planted in a shallow container, and trained to resemble a full-sized tree. The expression "bonsai" actually consists of two Japanese words: *bon* means a shallow container or tray, and *sai*, a plant or planting. However, the combined word *bonsai* means much more than this literal translation: it implies a stylish marriage of artistic expression and naturalistic effect that distinguishes a bonsai from a tree that is merely planted in a pot.

Your goal as a bonsai grower is an idealized recreation of nature, based on a careful study of the way trees grow in the wild. You should not aim for too realistic an approach, however, nor try to reproduce every twig and branch precisely. Rather, you should try to give a general impression of the way the tree grows in its natural state.

Bonsai may fulfil your artistic urges more than many other arts and crafts (painting, photography, pottery, wood carving, and the like), because the bonsai creation is constantly growing and changing. This unique blend of art and horticulture satisfies

An ever-changing landscape
All-season colour is provided by this mixed planting on tufa rock, with its Japanese white pine, a red 'Deshojo' maple, pink azalea, and quince, as well as low-growing Acaena, *heather, and mosses.*

English landscape in miniature
*The author's own collection, displayed on benches
at his nursery, reflects the natural beauty and variety
of the local English scenery.*

a love of nature, and trees in particular, so that you can enjoy the variety of the changing seasons, even if you live in a town. Moreover, if you group trees with rocks and other plants, you can create a wonderful impression of a landscape in miniature.

Bonsai for everyone

Many specialists feel that bonsai is a mystical art or discipline, requiring many years of dedication and practice to achieve worthwhile results, but the reality is that anyone can appreciate or create successful bonsai.

Bonsai cultivation does, of course, require a certain degree of both commitment and enthusiasm, and you will discover that you achieve better designs as your expertise increases. However, the beauty of bonsai is that it can be approached at a number of levels of interest and ability – as a fine art, a specialized type of horticulture, a consuming passion, a livelihood, or a hobby. Bonsai enthusiasts range from those with only one or two lovingly nurtured trees, to dedicated growers whose expertise and artistic expression enable them to produce large collections of exceptional trees.

Learning about bonsai

This book has been planned as a practical reference book to interest beginner and expert alike. It explains (*see pp. 14-35*) the origins and development of bonsai, and

Contrasting mood and style
The flamboyant exuberance of the Satsuki azalea 'Kaho' in bloom (top) gives a very different effect to the sturdy but sombre group of dwarf Japanese cedars planted in hollowed-out tufa rock (right).

describes the principles that underpin this fascinating art. Precise details are given on pp. 116–21 of the fifteen classic styles into which trees and shrubs can be trained, together with examples in the wild upon which they are based. Clear photographs show outstanding examples of the various styles.

At the heart of the book, an "A–Z of Bonsai Species" (*pp. 36–113*) provides a photographic catalogue of the cultivation and styling of different plants. Each entry is illustrated with a full-colour photograph of a superb specimen, fully annotated to demonstrate its salient features. This catalogue is supplemented by a dictionary of trees and shrubs that can be grown as bonsai (*pp. 184–209*), thus providing you with all the relevant details on over 300 suitable plants. The book contains comprehensive information on how to create a bonsai from a seedling, cutting or garden centre plant, with the basic techniques of pruning and wiring explained in carefully illustrated detail. Tools and containers are illustrated on pp. 122–9.

Follow the step-by-step projects on pp. 132–61, which show how superb, finished bonsai were created from initial raw material, and you should achieve a fairly reasonable result in a very short space of time. In fact, if you buy a plant from a garden centre and prune it to shape, you can produce a bonsai in minutes.

All this, however, is just the beginning. Gradually, like all artists and craftspeople, you will gain more skill, and learn how to refine and improve your bonsai. The maintenance

section (*pp. 170–83*) tells you how to keep your bonsai healthy, and the propagation section (*pp. 162–9*) how to create your own plant material and increase your stock.

How far you take the art of bonsai will depend on your own interest and dedication, how much effort you are prepared to put into learning to create and refine bonsai, and how much time you have for routine maintenance. Just as the bonsai will mature and improve as time goes by, so too will your pleasure and satisfaction in cultivating bonsai increase. The number of bonsai you can collect is bounded only by the space you have available, the designs only by your imagination or your wallet.

One final warning: bonsai are not likely to damage your health (unless you drop a very large specimen on your toes, or apply the pruners too near your fingers). The love of bonsai can and does, however, become an absolute obsession, although one that most bonsai enthusiasts are only too happy to endure.

Nature as an inspiration for art
*A frosted landscape gives an eerie emphasis to the hollowed-out oak trees and slender birches, whereas early morning mist (*inset*) creates an atmospheric backdrop to the tall Scots pines.*

CHAPTER ONE

THE ART OF BONSAI

A bonsai tree is infinitely changeable, both as the seasons come around, and as it matures over the years. It can never be described as complete, for there is always the possibility of improvement. The later chapters of this book detail the specifics of creating and maintaining a bonsai, but this chapter gives the general background to the subject. It describes bonsai's Eastern origins, and the traditions upon which modern enthusiasts base their work, as well as spelling out the general principles of choosing trees and shrubs for bonsai work, and the different sources from which you can obtain plant material. The vital importance of studying nature as a guide when creating a bonsai is constantly emphasized. Basic elements of bonsai design (branch spread, trunk form, the best view, sizes, and scale) are also defined. The pleasure that bonsai give at different seasons of the year is amply reflected in colourful illustrations and, finally, there are some hints on how to display bonsai for your own and other people's enjoyment.

A bonsai display
The varying levels of this bonsai collection allow each tree to be seen in its entirety. The wooden stands and fencing, and the ceramic containers, enhance the natural appearance of the trees.

Creativity in cultivation

The bonsai grower needs artistic ability similar to that of a sculptor or a painter, but blended with a love of plants and nature. Although bonsai is an art form, it is unique among other forms of artistic expression in that it includes the element of time: the design of the tree changes constantly and naturally as it grows, and as the seasons progress.

A classic bonsai has been described as ninety per cent art and only ten per cent horticulture, the latter being the cultivation skills necessary to keep the tree alive and growing, as well as to enable the design to take shape.

These artistic and horticultural skills are both necessary and complement each other. Not all bonsai growers are experienced gardeners; some come to the art with little knowledge of plant cultivation, but, as time passes, they acquire gardening expertise through daily watering, feeding, and grooming of their trees.

Other bonsai growers have an interest in horticulture, but little confidence initially in their artistic talents. They are very skilled at propagating material for bonsai, and then maintaining the trees in peak condition, and during this process they gradually learn the more creative aspects of bonsai design.

Natural beauty
The bonsai encapsulates all the characteristics of the tree throughout the seasons, but in miniature. This purple maple, *Acer palmatum* 'Dissectum atropurpureum', has foliage that opens in spring to a greenish-purple, becoming deep purple in summer, and orange in autumn. In winter, the leafless tree reveals an elegant structure.

Fact and fallacy

People often misunderstand the techniques of bonsai, suspecting that there is something unnatural about this form of cultivation, or that it is a process of stunting or damaging the trees. A bonsai is, of course, tiny if you compare it with a full-sized tree growing in the garden or the wild, but the small size is not the point of its creation, merely a way of making the process of cultivation more practical.

A better way of considering bonsai is to compare it with the ways in which garden trees and plants are trained. A fruit tree can be pruned into a cordon or an espalier; a rose or a fuchsia can be trained as a standard; evergreens are often trimmed as topiary, and so on. In bonsai, you prune and train the plant material to expose its natural beauty, while retaining its resemblance to a living, healthy tree.

Woodland effect
Over 18 years of cultivation, this group of Japanese larches, *Larix kaempferi*, has been extended by the introduction of additional trees to increase the perspective and depth of the design and enhance the impression of a natural copse.

The changing seasons
In autumn, the bright green summer foliage (*above*) is followed by the vivid straw-yellow of the needles (*left*).

Traditions of bonsai

The art of bonsai is usually linked with Japan, but it originated in China, and the concept of growing trees in containers may have been brought there much earlier from India. The Japanese probably adopted bonsai as an art form in the eighth century when they were greatly influenced by Chinese culture. Painted scrolls from the thirteenth century show many container-grown trees that look like bonsai, and there are many specific references to the art in later Chinese and Japanese books and paintings.

In oriental cultures, art brings order to the everyday world; real life is carefully structured according to specific principles. Bonsai sits very comfortably in such an artistic framework of beauty and correctness.

Japanese fashions in bonsai

The artistic rules and horticultural methods of bonsai derive from its long history in Japan. Over the many centuries that it evolved there, there were many different fashions at various times. Pines and bamboos have long been traditional bonsai material, and ornamental flowering trees were some of the earliest recorded bonsai subjects; later, magnificent flowering shrubs, such as azaleas, were cultivated. Growing trees like Japanese maples purely for the beauty of their leaves came relatively late, in the seventeenth century.

Bonsai in the Western world

Bonsai has become a real interest in regions such as Europe, America, and Australia only in the twentieth century. The Western tradition of bonsai is based on the Japanese vocabulary and classification of styles; most bonsai tools and containers are Japanese imports. Western growers have a wide range of interests and expertise; there are also great variations in climate, growing conditions, and the availability of trees. As a result, modern bonsai is perhaps more varied and less rigorously defined than the Japanese traditions of the art.

Japanese bonsai nursery
There are numerous specimens to be seen at this traditional bonsai nursery in Omiya.

Sources of bonsai material

Whether you plan to grow just one or two trees, or to cultivate a collection of bonsai, there are various ways of acquiring your plants. Each method has advantages and disadvantages, and each requires a different amount of effort and commitment.

Buying a bonsai
The quickest method of obtaining a bonsai is simply to buy one from a specialist nursery or garden centre. The main advantage is that you will instantly own a "ready-made" bonsai; however, the specimens may be very expensive, of poor quality, or even very difficult to obtain. Most bonsai trees sold in countries outside Asia have been imported from Japan, so their price includes transport and handling costs. In some areas, there are few bonsai outlets, and you may need to travel some distance to find one. Some plants sold as bonsai are not true bonsai, but merely young trees growing in pots.

Trees from the wild
There is no advantage in collecting seedlings or saplings from the wild, but often mature trees become naturally dwarfed by climatic conditions, an inhospitable habitat, or persistent grazing. It is sometimes possible to lift a dwarfed tree from the wild and replant it in a container. Such a tree may be quite old, with an attractively mature trunk, branches, and bark texture. It is more difficult to produce these "aged" characteristics in other ways.

The main disadvantage is that it can take you much time and effort to find a suitable tree, and then you require permission from the owner of the land on which it is growing to lift it. In some areas, it is illegal to remove living plants from their habitat.

It is also essential that you lift the tree at the right time of year, ideally in late winter, or in early spring before bud break. You should certainly not attempt it when the tree is in full leaf. It is also difficult to re-establish a mature tree as a bonsai. You will usually have to plant it out in a garden bed or suitable container to regain its vigour for four to five years.

Garden-centre bonsai
This triple-trunk *Juniperus × media* 'Blaauw', the Chinese juniper, was originally grown for garden use. It has been in bonsai training for four years.

Also, in the current climate of anxiety regarding conservation matters, it is now questionable whether trees should be collected from the wild at all, although there are some justifiable occasions, say, if the land is going to be cleared anyway for redevelopment.

Garden centre material
It can be a good idea to buy a plant from a garden centre or nursery and adapt it into a bonsai. There are plenty of species to choose from, and you can usually buy such plants fairly cheaply. Pruning the plant to shape takes very little time, so you can produce the

basic structure of an interesting bonsai in a few hours, or even in minutes.

The disadvantage is that garden centre and nursery plants may not be suitable for bonsai, as they have been developed for garden use. Tall-growing trees are especially problematic, but you can easily prune many specimens of smaller trees and shrubs into tree-like shapes.

Seeds

Growing material for a bonsai from seed (*see pp. 164–5*) is cheap, but has several serious disadvantages. It is time-consuming: firstly, some seeds take two years to germinate, and secondly, each seedling must be planted in open ground for several years before it has developed sufficiently for bonsai styling. Tree seeds do not stay viable for very long, and may not germinate well.

Trees grown from seeds often do not come true to their parent plant, and therefore a seedling may not display the same attractive characteristics, such as small fruits or leaves, that made you choose the species as suitable for bonsai in the first place.

Cuttings

Propagating cuttings to create your own bonsai material (*see pp. 166–7*) has several advantages. You can easily obtain the original material, even using shoots discarded from routine pruning of an existing plant. Cuttings are a speedy method: many root quickly, even within a few weeks, and may then put on as much growth in six months as a seedling would achieve in three or four years. Finally, cutting material does retain the parent's characteristics. The only disadvantage is that cuttings from some species either do not root or are difficult to cultivate.

Other propagating methods

Grafting, layering, and air layering (*see pp. 168–9*) are propagation methods that all produce offspring with exactly the same characteristics as the parent plant. As with cuttings, these methods are much quicker than growing from seed because they use material from a mature plant. For beginners or inexperienced growers, the main disadvantage with grafting is that it needs a considerable degree of technical skill and dexterity.

Grafting bonsai pines has one unique advantage. If you graft *Pinus parviflora*, the Japanese white pine, which has attractive needles, on to *Pinus thunbergii*, the Japanese black pine, you will gain a strong root system, and a bonsai with more character, as the black pine has a rugged, aged-looking trunk, while that of the white pine is smooth.

Group from cuttings
This planting of six-year-old shrubby honeysuckle, *Lonicera nitida*, was grown from cuttings. The effect of a natural, open landscape is enhanced by planting the group on an artificial stone slab.

Choosing trees and shrubs for bonsai

In theory, it is possible to use any type of tree or shrub for bonsai, although some subjects are more suitable than others. The principal characteristics you should look out for, when selecting a plant, are an interesting trunk and good arrangement of branches, attractive bark colour and texture, and compact and finely textured foliage (preferably with small leaves). If you want a subject with flowers or fruits, these must be small.

Many very beautiful trees, including the colourful maples, crab apples, and graceful larches are ideal. So too are evergreens with finely textured or needle-like foliage, such as cedars, pines, and junipers.

Large and small subjects

Many dwarf forms, such as the dwarf birch, *Betula nana*, adapt readily to bonsai, particularly as small-scale trees. A number of readily available and fast-growing garden shrubs, such as quince, cotoneaster, and pyracantha, are easily pruned to tree-like shapes. At the other end of the scale, there is the real challenge of trees like the English oak, *Quercus robur*, that in nature grow to huge proportions.

Seasonal effects

Some exceptions to the bonsai ideal of small leaves and fine twigs, such as the ornamental cherries, *Prunus*, provide wonderful seasonal effects with their lush flowers. However, if you have a restricted space that will accommodate only one or two bonsai, do not choose species that make a short-lived display in one season, and afterwards lack interest.

For year-round interest, you need not necessarily choose evergreen species, because deciduous trees such as elms and maples make a particularly impressive sight in the winter months, when their fine branch and twig structure is fully revealed.

"Rescued" for bonsai
This 20-year-old, garden-grown Kurume azalea, *Rhododendron obtusum*, had been sawn down to a stump prior to being thrown away. Luckily, it was preserved for bonsai training instead.

Inspiration from nature

Many people are attracted to bonsai through a love of nature. Even if you live far from open landscape, with bonsai you can enjoy the magnificence and beauty of nature recreated on a manageable scale, because the specimens have been inspired directly by the way in which trees grow in the wild.

Observing nature

Whatever you do in bonsai should reflect your observations of nature, related to the basic guidelines of bonsai cultivation. In nature, there is a wide variety, not only of different species, but also of different ways in which trees grow depending on their environment and weather conditions. While the same species of tree will always exhibit similar basic features (such as leaf shape and bark texture),

it will develop very differently depending on whether it grows by itself or in a group, is sheltered or exposed to strong winds, is surrounded by plentiful soil and moisture, or has to extend its roots to seek nutrients.

Bonsai can reflect the entire range of ways trees grow in nature, from a striking single specimen or a dense forest of trees, to a wooded landscape on grassland or a craggy mountainside. The basic principles of styling and planting, explained in later chapters, help to create a sense of perspective, and an impression of scale and space.

It is essential to study trees in nature when "training" yourself as a bonsai grower. It is not a good idea to use even a fine bonsai as a model for your own tree. That design worked well because of the specimen the grower

Roots growing over a rock
Growing wild in the Welsh mountains, this *Betula pendula*, the silver birch, owes much of its impact to the way the tree has established itself over its rocky base, with exposed roots gripping the stone.

started with, and the way in which it was trained. You will not be able to reproduce all these elements to "copy" a successful bonsai; instead, you should consider the material you have, and use your experience of natural growth patterns and bonsai training to bring out its full potential.

Styles of bonsai
The categories of bonsai styles (*shown on pp. 116–21*) have been based on specific elements in nature. Often the names of the styles explain the origin of the design and its aims: slanting style, for example, gives the effect of a tree exposed to strong wind, the trunk leaning at an angle. Some trees suggest a style – *Picea abies*, the Norway spruce, naturally looks formal and upright, whereas an oak grows in an informal arrangement. Most trees and shrubs that are suited to bonsai can be developed in any of several styles.

Mixing species
In nature, different types of tree frequently grow together, like the Scots pines and English elms shown on the *left*. In bonsai, both the scale and horticultural requirements limit the possibilities for mixing species. The example *above*, however, successfully combines some *Juniperus × media* 'Blaauw', Chinese juniper, and *Larix kaempferi*, Japanese larch.

Design principles

A bonsai design encompasses the style and condition of the tree; the container's size, shape, and finish; and the relationship of tree and container. Some basic elements apply to all bonsai, the main ones being root spread, trunk form, and the arrangement of branches.

Root spread
In both nature and bonsai, an interesting root formation exposed above the soil gives a sense of maturity and stability, whereas a young tree's roots are typically concealed beneath the ground. Ideally, roots should extend in all directions from the trunk, but need not be evenly spaced or arranged symmetrically, as long as there is a good visual balance. Roots can give a naturalistic impression of stability and balance, even though they are heavier on one side of the tree, or their complex textures and divisions can break up the tree's structural lines. The way the roots connect to the trunk, whether they radiate or flow from its base, or seem a firm anchorage, forms another natural and artistic element of bonsai design.

Trunk form
Bonsai trees may have straight, curved, angled, or divided trunks, just as trees in the wild do, but the most important trunk feature is a good taper, with the diameter diminishing smoothly towards the top. Thickness at the base adds to an impression of age, but a parallel trunk line passing into the tree's apex destroys balance. The trunk's thickness should suit the species' characteristics, whether a delicate maple or a heavy oak. Some trees need several years of growth and training to develop an ideal form.

It is also important to see the trunk, even if the foliage masses cut across it; a trunk's shape, bark texture, and colour add character. A very aged or weathered trunk can be an advantage, but avoid a tree with a distinctly scarred trunk unless it can be made a feature.

Branch arrangement
Branches form the basic structure of a tree's silhouette. Their arrangement as they emerge from a bonsai trunk should be well balanced,

in harmony with the general character of the tree, and visually complementing the trunk line. You can adjust the outline and structure quite radically by pruning and wiring, but you must remember the following basic rules when considering a tree or shrub for bonsai.

A spiral staircase is a good model for the ideal arrangement of branches, creating a balanced, although not necessarily symmetrical, pattern around and up the trunk. The first branch should be roughly one-third up the trunk, with the heaviest branches at lower levels. Branches are usually thicker near the trunk and taper along their length. Bonsai trees are normally pruned to an approximately conical spread, with the most delicate twigs at the top.

Balance and harmony
Careful training of the shape and structure of a tree, and detailed consideration of the relationship between it and its container are necessary to create a well-balanced design. This Japanese white pine, *Pinus parviflora*, is an excellent example of a successful bonsai.

Branches at the apex are pruned more closely; sometimes the lower branches may extend quite far before being pruned, so they thicken at the trunk. Prune out branches that cross, spread out from the same point on the trunk, or grow directly opposite one another. Wiring can often adjust a branch's position to fill a gap.

Exposed roots

The shapes and textures of exposed roots are an interesting aspect of bonsai, and the visible spread of roots adds to the impression of age, as can be seen with this *Quercus robur*, the English oak.

Spread of branches

The arrangement of branches visually balances the sinuous line of the trunk and creates an attractive triangular silhouette for the bonsai.

Substantial trunk

The strong roots and the rugged bark of this 50-year-old tree are the result of grafting it on to a lower trunk of the Japanese black pine, Pinus thunbergii. *It was field-grown for a number of years to thicken the trunk.*

Root interest

Exposed roots add to the craggy, mature feel of this handsome tree and visually anchor it in its chunky, unglazed container.

The front view

Bonsai are always designed with a "front" view, or preferred viewing angle, even though they can be viewed from all sides. A bonsai should be viewed with eye level corresponding to a point about halfway up the trunk. It should highlight the most attractive branch arrangement, allowing you to "look into" the tree while creating a pleasant silhouette. The front view should let you see the most pleasing part of the roots, and the most graceful angle and best taper of the trunk.

Curves in the lower part of the trunk can be best seen when they veer to one side, not towards the viewer: a tree with a forward curve is called "pigeon-breasted", an undesirable trait. Only the upper third of the tree should contain branches that grow directly forwards; to achieve depth and perspective, branches at the back should extend away from the viewer. Beginners who study photographs instead of live trees make the mistake of neglecting the back branches, invisible in photographs. The apex, or top of the tree, should incline towards the viewer, or "bow" to you, as the Japanese say. An apex leaning away never looks right (*see below*).

Choosing the front view means assessing roots, trunk, apex, and branches from various angles to find

Acer palmatum 'Seigen'
Front view of maple

MAPLE SEEN FROM DIFFERENT VIEWPOINTS

| **Left side view** | **Right side view** | **View from the back** |

the best combination. Pruning and wiring can adjust the apex and branches, so the trunk and roots are more crucial to your decision; the most critical are the roots as they are most difficult to change.

Bonsai sizes

Bonsai is not about "making trees small": the tree is smaller than in nature mainly to make it more convenient to work on. Sizes range from a tiny tree that you can balance on your hand to one taller than a man. Most bonsai fall within a middle range of 15cm (6in) to 60cm (2ft), because very large or very small specimens present special problems.

Large trees, over 2m (6.5ft), are impressive, but difficult to transport safely, or even to move for grooming. There is also the expense of a large container, and the problem of where to display them. Very small trees in tiny containers may need watering several times a day in warm or dry weather. Design is also difficult: in a medium-sized bonsai, one leaf may represent a cluster of leaves in scale with the natural size, but one leaf in a tiny tree must represent a branch or whole apex. You may be able to represent only two branches and the apex – very small bonsai require a minimalist approach with the principle of

"less is more". However, the scale of miniature bonsai (also called *mame* bonsai) does allow a large collection to be housed in a limited space.

A sense of scale

Whatever size your bonsai, its scale must create a realistic impression. Small-leaved trees are more adaptable in terms of scale. The larger a tree's leaves and the coarser its foliage and twigs, the more difficult it is to make them represent a full-sized tree. Some trees are simply not adaptable to very small bonsai; others are quite unsuitable for extra-large specimens; but many species grow readily as medium-sized bonsai. There is often more scope for adjusting the sense of scale in group and landscape plantings, where the trees relate to each other and to the added rocks or ground-cover plants (*see pp. 148–61*).

A realistic feeling of scale
The small foliage and compact silhouette of a dwarf tree, such as this little Japanese white pine, *Pinus parviflora* 'Yatsubusa', achieve a much more convincing impression of distance than could be created with a full-sized tree.

Spring colour

S pring, with its welcome return of colour and growth after the bleakness of winter, is a particularly exciting time in the bonsai world. New buds begin to swell and break, furnishing fresh new foliage and some of the earliest flowers. Gradually, the rate of growth quickens, until every tree and shrub is bursting with life and vigour.

In early spring, the Japanese larch, *Larix kaempferi*, is one of the first trees to break into leaf, its bright green new needles heralding the coming season. The Japanese maples, *Acer palmatum*,

especially the red-leaved cultivars 'Seigen' and 'Deshojo', and the lime-green 'Ukon', unfold their leaves into a brilliantly colourful display. Even those deciduous and evergreen species that have green leaves exhibit a breathtaking range of different hues and textures.

In mild weather throughout winter and spring, the autumn cherry, *Prunus subhirtella* 'Autumnalis', can be relied on to produce flushes of white or pale pink blossoms. Flowers in vivid reds and pinks, and pure white, adorn the flowering quinces, *Chaenomeles japonica*, *C. speciosa*, and

Yellow catkins
Complemented by the light tone of a cream, matt-glazed container, these yellow catkins are a striking spring feature of the dwarf willow, *Salix repens*.

C. × *superba*. As the weeks pass, other trees start to unfurl their leaves, while beautiful flowers clothe the branches of crab apples and cherries.

The wisteria makes a lavish show with its cascading clusters of fragrant blue, mauve or white, pea-like flowers against a background of fresh green foliage. Finally, in late spring, the many spectacular cultivars of the azaleas, *Rhododendron*, burst into richly coloured flower.

Bright leaves
This maple cultivar, the beautiful *Acer palmatum* 'Deshojo', is prized for its vivid red foliage. To bring on a second crop of these brilliant leaves late in the summer, use the technique of leaf cutting a bonsai (*see p. 181*).

Fine blossom
The cascading racemes of the wisteria make it one of the most attractive of spring-flowering trees, in bonsai as well as in nature.

Fragrant flowers
The blossoms of the crab apple, *Malus cerasifera*, are highly perfumed, in addition to forming a pleasing display.

Summer glory

One of the greatest attractions of summer for bonsai enthusiasts is the variety of greens produced by the leaves of the various trees and shrubs. Other bonsai provide a striking contrast with their coloured or variegated foliage. By midsummer, the deciduous trees and shrubs are in full leaf, and the evergreens look noticeably fresher for the addition of new foliage.

As the summer advances, all bonsai are growing very vigorously and changing constantly. Flowering trees are especially attractive now. The sensational blossoms of the brilliant Satsuki azaleas, or *Rhododendron*, are one of the glories of early summer. The

different varieties of the pomegranate, *Punica granatum*, produce scarlet, white, yellow, or pink flowers in high summer, and the potentilla is spangled with small blossoms in a similar variety of shades. Cotoneaster and pyracantha species also flower in summer, and by the end of the season have begun to form their colourful fruits, as has the crab apple, *Malus*.

Early in the season, you can leaf cut some deciduous trees, particularly maples, *Acer*, and by late summer new leaves will sprout to give a second display of the glorious colours of spring.

Striking features
The coral-pink bark and twigs echoing the pink tinge of the foliage are characteristic of the 'Sango Kaku' maple, proving that it is not only flowers and leaves that give a tree summer interest. The compact habit of this cultivar of *Acer palmatum* adds to its attraction as a subject for bonsai.

Covered in bloom
The flowers of the Satsuki azalea, *Rhododendron indicum* 'Kaho', as with most azaleas, are relatively large for bonsai. Because they are so abundant, completely clothing the branches, the effect is of one richly coloured mass of delicate blossom.

Spectrum of colours
As can be seen here, the Satsuki azalea cultivars often have multicoloured or striped flowers, creating an intensely vibrant effect on a single bonsai plant.

Versatile shrub
The potentilla is as popular as bonsai material as it is as a flowering garden shrub. This example (*Potentilla fruticosa*) has bright yellow flowers, but the range of colours available in various forms spans white, cream, yellow, pink, and orange.

Autumn tints

The season of autumn is as colourful as spring, but its brilliance lasts longer, allowing more time to appreciate its beauty. The leaves of some deciduous species may be changing colour and beginning to fall, while others have not yet begun their most striking colour changes, and still others have already fallen to the ground.

The rich, strong colours – yellow, orange, red, and purple – of the maples, *Acer*, are sensational in autumn.

The euonymus and stewartia produce even brighter reds, while the leaves of the gingko change to a distinctive buttercup yellow, and the needles of the larch turn from bright green to vivid gold. The leaves of beech, *Fagus*, become a russet brown, while those of the birch trees, *Betula*, take on a rich golden hue. The luscious red berries of the rowan or mountain ash, *Sorbus aucuparia*, cluster decoratively among its orange and golden foliage. As the leaves fall from other fruiting species, such as crab apples, *Malus*, the Japanese deciduous holly, *Ilex serrata*, and some cotoneasters, the structure of their branches is exposed, covered with bright fruits.

Spectacular display
The individual trees in this dense group of trident maples, *Acer buergerianum*, are at different stages of turning colour, thus providing a stunning range of tints from green and orange to brilliant scarlet.

Fruiting specimen
Berries are an additional source of
autumn colour, as can be seen with this
cotoneaster, displayed on lava rock. The
blue-green, glazed pot contrasts very
attractively with the bright red
of the fruit and leaves.

Mellow tones
The dark grey-brown of the trunk
and the greenish-grey of the pot
complement the soft yellow of the
leaves of this English elm, *Ulmus
procera* (*above*).

Turning colour
This group planting of *Fagus crenata*
realistically captures the effect of a
beech wood in autumn. Leaves in all
shades from yellow to brown show
up well against the pale tree trunks.

Winter interest

Winter is an important season in the world of bonsai, for it is considered that many bonsai can be best appreciated when the structure of deciduous trees is unobscured by foliage. The Japanese traditionally display their bonsai, and hold major exhibitions, at this time of year.

Winter is also a prime time for viewing evergreens, which seem to express an air of strength and perseverance throughout the harshest conditions, as well as providing a pleasing contrast to the lighter, more fragile tracery of deciduous trees.

When bare of leaves, deciduous trees, such as the Chinese elm, *Ulmus parvifolia*, and trident maple, *Acer buergerianum*, reveal their mass of delicate twigs. Others, such as the crape myrtle, *Lagerstroemia indica*, and stewartia display their fascinatingly textured and coloured bark. Fruit hangs on some trees throughout the winter, enlivening the sombre scene with splashes of vivid colour. The Chinese quince, *Chaenomeles sinensis*, looks especially attractive with its winter combination of strongly patterned branches, decorative bark, and bright fruits.

In late winter, the pale, fragrant blossoms on the bare wood of the flowering apricot, *Prunus mume*, herald the coming spring. They are followed shortly afterwards by the cheerful yellow flowers of the winter jasmine, *Jasminum nudiflorum*, also carried on leafless branches.

Refined detail
In winter, with no leaves to mask their delicate traceries, fine-twigged species such as these Korean hornbeams, *Carpinus turczaninowii*, really come into their own.

Impression of substance
Colour and mass are provided by evergreens such as this Japanese black pine, *Pinus thunbergii*. Erect, bright green needles and rugged bark on this species give year-round impact, but are particularly striking at a time when many other trees are bare.

Rare blossoms
One of the few trees that flowers in winter is *Prunus mume*. This attractive cultivar has a bonus of flowers in a range of different colours, from white to deep pink, on the same plant.

Dramatic silhouette
After leaf fall, mature, deciduous trees, such as this gnarled, aged oak, *Quercus robur*, are particularly striking when their beautiful structure becomes more visible.

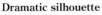

How to display bonsai

Most bonsai are hardy trees that must live permanently outdoors. Ideally, they should be viewed against a plain background (rarely possible in a garden). They need good light and protection from any fierce winds. Displaying them on shelves against a wall meets these criteria, but the wall should be in good light and must not cast a shadow on the trees. Rotate the bonsai occasionally: if the trees are left in one position, with the front view permanently on display, rear branches can die from lack of light and from the intensity of heat reflected off the wall.

Rock plantings need more humid conditions. You can keep one or two trees outdoors in water trays. A larger collection needs to stand on a bench or shelf that can form a water basin with a larger surface area in summer.

How you arrange the bonsai is a personal decision, taking into account the viewpoint, the relationship of trees to each other within a group, and their seasonal features.

The height of displays

The level for a bonsai display is usually a compromise between a practical height for easy maintenance, and the best viewing position (at eye level). Usually, bonsai are arranged on benches at tabletop height, or on shelves attached to a garage or extension wall. Those on a patio, viewed from a sitting position, may be sited a little lower, on a paving slab supported on bricks for example. Bonsai can also stand on a garden wall.

Never place a bonsai so that you have to look down on it: keeping it off the ground also avoids mud splashes, and discourages insects from entering the pot, although a large tree may stand on the ground at a distance. Use a "monkey pole", a platform on a single vertical pole, for an individual tree.

Contrast of heights in display

In this garden, the bonsai are set at varying heights against a dark fence for greater impact.

Japanese setting
Bamboo screens are perfect backgrounds for bonsai.

Reflected in a pool
Rock plantings stand in a shallow water basin.

Traditional display
In this classic *tokonoma* display, a tree is set in an alcove with an accessory rock.

Displaying bonsai indoors

Sometimes you will want to bring an outdoor bonsai indoors temporarily for your own enjoyment or a special occasion. Place the tree in a bright position, but not on a windowsill with full midday sun. Keep it away from heat sources such as an open fire or a radiator, and be cautious of electrical appliances: a tree placed on top of a television is exposed to heat from the back of the set.

Even the most informal indoor display needs space to set off the tree. The best background is a plain, pale wall: patterned wallpapers or fabrics detract from the tree's natural beauty. In Japan, the traditional space was a *tokonoma* alcove.

Watering bonsai indoors can be a problem. As tree and container together form the design, do not alter this relationship by standing the pot in a tray or dish for drainage. Simply take the bonsai to the kitchen or outdoors for watering, and drain it well before replacing it. Protect furniture from the feet of the pot with a rush mat or another discreet base.

Preparing bonsai for exhibition

There are few opportunities to exhibit bonsai, and conditions vary according to the dictates of the specialist bonsai or general horticultural societies in your region. At the national level, growers submit their best specimens, and the organizers then choose overall examples of excellence (rather than mark them competively). At local level, the standards will be very different from those of a specialist society.

It is important to prepare both tree and container, so that the bonsai is in the best condition for display. Groom the tree to refine the silhouette and remove any dead leaves. Weed the soil surface and remove plant debris from the container. Freshen or renew mosses, grasses, or ground-cover plants. Clean off dirt and water marks from the pot and rub up the surface to a smooth finish. You can leave neat and effective wiring in place.

If you enter one or two bonsai, you are unlikely to have any influence on how or where they are displayed, so this preparation is your final chance of presenting the tree at its best. If exhibiting *mame* (miniature bonsai), you may be given a space to arrange the group.

CHAPTER TWO

A-Z OF BONSAI SPECIES

Attractive bonsai subjects can be trained from a wide
variety of trees and shrubs, and this chapter gives
detailed information on about 80 different species and
forms. The trees and shrubs are listed in alphabetical
order of their botanical names, followed by their common
names. The concise but informative text describes the
characteristics of each plant, its origin, and habitat, and
any special features that make it ideal as a bonsai.
Full-colour photographs illustrate top-quality bonsai
examples of each tree or shrub, fully captioned and
labelled to point out the salient features. A separate
photographic detail indicates the size of a typical leaf
from each bonsai, and helps with its identification.
Advice is given on how to create and care for a bonsai
specimen, together with suggestions for the styles and
sizes that are most appropriate to it.

Choosing an appropriate species
*Part of the art of bonsai lies in selecting a tree or shrub to grow
in a style that suits its natural characteristics. Here, a dwarf spruce that
lends itself to rock plantings,* Picea abies *'Little Gem', is used to achieve
a realistic impression of mature, windswept trees on a mountain with
specimens less than 8cm (3in) high.*

How to use the A-Z species guide

These pages explain how this species guide was devised to help you; the annotated sample page opposite demonstrates the system used. There is also a fuller dictionary of 300 or so species suitable for bonsai on pp. 184–209. This offers a greatly extended range of garden shrubs and trees which you can train into bonsai, as well as many additional varieties and cultivars.

Finding your way around the guide

The 80 or so different trees and shrubs shown in the guide are given in alphabetical order of their genus and species names, with the common name following each botanical name. If a species has two botanical names or has been reclassified, it is included under the most commonly used name, with the synonym in brackets and smaller type.

Description of each species

The introductory text on each plant describes its origins and native habitat, as well as any interesting historical details of the plant, in the wild or in bonsai culture. The plant's natural shape, structure, and growing pattern will help you plan the most suitable style of bonsai for it. Also indicated are outstanding features like textured bark, or seasonal effects like flowers, fruit or colourful autumn tints.

Any interesting cultivars, forms or related species that make good bonsai are also mentioned, especially if they are better suited to a particular style or size than the main species. The naturally finer leaves and twigs of dwarf forms make them suitable for smaller bonsai sizes. An alternative species or subspecies may be more drought- or frost-resistant, and therefore more tolerant of a difficult climate.

Styles and sizes

The appropriate styles for each of the species are listed, such as formal or informal upright, cascade or multiple-trunk. Past experience has proved the suggested styles to be practical and most likely to be successful; a species that grows naturally upright is likely to succeed as a bonsai in that style. Which style you select

for a bonsai must also depend on the original form of the individual plant. For additional information on styles, see pp. 116–21.

Its natural twig structure, leaf size, and rate of growth make each plant most suited to a particular size or sizes; you will find it difficult, for example, to grow a large-leaved species as a tiny bonsai. The recommended sizes are: extra-large, over 90cm (36in); large, 45–90cm (18–36in); medium, 20–45cm (8–18in); small, 10–20cm (4–8in); extra-small, up to 10cm (4in). These sizes are, however, only approximate, and have been included to give a consistent guide to the height of the bonsai.

Cultivation details

Concise notes on cultivation cover the main principles of maintaining and propagating the bonsai. Best times and methods for every aspect of care are given for each featured tree or shrub. The cultivation notes are placed in a box and categorized under symbols for quick and easy reference (*see box opposite*). More detailed information on routine care is given on pp. 170–83, and on propagation on pp. 162–9.

The illustrations

Each specially taken photograph of a bonsai is fully captioned and annotated to give the tree's age, height, and style, its structure or seasonal characteristics, and the bonsai method used to achieve the effect. Remember, however, that it is impossible to "copy" a photograph of a successful bonsai or even an actual example. Instead, you must study the individual plant material, and enhance its natural features with training so that it becomes a unique specimen.

Choosing a container

The styles and materials of the pots are described, because a well-chosen container is an integral part of a good bonsai design. The illustrated containers range from handmade pots to Japanese Tokoname ware and, in one case, a slab of rough stone. The reasons for choosing the size, shape, and finish of each container give you pointers for selecting your own pot. For more on containers, see pp. 122–5.

The leaf details

Each bonsai entry has a separate, close-up photograph of an individual leaf, shown at a specified reduction from its life size. The leaf details will help with identification of the tree or shrub, because the bonsai may have been photographed in spring when flowers hide its leaves, or in the autumn or winter in order to depict its twig structure after leaf fall. The leaf details also more clearly indicate the actual size of the plant which, of necessity, is often shown greatly reduced.

Cultivation box symbols

⊙ Position: best light level; special winter or summer care (*see also pp. 172–3*).

◩ Watering: rate and amounts (*see also p. 174*).

⊡ Feeding: correct frequency, amounts, and type of fertilizer (*see also p. 174*).

▣ Repotting: best time of year; frequency of repotting as bonsai matures (*see also pp. 176–7*).

◩ Pruning: best times for maintenance pruning (*see also pp. 178–81*).

◪ Propagation: most reliable methods; best times of year (*see also pp. 162–9*).

Identification
The botanical name, by which the "A–Z Species Guide" is ordered, is shown in Roman type, with synonyms, where applicable, in brackets. The common name appears in italic type.

Cultivation box
Notes on the care and propagation of the featured plant are given point by point. For instant recognition, each topic covered has its own identification symbol.

General description
This covers the history and special features of each tree or shrub, and lists forms, cultivars, and related species suitable for bonsai.

Bonsai suggestions
This gives appropriate styles and sizes for the plants in the entry.

Leaf detail
For easy reference, the leaves of each illustrated plant are shown either at a specified reduction or at life size.

A-Z OF BONSAI SPECIES   61

Crataegus *Hawthorn*

These small deciduous trees have dense growth and prickly branches which make them ideal for use in hedges, and small leaves, so they are especially suited to bonsai. They often grow wild across North America, Asia, and Western Europe. In spring, they bear clusters of white, pink or red flowers, followed by orange or red berries in autumn. The common hawthorn, *Crataegus monogyna*, has white, strongly scented flowers. *C. laevigata* is less common in the wild, but has many hybrids: 'Paul's Scarlet' is very beautiful, with double scarlet flowers. The Japanese hawthorn, *C. cuneata*, has large, rosehip-type berries and white flowers.

CULTIVATION

⊙ Site in full sun. Protect small sizes from frost.
◩ Water daily throughout growing season, in generous amounts. Keep moist at all times. Spray regularly against mildew.
⊡ Feed twice a month during growing season.
▣ Repot once a year, in early spring or early autumn. Use basic soil mix.
◩ In spring, pinch out terminal shoots to two or three leaves. Prune branches after flowering or after leaf-fall.
◪ To propagate species: seeds stratified in winter, sown in spring; softwood cuttings in summer. Hybrids: graft in late winter or early spring.

Bonsai suggestions
Hawthorns can be grown in all bonsai sizes and styles, except formal upright and broom.

Crataegus laevigata 'Paul's Scarlet'
This informal upright, now 12 years old, is 65cm (26in) tall.

Crataegus laevigata 'Paul's Scarlet', leaf
one third life size

Spring flowers
This is a prolific cultivar and, in spring, is covered in bright red flowers for a magnificent display.

Field-grown specimen
The grafted tree was allowed to grow in the field for five years to develop the trunk. It has then had four years' training as a bonsai.

Tokoname pot
The shallow, unglazed, oval pot from Japan balances the informal shape of this tree, and its soft colours is a foil for the bright flowers.

Exposed roots
Strong visual interest is created at the base of the tree by the knotted, exposed roots.

Main caption
This gives the height, age, and style of the bonsai, and points out its particular features.

Seasonal features
Each specimen is shown at a time of year that highlights its special features, such as spring flowers or brilliant autumn leaves.

Special interest
Details of the way the example was created, or particularly interesting features, are also explained.

Container
Concise information covers the type and style of container, and gives reasons for the choice of a particular shape or colouring.

Acer buergerianum (A. trifidium) *Trident maple*

The trident maple is a deciduous tree with naturally upright growth. It is tolerant of pruning, dry soil, and air pollution, and for this reason it is grown as a "street" tree in many cities around the world. In autumn, its foliage develops spectacular tints of orange and red. Unlike many maples, however, its roots need protection in winter, as their high moisture content makes them very susceptible to damage by frost. *A. b. formosanum* is an interesting sub-species that does not grow as tall as the main species, but carries a dense growth of leathery leaves. An unusual cultivar for bonsai is *A. b.* 'Mino Yatsubusa', a dwarf form with a pointed apex. In autumn, its long, narrow, shiny leaves look as though they have been lacquered scarlet and orange. *Acer ginnala*, the Amur maple, is a good alternative for harsh winter conditions, as its roots are more resistant to frost damage.

Bonsai suggestions
Trident maples can be grown in every style except broom, and in all sizes. A web-like root structure makes these trees especially suitable for root-over-rock designs.

Acer buergerianum,
leaf one-third life size

Structure of branches
Since the formation of its trunk, the tree has been grown in a container for five years and the structure of its branches has been refined.

Leaf colour
The foliage is a fresh green until the autumn, when the rich colouring of the leaves varies from orange to red.

Shaping the trunk
The solid trunk, with its tapering top, was created by growing the tree in the ground for a number of years and giving it a severe annual pruning.

Tokoname ware
The proportions of this tree are balanced by the size of its grey, unglazed container.

Acer buergerianum
TRIDENT MAPLE
This tree is 20 years old and 55cm (22in) high. It has been trained into an informal upright.

Acer buergerianum
TRIDENT MAPLE
A root-over-rock style features the sturdy cascade of roots from this 25-year-old tree, which is 38cm (15in) high. The thick mass of leaves balances the texture and weight of the supporting rock.

CULTIVATION

⦿ Position in full sun. Protect from frost.
◔ Water daily throughout growing season. In winter, keep relatively dry to minimize risk of frost damage to roots.
⦂ Feed weekly for first month after leaves appear, then every two weeks until late summer.
▣ Repot annually in early spring as buds swell, but before bud burst. Cut frost-damaged roots back to older woody growth: new roots will grow quickly. Use free-draining soil mix.
▧ Trim new shoots to one or two sets of leaves throughout growing season. Vigorous, well-fed plants can be leaf-cut in midsummer.
▤ Sow seeds in late autumn (protect from frost). Take softwood cuttings in midsummer. Hardwood cuttings (as thick as a pencil, a broom handle, or even a wrist) between late winter and early spring. Air layering in spring.

Acer ginnala
AMUR MAPLE
This is a hardy species that is often substituted for *A. buergerianum* in locations where winter conditions are harsh. This group planting is now 15 years old and has reached a height of 60cm (24in).

Three-pointed leaves
In the autumn, the foliage turns from green to brilliant crimson.

Shallow, oval pot
The brown, unglazed, Japanese Tokoname container is displayed on a wider, varnished wood base to balance the grouping.

Asymmetrical shape
This is achieved by planting the tallest trees off-centre, with smaller specimens at the sides and back, to give a sense of perspective.

Acer campestre *Field maple*

The leaves of the field maple have an attractive shape and turn a bright buttercup yellow in autumn. It is a small deciduous tree, and the native European maple. Like other maples, *Acer campestre* is a good choice for training as bonsai, although it is not cultivated as frequently as its Japanese cousins (*see opposite and pp. 44–5*). Its relatively coarse twigs make it unsuited to smaller bonsai sizes, except the extra-small size, when a single leaf can represent the mass of foliage and twigs on a single branch.

Bonsai suggestions

Field maples are suitable for every style of bonsai, except literati. The best sizes are medium to large, but you can also grow these trees as extra-small bonsai.

Acer campestre
FIELD MAPLE
This 13-year-old group, grown from cuttings, has an overall height of 53cm (21in).

Acer campestre, *leaf one-third life size*

Strong leaf colour
This vivid, bright green summer foliage turns to clear yellow in autumn.

Creating visual space
A sense of space is achieved by varying the height and thickness of the trunks in this asymmetrical group.

Shallow container
A brown, unglazed, Japanese Tokoname oval forms a broad, low base for this group of trees.

Acer palmatum *Japanese maple*

The many attractive qualities of this elegant tree make it one of the classic bonsai trees. It responds well to bonsai cultivation, and has a graceful branch structure, delicately shaped leaves with five lobes, and seasonal variation of foliage (from the greens of spring to autumn reds and russets). The bark of older specimens develops beautiful silver colouring. This species, also native to China and Korea, has been cultivated in Japan for centuries: there are now over 250 cultivars.

Bonsai suggestions

Japanese maples are suitable for every style of bonsai cultivation, except literati. They can be grown in all sizes.

CULTIVATION

◉ Position in full sun, slight shade in summer to avoid leaf scorch. Protect from severe frost: below –10°C (–14°F).

◻ Water daily during growing season, but keep water off leaves in bright sun to avoid scorching. Sparingly in winter, but keep soil moist.

⋯ Feed weekly for first month after leaf buds open, then fortnightly until late summer.

▣ Repot every two years in early spring until ten years old, then as necessary. Use basic soil mix.

▧ In spring, trim new leaves to one or two pairs. Remove large leaves during growing season. Cut back long internodes. For small leaves and good autumn colour, leaf cut totally in midsummer. Wire after leaf cutting.

▨ Sow seeds in winter. Softwood cuttings in summer. Layering or air layering in spring or summer.

Acer palmatum
JAPANESE MAPLE
This specimen was grown from seed and has been styled as an informal upright. It is eight years old and measures 53cm (21in) high.

Acer palmatum,
leaf one-third life size

Autumn shades
The graceful, five-lobed leaves turn rich red and russet, replacing the fresh green colour of spring and summer.

Pruned to shape
The fine trunk is the result of five years in open ground. The tree was in its pot for one year and shaped only by pruning.

Matt-glazed oval
The natural earth colour of this container by Bryan Albright offsets the darker hues of the foliage.

Acer palmatum cultivars *Japanese maples*

The cultivars of *Acer palmatum* are so diverse they could furnish an entire and splendid collection. In spring, the colours of their foliage rival the brilliance of most flowers and the leaf shapes and sizes are astonishingly varied. Some leaves are small and compact, in shades of ruby-red or scarlet. The large cut-leaf shapes of other cultivars create a tranquil floating or weeping effect with their lacy patterns of green or purple. Whatever their spring or summer hues, the leaves of all varieties change in autumn into a startlingly wide range of tints, from palest yellow, through oranges and reds, to purple. As a bonus, some varieties have colourful trunks and stems, others have interesting textures and muted shades.

Bonsai suggestions

All Japanese maple cultivars are suitable for every style of bonsai, except literati. They can be grown in all sizes.

Acer palmatum **'Deshojo'**, *leaf one-third life size*

***Acer palmatum* 'Deshojo'**
JAPANESE RED MAPLE
This specimen is 40 years old, 80cm (32in) tall, and has been grown in twin-trunk style.

Brilliant spring colour
Bright red foliage turns to green in summer, then to vivid shades of red and orange in autumn.

Twin-trunk style
A strong, interestingly shaped root spread gives stability to the graceful trunk, which has been thickened by being grown in open ground.

Green, glazed pot
The colour of this Japanese container complements the red hues of spring and autumn and also echoes the hue of the summer foliage.

Acer palmatum 'Ukon'
UKON MAPLE
The trees were planted as a group six years ago from nine-year-old grafted plants. The overall height is 75cm (30in), and the curved trunks have been carefully arranged to allow some crossing, for a natural, uncontrived effect.

Fresh summer colour
The foliage is lime green in summer, giving the group a light and airy feel.

Discreet simplicity
This Japanese Tokoname, shallow oval is brown and unglazed, and ensures that attention is focused on the group of trees.

Acer palmatum 'Dissectum atropurpureum'
CUT-LEAF PURPLE MAPLE
The elegance of this cultivar is evident in the light, spreading structure of this 30-year-old informal upright, which is 65cm (26in) tall. The finely cut leaves change from purple to bright orange in autumn.

CULTIVATION

◉ A position in full light best displays the spectacular autumn colour, but shield from hot summer sun to avoid leaf scorch. Protect against severe frost: below –10°C (–14°F).

◇ Water daily throughout growing season but, to prevent scorching, do not let water fall on leaves exposed to bright sun. Sparingly in winter, but keep soil moist.

⁙ Feed weekly for first month after leaf buds open, then fortnightly until late summer.

▭ Repot every second year in early spring, until tree is about ten years old, then as necessary. Use basic soil mix.

▧ Trim new growth to one or two pairs of leaves in spring. Remove large leaves throughout growing season. Cut back long internodes to maintain short internodal distances. Total leaf cutting in midsummer for small leaves and good autumn colour. Wiring is best done immediately after leaf cutting.

✂ Take softwood cuttings in summer. Layering or air layering in spring or summer.

Arundinaria *Bamboo*

The graceful bamboo canes give an oriental feel to any garden as their grass-like leaves tremble in the gentlest breeze. Bamboos come from the East, especially China and Japan. They are often wrongly named. The common "sacred bamboo" is not a bamboo at all, but *Nandina domestica*, a shrub related to *Berberis* (*see p. 189*). *Arundinaria, Sasa,* and *Phyllostachys* are the species most used for bonsai; they are usually grown as a group to represent a bamboo grove, or to accent or complement other species.

Bonsai suggestions

Multiple-trunk is the best style. Single-trunk style is sometimes used for varieties with strong, interesting stems but, as individual stems only live for five to six years, replacement shoots must be grown. The sizes usually range from small to medium.

CULTIVATION

● Keep in partial shade. Protect from frost.
◊ Bamboos love moisture, so water daily at least, more often for plants grown on slabs or in shallow pots. Do not allow to stand in water.
⚡ Feed every two weeks in spring and summer, preferably with a feed high in nitrogen.
▬ Repot every second year in late spring. Use basic soil mix on slabs and in shallow containers, free-draining mix in deeper pots.
✎ Cut dwarf forms right back to ground level in early spring. Larger forms can be controlled by systematic peeling of leaf sheaths, but this is not essential.
✦ To propagate, divide rhizomes in early spring.

Arundinaria nitida, leaf one-third life size

Multiple-trunk
The canes are cut right down to ground level every second year in spring, in order to renew the stems.

Arundinaria nitida
BAMBOO
This six-year-old specimen has been grown in multiple-trunk style. The height is 25cm (10in).

Grass-like stems
The fresh green foliage is carried on graceful, arching stems.

Drum-shaped container
The chunky shape of the glazed, Japanese Tokoname pot visually anchors this light and airy specimen to the ground.

Nandina domestica
SACRED or HEAVENLY BAMBOO
In size and style, this bonsai can be
compared with the *Arundinaria*, but this
bamboo has been planted with rock to
represent trees in a landscape.

Delicate compound leaves
*This foliage turns to brilliant scarlet
in the autumn, before it falls.*

Oval pot
*The striking, blue, glazed, Japanese
Tokoname container complements
the fine structure of the plant.*

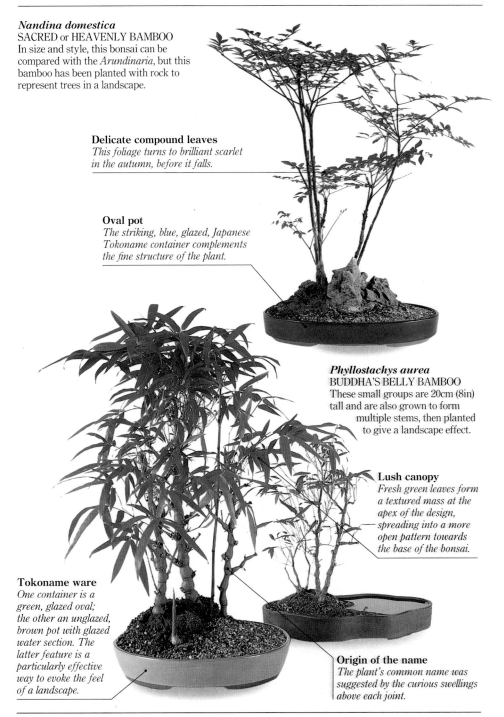

Phyllostachys aurea
BUDDHA'S BELLY BAMBOO
These small groups are 20cm (8in)
tall and are also grown to form
multiple stems, then planted
to give a landscape effect.

Lush canopy
*Fresh green leaves form
a textured mass at the
apex of the design,
spreading into a more
open pattern towards
the base of the bonsai.*

Tokoname ware
*One container is a
green, glazed oval;
the other an unglazed,
brown pot with glazed
water section. The
latter feature is a
particularly effective
way to evoke the feel
of a landscape.*

Origin of the name
*The plant's common name was
suggested by the curious swellings
above each joint.*

Betula nana *Dwarf Birch*

In autumn, the tiny leaves of the dwarf birch turn a rich gold, in winter, its delicate twigs are very decorative and, all year, the coppery, shiny trunk is as pleasing as the silver birch's white trunk (*see opposite*). These features make *Betula nana* an excellent tree for bonsai, although in gardens it can become very straggly without clipping. As its other common name of Arctic birch implies, this native of northern temperate regions can survive the extreme cold up to the Arctic circle, and grow on mountains that are free of ice and snow for only three months of the year.

Bonsai suggestions

Betula nana is suited to informal upright, slanting, broom, root-over-rock, clasped-to-rock, twin-trunk, clump, straight line, and sinuous styles, and is extremely useful in saikei plantings. It is excellent in extra-small and small bonsai sizes.

CULTIVATION

⬤ Position in full sun or partial shade. Protect from frost to prevent twig die-back.

◔ Water daily throughout growing season. Sparingly in winter, but keep moist.

⬚ Do not feed until one month after leaves have opened, then every two weeks in growing season.

▣ Repot every second year, in early spring before bud burst. Use basic soil mix.

◩ Trim new shoots constantly to one or two leaves throughout summer to create compact foliage masses. Trim out crossing branches and tidy up shape while tree is leafless in winter.

▣ Take softwood cuttings in spring and summer. Cuttings root very easily.

Betula nana, *leaf two-thirds life size*

Betula nana
DWARF BIRCH
Twelve-year-old trees, which have been grown from cuttings, form a compact group 35cm (14in) high.

Tiny serrated leaves
The glossy, green foliage takes on lovely orange hues in autumn.

Composition
The trunks of 21 trees are planted on a slab of rock at various angles to fan out the mass of delicate twigs and leaves.

Betula pendula *Silver Birch*

Birches are among the most tolerant and hardy of deciduous trees, being native to the temperate and cold areas of the northern hemisphere. The species most often grown as bonsai is the silver birch, which has the well-known white trunk, elegant twigs, and leaves that turn golden brown in autumn. You may need to grow a young tree in a pot for many years before the bark on its shiny, copper-brown trunk changes to a shimmering silver-white, scored and cracked with black lines. Two to three years in open ground, however, can have the same effect.

Bonsai suggestions
Informal upright, twin-trunk, and group are good styles for silver birches. The best sizes are small to extra-large.

CULTIVATION

● Position in full sun or partial shade. Protect from severe frost to prevent twig die-back.
◌ Water daily throughout growing season. Keep moist in winter.
⋮ Feed every two weeks from one month after leaves open, until late summer.
▣ Repot every second year until ten years old, in early spring before bud burst, then as roots develop. Use free-draining soil mix.
▧ Trim back new shoots to two or three leaves in spring and at successive flushes of growth. Remove large leaves throughout growing season. Birches bleed copiously, so use a wound sealant.
▣ Sow seeds in winter or spring.

Betula pendula, leaf
one-third life size

Shapely foliage
The leaves are attractively serrated and turn in autumn from green to rich yellows and oranges.

Betula pendula
SILVER BIRCH
This informal upright is 35 years old and 75cm (30in) tall. It was collected from the wild, then trained as a bonsai for 20 years.

Twisting trunk
The overall impression is of a strong, erect tree, but the gentle curving and twisting of the trunk adds visual interest.

Semi-matt, glazed container
The rectangular pot by Petra Engelke provides horizontal balance for the curving trunk.

Caragana arborescens *Chinese pea tree*

Caragana species are tough, adaptable trees, surviving windy, freezing conditions and poor soil in the wild. Curiously, they grow well as indoor bonsai, even in very warm rooms. They belong to *Leguminosae*, the pea family, and are natives of central Asia. *C. arborescens*, the deciduous Chinese pea tree from Siberia, is often grown as bonsai; its fragile and graceful appearance belies its tough nature. Many specimens of *C. sinica* (*C. chamlagu*), the Mongolian red shrub, are exported from China and Taiwan. Indoors or in mild areas, the leaves are often semi-evergreen.

Bonsai suggestions
These trees are suitable for every style except formal upright, and look equally attractive in all sizes.

CULTIVATION

◉ Position in full sun indoors or out. Indoor plants placed outside need frost protection.

◌ Water daily or every two days during growing season. Keep relatively dry in winter.

⚡ Feed every two or three weeks throughout growing season.

▣ Repot every second year in winter or early spring. Use free-draining soil mix.

▧ As young tree develops, in winter prune hard or remove branches. Shorten new shoots in summer. Beware sharp spines.

▨ Sow stratified seeds in spring. Softwood cuttings in summer.

***Caragana arborescens**, leaf one-third life size*

Dainty foliage
The symmetrical, compound leaves change from fresh green to yellow in autumn.

Caragana arborescens
CHINESE PEA TREE
This small, informal upright bonsai is four years old. Its height is 15cm (6in).

Shaping an upright
The tree was grown from seed until 90cm (36in) tall, then pruned to 8cm (3in) and potted. It has been in bonsai training for just one year.

Cream, glazed ware
The round, chunky pot enhances the proportions of this small specimen.

Carmona microphylla (Ehretia buxifolia) *Fukien tea*

This large shrub is well known to bonsai growers as *Carmona microphylla*, but the correct botanical name of *Ehretia buxifolia* more accurately describes its small, evergreen, box-like leaves (*see p. 190*) and compact habit. You can clip it into a bonsai very easily, without wiring. It makes a very convincing, "tree-like" tropical plant, and in temperate areas grows well as an indoor bonsai. In spring and early summer, white flowers nestle among its shiny, dark green leaves. The green berries ripen into red. Most bonsai plants of this species come from southern China.

Bonsai suggestions
The Fukien tea can be easily trimmed into any style of bonsai. It is equally suitable for growing in all sizes.

CULTIVATION
● Position in full sun, slight shade in hot summers. Minimum temperature 15°C (60°F).
◫ Keep soil moist at all times. Water sparingly in winter.
⣿ Feed every two weeks from early spring to early autumn. Every four to six weeks in winter.
▦ Repot every second year in early spring, at start of growing season. Use basic soil mix.
▨ Trim new shoots constantly to two or three leaves once six to eight leaves have formed. Wire woody branches at any time.
☒ Sow seeds in greenhouse conditions at any time. Softwood cuttings in spring or summer.

Carmona microphylla, leaf one-third life size

Carmona microphylla
FUKIEN TEA
This 30-year-old specimen is a Chinese-styled twin-trunk. Its height is 87cm (35in).

Box-like leaves
The glossy, green foliage completely clothes the branches of the tree.

Twin-trunk style
A low branch, trained as a twin-trunk, emphasizes the dramatic line of the weighty main trunk.

Green, glazed pot
The shade and shape of this Chinese container complements the tree's colouring and silhouette.

Carpinus *Hornbeam*

Natives of the cool temperate regions of Europe and eastern Asia, hornbeams are small trees with oval leaves on long, slender branches. The European hornbeam, *Carpinus betulus*, has distinctive striped and ridged grey bark; its bright green foliage turns a clear yellow in autumn. *C. laxiflora*, the Japanese loose-flowered hornbeam, bears prominent autumn catkins. A favourite for bonsai is *C. turczaninowii*, the Korean hornbeam. It has delicate, branching twigs, and tiny leaves which turn a splendid orange-red in autumn.

Bonsai suggestions
All sizes, and all styles except formal upright, are suitable when you grow hornbeams as bonsai subjects.

CULTIVATION
● Position in sun or slight shade. Protect from frost to avoid twig die-back.
◌ Water daily in summer, more sparingly in winter. Keep soil moist at all times.
⚘ Feed weekly for first month after leaves appear, then every two weeks until late summer.
▣ Repot in every spring, every second year until tree is ten years old, then as necessary when roots fill pot. Use basic soil mix.
✄ Trim new shoots to one or two leaves. Remove large leaves during growing season.
☑ Sow fresh seeds in autumn, stratified seeds early spring. Softwood cuttings in midsummer.

Carpinus laxiflora,
leaf one-third life size

A profusion of foliage
The tree is covered with ribbed, serrated, pointed leaves in a bright green.

Carpinus laxiflora
JAPANESE LOOSE-
FLOWERED HORNBEAM
This 30-year-old tree has been grown into an informal upright style. It is 75cm (30in) high.

Well-balanced form
The trunk has a good taper and supports a regular foliage mass.

Tokoname container
This shallow, matt-glazed, speckled, cream oval complements the tree's spreading shape.

Cedrus *Cedar*

These impressive evergreen conifers are all suited to bonsai. The genus has only four species. *Cedrus atlantica*, the Atlas cedar, with green foliage and dark grey bark, comes from the Atlas mountains of Algeria and Morocco. Its attractive form *C. a. glauca*, the blue cedar, has blue-grey foliage and paler grey bark. *C. brevifolia*, the Cyprus cedar, bears clusters of dark green needles. *C. deodara*, the Deodar or Indian cedar, has larger needles and a drooping leader stem, while spreading horizontal branches make *C. libani*, the cedar of Lebanon, unmistakable.

Bonsai suggestions

Grow cedars in formal and informal upright, twin-trunk, or group styles. *C. brevifolia* works well in extra-small to large sizes, other species in medium to extra-large.

Evergreen foliage

This conifer bears small, fresh green needles in compact clusters.

Cedrus atlantica,
leaf one-third life size

Cedrus atlantica
ATLAS CEDAR
The overall height of this very fine group planting of 20-year-old trees is 105cm (42in).

Elegant spacing

The wide spacing of the tall, straight trunks, subtly bonded by the network of branches, gives this group grace.

Enhancing perspective

This brown, unglazed, Japanese Tokoname oval pot is shallow and makes a natural-looking low base.

Celastrus orbiculatus *Oriental bittersweet*

A native of China and Japan, this vigorous deciduous climbing shrub is grown mainly for the beauty of its fruits. These woody green capsules split open to reveal a golden yellow lining and three brilliant red seeds. They remain on the tree for much of the winter. The mid green leaves are oval and toothed, the flowers green and inconspicuous. Relatively small leaves and fruits, and supple, easily wired branches make this shrub very suitable for bonsai, if thoroughly pruned.

Bonsai suggestions

Bittersweet is suitable for informal upright, slanting, semicascade, cascade, root-over-rock, clasped-to-rock, twin-trunk, clump, straight line, and sinuous styles.
The best sizes are small to medium.

CULTIVATION

⬤ Site in full sun to encourage autumn fruiting. Protect small sizes from frost and freezing winds.
◊ Water daily and generously throughout growing season. Less frequently in winter, but keep moist at all times.
⊡ Feed twice a month in growing season.
▣ Repot annually or every second year, in early spring. Use basic soil mix.
▧ After flowers have appeared in spring, trim back new shoots to one or two leaves. Trim again to two or three leaves in late autumn. Wire in summer.
▣ Take softwood cuttings in summer. Layering or air layering in spring or summer.

Oval leaves
The bright green of the foliage changes to yellow in the autumn.

Celastrus orbiculatus
ORIENTAL BITTERSWEET
The style of this eight-year-old tree is root-over-rock. Its height is 20cm (8in).

Celastrus orbiculatus,
leaf one-third life size

Root feature
A dramatic effect is created by the heavy roots gripping the highly textured surface of the grey, Japanese Ibigawa rock.

Speckled, cream pot
This semi-matt, Japanese Tokoname oval gives depth and balance to the base of the design.

Chaenomeles *Flowering quince*

Some of the loveliest and easiest bonsai plants are the flowering quinces, natives of China and Japan. Most produce spectacular blossoms in white, pink, orange, or red on bare branches in early spring. The white-flowered *Chaenomeles speciosa* 'Nivalis' is especially good as a bonsai, as are the many cultivars of *C. × superba* – among the best are 'Etna', with rich vermilion flowers, and 'Pink Lady', a clear rose pink. Maul's flowering quince, *C. japonica*, bears red flowers, and its prized dwarf form, *C. j.* 'Chojubai', produces smaller red or white flowers all year round.

Bonsai suggestions
Flowering quinces are suitable for all styles, except formal upright and broom. Sizes can be extra-small to medium.

CULTIVATION

◉ Position in full sun. Protect from frost.
◌ Water daily throughout growing season; mist-spray except when in flower or fruit. Sparingly in winter, but always keep soil moist.
⚘ Feed every two weeks from end of flowering until the leaves fall.
▣ Repot every year or two years in mid autumn; or, with care, in early spring before bud burst. Use basic soil mix.
▨ In mid autumn, trim current season's growth to two nodes. Remove basal shoots.
☑ Sow seeds in early spring. Softwood cuttings in midsummer, hardwood cuttings in winter. To produce a bonsai in one year, select a hardwood cutting for a preformed trunk. Division, especially dwarfer forms. Grafting, often for named hybrids of *C. japonica*.

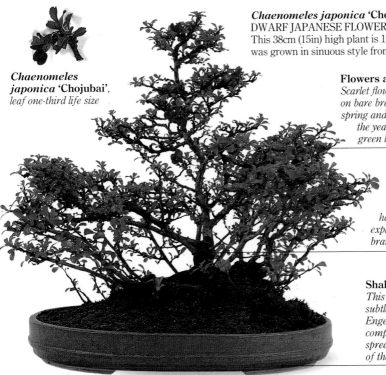

Chaenomeles japonica 'Chojubai', *leaf one-third life size*

Chaenomeles japonica 'Chojubai'
DWARF JAPANESE FLOWERING QUINCE
This 38cm (15in) high plant is 12 years old and was grown in sinuous style from a cutting.

Flowers and foliage
Scarlet flowers are borne on bare branches in early spring and reappear through the year among the bright green leaves.

Multiple trunks
To achieve this effect, the shrubby habit of the species was exploited by layering low branches along the soil.

Shallow, oval pot
This container with its subtle glaze is by Petra Engelke. Its shape complements the broad spread and sinuous style of the bonsai.

Chaenomeles sinensis (Pseudocydonia sinensis) *Chinese quince*

The Chinese quince from China and Korea has an attractive, flaky bark and a mass of glossy, green leaves that in autumn turn through shades of gold, orange, red, and purple. Small, pink, spring flowers are followed by fragrant, yellow, autumn fruits. The tree is particularly striking in winter, when the bold pattern of contorted branches is set off by decorative bark and fruits. Now correctly classified as *Pseudocydonia sinensis*, the Chinese quince has had many identities, and is included here under its best-known pseudonym for comparison with *Chaenomeles* (*see p. 55*).

Bonsai suggestions

The Chinese quince looks best in informal upright, twin-trunk, and group styles. It is suited to medium to large sizes.

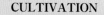

CULTIVATION

- Position in full sun. Protect from frost.
- Water daily throughout growing season, and give plenty of water when fruit is swelling. Sparingly in winter, but keep moist.
- Feed every two to three weeks throughout growing season.
- Repot every second year, in autumn after root pruning. Use basic soil mix.
- Shorten new shoots to two or three leaves in summer; wire while still flexible. Prune heavy branches in autumn.
- Sow stratified seeds in early spring. Softwood cuttings in summer.

Chaenomeles sinensis
CHINESE QUINCE
At 25 years old, this twin-trunk bonsai has reached a height of 90cm (36in).

Chaenomeles sinensis,
leaf one-third life size

Variable foliage
The thick, glossy, oval leaves gradually turn from fresh green to a range of warm shades in autumn.

Twin-trunk style
Colourful, flaky bark, which is characteristic of this species, shows off the well-balanced trunks.

Blue, glazed ware
The Japanese Tokoname oval provides a colour contrast to the leaves as they change.

Chamaecyparis *False cypress*

Natives of Japan and North America, the false cypresses are tough, long-lived evergreens that usually grow in conical or columnar shapes. Their flat, fan-shaped branches bear scale-like leaves. The most widely used bonsai species is *Chamaecyparis obtusa*, the Hinoki cypress. Its deep green, blunt-ended leaves are edged with blue around the undersides. Two dwarf cultivars are excellent for bonsai: *C. o.* 'Nana Gracilis' is the most popular in Europe and North America, but 'Yatsubusa', the Japanese dwarf form, is better, as it is neater and more compact.

Bonsai suggestions
Chamaecyparis species look good in every style of bonsai, except broom. They are suitable for all sizes.

CULTIVATION

⦿ Keep in good light, but shield from full summer sun to avoid leaf scorch. In cold conditions, particularly when soil is frozen, protect foliage from drying winds.

◇ Water and give foliage a mist-spray daily, from late spring to early autumn. Do not allow soil to dry out.

⦿ Feed every two weeks from early spring to late autumn.

⬛ Repot every second year in early to mid spring, for young trees. Repot trees over ten years old when roots fill pot. Use basic soil mix.

◪ Pinch out tops of foliage sprays during growing season.

▣ Cuttings are best rooted in sharp sand in summer or autumn. Grafting in late summer, except for the 'Yatsubusa' cultivar.

***Chamaecyparis obtusa* 'Yatsubusa'**, *leaf two-thirds life size*

Dense foliage
A profusion of fine-textured, dark green leaves fills out the silhouette.

***Chamaecyparis obtusa* 'Yatsubusa'** DWARF HINOKI CYPRESS
This group of ten-year-old trees, grown from cuttings, is 30cm (12in) in height.

Landscape effect
The five trees, planted on a low ceramic base, are arranged to create the impression of an open landscape.

Irregular shape
A free-form pottery slab by Petra Engelke gives an interesting, natural contour around the base.

Cotoneaster *Cotoneaster*

The small leaves, flowers, and fruits of the numerous members of the cotoneaster family make them ideal for bonsai cultivation. Cotoneasters can be deciduous or evergreen shrubs and are often grown in gardens. They include varieties with a prostrate, spreading, or upright habit, so they are suitable for growing in a wide range of bonsai styles.

The deciduous *Cotoneaster horizontalis*, with its dark green, shiny leaves, pink flowers, and bright orange-red berries is often trained as a bush in bonsai. Another deciduous shrub, *C. adpressus praecox*, is a fine sight in autumn when its leaves turn scarlet and complement its bright red berries. Many evergreen cotoneasters also make good bonsai. *C. microphyllus* has slender leaves,

white flowers, and large red berries, while the more compact *C. conspicuus decorus* bears fragrant masses of white, spring flowers.

An attractive dwarf variety is *C.* 'Skogholm', its large fruits contrasting with the small leaves. The tiny *C. congestus* is ideal for training as a very small bonsai.

Bonsai suggestions

Cotoneasters are suitable for growing in informal upright, slanting, semicascade, cascade, root-over-rock, clasped-to-rock, twin-trunk, and clump styles. They are suitable for extra-small to medium sizes.

Cotoneaster horizontalis
ROCKSPRAY COTONEASTER
This informal upright is now eight years old and has reached a height of 25cm (10in).

***Cotoneaster
horizontalis**, leaf
two-thirds life size*

Angular shape
*The balanced silhouette and
the angular movement of trunk
and branches was created by
careful wiring.*

Colourful fruits
*When the leaves fall in
autumn, the bright red
berries continue to lend
interest to the tree.*

Blue, glazed pot
*A dramatic colour contrast
with the autumn leaves and
brilliant fruits is provided by
the cloud-shaped, Japanese
Tokoname container.*

Cotoneaster 'Skogholm'
COTONEASTER
'Skogholm' is a useful dwarf cotoneaster.
This semicascade, grown from
a cutting, is eight years old
and only 12cm (5in)
high. The pale blue
pot complements
the evergreen
leaves and bright
red berries.

CULTIVATION

◉ Position in full sun. Protect from frost.
◌ Water daily throughout growing season.
Keep moist at all times: in winter, water
sufficiently to prevent soil from drying out,
especially with evergreen varieties.
⬙ Feed every two weeks until flowering, and
then once a month until late summer.
▣ Repot in early spring, annually until plant is
ten years old, then as necessary when roots fill
pot. Use basic soil mix.
▧ In early spring, cut back old branches.
Scissor-trim new shoots constantly in growing
season for denser twig growth.
☑ Sow stratified seeds in spring. Softwood
cuttings in summer, or hardwood cuttings in
autumn or winter.

White blossom
*In the spring, the glossy, green
foliage is spangled with small,
star-like flowers.*

**Cotoneaster
conspicuus decorus**
COTONEASTER
This specimen has been
trained as an informal
upright. It is ten years
old and 20cm (8in) high.

Pruned to shape
*A period in open ground allowed
the shrub to make prolific growth.
Then the shape of the bonsai was
created by pruning.*

Grey-brown, round pot
*The deep Japanese Tokoname pot
gives stability to the delicate,
asymmetrical shape of the tree.*

Crassula arborescens *Jade tree*

In its native South Africa, this evergreen succulent can become a tree three metres (ten feet) tall, with thick branches and smooth, rounded, fleshy leaves. In temperate regions, it is often grown as a houseplant, and is easily propagated by rooting a single leaf in sandy, well-drained soil. The jade tree makes an interesting, tree-like indoor bonsai. The leaves of *Crassula arborescens*, the species most commonly cultivated as bonsai, are a striking jade green, and develop a red tinge in full sun. Small, pale pink flowers adorn the tree in winter or, in some regions, in early spring.

Bonsai suggestions
The jade tree can be grown in informal upright, twin-trunk, or clump styles. It is suitable for medium to large sizes.

Crassula arborescens
JADE TREE
This 20-year-old tree, grown as an indoor bonsai in clump style, is 70cm (28in) tall.

Crassula arborescens,
leaf one-third life size

Tree-like appearance
Stout, fleshy stems make this specimen
look like a multi-stemmed tree.

CULTIVATION
● Position in full sun, warm location. Minimum temperature 10°C (50°F).
◌ Water moderately in summer. Every three to four weeks in cool conditions, so as to prevent leaves wrinkling.
⁙ Feed monthly from late spring through to early autumn.
▦ Repot every other year in spring. Use free-draining soil mix.
◪ Pinch back new shoots in spring; prune branches throughout growing season. For a tree-like effect, remove leaves from the trunk and the bases of old, lower branches.
◪ Take cuttings or a single leaf at any time. Use sandy, well-drained soil mix.

Red-edged foliage
The massed succulent
leaves are bright green,
and become strikingly
edged with red if the
tree is grown in full
sunlight.

Traditional, glazed Chinese pot
The sturdy, round pot complements
the stout trunks, and highlights the way
they converge at the base of the tree.

Crataegus *Hawthorn*

These small deciduous trees have dense growth and prickly branches which make them ideal for use in hedges, and small leaves, so they are especially suited to bonsai. They often grow wild across North America, Asia, and Western Europe. In spring, they bear clusters of white, pink or red flowers, followed by orange or red berries in autumn. The common hawthorn, *Crataegus monogyna*, has white, strongly scented flowers. *C. laevigata* is less common in the wild, but has many hybrids: 'Paul's Scarlet' is very beautiful, with double scarlet flowers. The Japanese hawthorn, *C. cuneata*, has large, rosehip-type berries and white flowers.

Bonsai suggestions
Hawthorns can be grown in all bonsai sizes and styles, except formal upright and broom.

Crataegus laevigata
'Paul's Scarlet', *leaf
one-third life size*

***Crataegus laevigata* 'Paul's Scarlet'**
DOUBLE RED FLOWERING HAWTHORN
This informal upright, now 12 years old,
is 65cm (26in) tall.

Spring flowers
*This is a prolific cultivar
and, in spring, is covered
in bright red flowers for
a magnificent display.*

Field-grown specimen
*The grafted tree was allowed to
grow in the field for five years to
develop the trunk. It has then had
four years' training as a bonsai.*

Tokoname pot
*The shallow, unglazed,
oval pot from Japan
balances the informal
shape of this tree, and
its soft colour is a foil
for the bright flowers.*

Exposed roots
*Strong visual interest is
created at the base of
the tree by the knotted,
exposed roots.*

Cryptomeria japonica *Japanese cedar*

This evergreen genus has only one species, *Cryptomeria japonica*, but many cultivars have been developed from it. *C. japonica* is a tall tree with a straight trunk grown as an ornamental in Europe and North America, and for timber in Japan. It is usually conical in shape. It has fine colour: the pointed, needle-like foliage is a bright blue-green, and the bark is red-brown and peels off in strips. In cold, frosty conditions, the hue of the foliage may change from fresh green to olive green, brown or almost purple, but the bright colouring quickly returns when the weather turns warmer. A dwarf Japanese cultivar, *C. j.* 'Yatsubusa', is often used for bonsai. It grows naturally in a narrow, conical shape, and its foliage is tight and compact in form.

Bonsai suggestions
Formal upright, clasped-to-rock, twin-trunk, clump, and group styles are all suitable. Dwarf forms are especially good for rock planting and saikei. *C. japonica* is best grown in medium to extra-large sizes, dwarf forms in extra-small to medium sizes.

Cryptomeria japonica **'Yatsubusa'**
DWARF JAPANESE CEDAR
After growing together in this design for four years, this group of 10- to 15-year-old trees has reached an overall height of 63cm (25in).

CULTIVATION

⬤ Position in full sun, slight shade in summer. Protect from frost and drying winds. Leaf colours may change in frost (*see left*).
◿ Water freely once a day, and mist-spray daily, throughout growing season. Water sparingly in winter.
◔ Feed fortnightly from spring through to late autumn.
▣ Repot every second year, in mid spring. For older trees, according to root development, every five years in mid spring. Use basic soil mix.
◩ Pinch back new shoots when about 12mm (½in) long, throughout growing season.
✂ Take softwood cuttings in summer.

Perspective effect
There are two groups in this design, with the smaller, more slender trees in the background lending an illusion of distance.

Slate slab
This natural material with its irregular outline provides a realistic landscape setting.

Cryptomeria japonica
'Yatsubusa', *leaf*
two-thirds life size

Fine-textured foliage
The foliage closely follows the
line of the trunk. In autumn, the
needles become a rich bronze.

Elaeagnus *Elaeagnus*

The elaeagnus family includes evergreen or deciduous shrubs and small trees; most grow quickly and are wind-resistant. They are native to Asia and North America, but are cultivated elsewhere. Some are deciduous, others evergreen. *Elaeagnus multiflora* makes a good bonsai, with deciduous leaves that are green above and silver underneath. The small, fragrant flowers, which bloom in spring, are followed in summer by blood-red, oblong fruit. The evergreen foliage of *E. pungens*, the thorny elaeagnus, is shiny green above, with white undersides speckled brown. It produces scented white flowers in autumn.

Bonsai suggestions
Informal upright, slanting, semicascade, and cascade styles are suitable for elaeagnus, in small to large sizes.

Leaf interest
The undersides of the leathery, bright green leaves are silvery, and some are finely speckled with brown.

*Elaeagnus
multiflora, leaf
one-third life size*

**Elaeagnus
multiflora**
ELAEAGNUS
A sturdy ten-year-old specimen, which has been trained from a young graft, is now 20cm (8in) high.

Upward growth
The tree has been styled only by pruning; the twig growth has a natural upward bias, making wiring unnecessary.

Blue, glazed pot
The colour of this cloud-shaped, Japanese Tokoname ware complements the tree's mass of bright foliage.

Euonymus *Euonymus*

These shrubs and small trees, known as spindles, grow on all continents except South America and Africa. They are very varied and may be evergreen or deciduous. The foliage and fruits of deciduous species provide a dazzling display of colour in autumn. The finest is *Euonymus alatus*, the winged spindle. Two species that make very attractive bonsai are *E. europaeus*, the European spindle, with striking scarlet seed pods, and the Japanese spindle, *E. sieboldianus*. Its pale green flowers turn into pinkish-white fruits with red seeds.

Bonsai suggestions

Euonymus trees and shrubs suit every bonsai style, except broom. They can be grown in all sizes.

CULTIVATION

◉ Position in full light with some sun. Protect small sizes in winter.

◌ Water daily in summer, less frequently in winter, but do not allow soil to dry out. Mist-spray leaves during growing season.

⦂ Feed every two weeks from late spring to late summer.

▣ Until the tree is ten years old, repot annually in early spring, then every two years, or when roots fill the pot. Use basic soil mix.

▨ In spring, trim new growth to two or three leaves. Repeat twice in the growing season. In autumn or early spring, prune old branches.

▥ Propagate by softwood cuttings in summer, hardwood cuttings in autumn. Layer in spring or summer.

Euonymus alatus, *leaf two-thirds life size*

Euonymus alatus
WINGED SPINDLE
Trees grown from three- to five-year-old cuttings form a group that stands 20cm (8in) high.

Compound leaves
The fresh green foliage becomes tinted with red in autumn.

Dainty group
This planting has been trained as a group for one year. Slender, angled trunks and crossing branches give a natural look.

Irregular bark
Corky, wing-like growths give the trunks an unevenly toothed outline.

White, glazed oval
This simple container sets off the pattern of dark trunks and brightly coloured foliage.

Fagus crenata *Japanese white beech*

The impressive beeches are deciduous trees that grow in the northern hemisphere. The tranquil air of a beech wood is often recreated in bonsai by grouping the plants in a forest planting. The russet-brown dead leaves of the Japanese white beech stay on the tree all winter, only falling when new buds force them off in spring. This beech has more pointed, smaller and narrower leaves than the European species (*see opposite*), and has a pale, slender trunk. It is customary to scrub the trunk whiter with water and an old toothbrush, but the lime-sulphur spray sometimes used in winter to kill pests will also bleach the bark almost white.

Bonsai suggestions

Formal and informal upright, slanting, twin-trunk, clump, and group styles are all suitable. Medium to extra-large sizes are preferable because of the leaf size.

CULTIVATION

◉ Position in full sun, but partial shade in summer. Protect young foliage from wind.

◌ Water daily throughout growing season. Foliage scorches easily, so on sunny days avoid water on leaves. Water sparingly in winter, but do not allow soil to dry out.

⁙ Feed fortnightly, from one month after leaves appear until late summer.

▣ Repot every second year in spring, until tree is ten years old, thereafter as necessary when roots fill pot. Use basic soil mix.

◩ Pinch back growing tips to two sets of leaves in spring. Remove large leaves only throughout growing season; total leaf cutting is not recommended.

☑ Sow fresh seeds in autumn, stratified seeds in spring.

Fagus crenata, *leaf one-third life size*

Fagus crenata
JAPANESE WHITE BEECH
This group of 15-year-old trees has an overall height of 75cm (30in).

Ribbed oval leaves
The foliage turns from fresh green to russet in autumn and is retained through the winter.

Closely planted groups
The design is made up of three groups of tightly planted trunks.

Colour contrast
The almost white bark of the mature tree contrasts well with the warm autumn leaf colour.

Oval, unglazed container
A shallow, rounded pot enhances the illusion of a natural landscape.

Fagus sylvatica *European beech*

The native European beech is a majestic tree with graceful, spreading branches. Its dense foliage turns from a fresh, light spring green through the darker green of summer to autumnal shades of russet and gold. It is widely grown as a timber and ornamental tree, and for hedging. Beeches are slow-growing: it takes a very long time for a single, large-trunked bonsai to develop, although the result will be hugely rewarding. Beeches are often grown as group plantings, because they look mature when only a few years old. The purple, weeping, and cut-leaf forms of *F. sylvatica* are best grown as single specimens.

Bonsai suggestions
Formal and informal upright, slanting, twin trunk, clump, and group are all good styles. Medium to extra-large bonsai sizes are best because of the largish leaves.

<table>
<tr><td colspan="2" align="center">CULTIVATION</td></tr>
</table>

■ Site in full sun, but shade from strong summer sun. Protect young foliage from wind.

◌ Water daily throughout growing season. In bright sun, do not let water fall on leaves as they will scorch. Water sparingly in winter, but keep soil moist always.

⁙ Feed every two weeks, from one month after leaves appear until late summer.

▦ Repot until tree is ten years old, every second year in spring, then as roots develop. Use basic soil mix.

▧ In spring, pinch back growing tips to two sets of leaves. Remove large leaves at any time during the growing season, but avoid extensive leaf cutting.

☑ Sow fresh seeds in autumn, stratified seeds in spring.

Fagus sylvatica,
leaf one-third life size

Shapely foliage
The silky textured, serrated, oval leaves are green in summer and take on golden tints in autumn.

Typical shape
The silhouette shows the characteristic, upright, spreading growth of a beech tree.

Fagus sylvatica
EUROPEAN BEECH
This handsome, informal upright has been trained as a bonsai for 20 years. It is 35 years old and 90cm (36in) tall.

Unglazed, oval pot
The warm Goma tones of this Japanese Tokoname ware complement the spring and summer greenery, and enhance the rich autumn foliage.

Ficus *Fig*

The figs are mostly tropical plants, growing wild in the south-east Asian jungles. Many hundreds of species make up this large tree family. *Ficus elastica*, the familiar rubber plant, is popular as a houseplant, but the smaller-leaved forms make better bonsai. In Europe and North America, the species grown most as bonsai are *F. benjamina*, the graceful weeping fig, and the upright *F. retusa*, or Banyan fig. In Australia, with its warmer climate, more species can be grown, such as *F. macrophylla*, *F. rubiginosa*, and *F. platypoda*.

Bonsai suggestions

Small-leaved forms are best as small-scale bonsai, although figs can be grown in all styles, except literati, and all sizes. The striking aerial roots of banyan types like *F. retusa* are often featured in clasped-to-rock styles.

CULTIVATION

◉ Tolerates low light. Protect from frost and draughts. Minimum 15°C (60°F). Avoid fluctuations in temperature and soil moisture.

◊ Water generously in summer. Keep moist otherwise, especially in low light (e.g. bonsai in normally lit room). Mist-spray for humidity.

⚘ Feed every two weeks in growing season.

▣ Repot every second year in spring. Use basic soil mix.

▧ Trim new shoots back to two or three leaves during growing season, unless you want extension growth. Leaf cut strong plants completely in summer. Cuts exude milky latex, so prune larger branches in winter; seal wounds with cut paste. Wire at any time, but remove if wire bites into stems, as they mark easily.

▣ Take softwood cuttings in summer. Air layering in spring.

Ficus retusa
BANYAN FIG
This 25-year-old, informal upright specimen is 75cm (30in) high.

Ficus retusa, leaf one-third life size

Evergreen leaves
A profusion of glossy foliage clothes the divided branches.

Complex root network
The heavy, aerial roots swathe the base of the trunk of this healthy, vigorous tree.

Powerful trunk
An interesting arrangement of branches, at varying angles, is supported by a weighty trunk.

Green, cloud-shaped pot
The design is balanced by the shape and dimensions of this glazed, Chinese container.

Fuchsia *Fuchsia*

Many people are intrigued by these shrubs with their wonderful flowers. Fuchsias are sub-tropical plants from South and Central America, although many can withstand a light frost. They are often grown as "standards": the stem is tied to a cane, and the side shoots are rubbed off to make a trunk. Then new shoots are trimmed and pinched to make a weeping head. You can create tree-like forms with the same technique. Fuchsias with small leaves and flowers are best for bonsai. Examples are *Fuchsia microphylla*, *F. × bacillaris*, and the cultivars 'Tom Thumb' and 'Lady Thumb'.

Bonsai suggestions

Grow fuchsias in informal upright, semi-cascade, cascade, slanting, and root-over-rock styles, and in extra-small to medium sizes.

CULTIVATION

◉ Site in full sun. Indoor fuchsias need a bright position. When they are grown outdoors, the minimum temperature required is 7°C (45°F).

◌ Water every day during growing season. In winter, keep soil barely moist, or allow it to dry out between waterings; mist-spray to maintain humidity.

⦂ Feed every two weeks throughout growing season.

▣ Repot once a year in early spring. Use basic soil mix.

▨ Constantly pinch out new shoots throughout growing season. Prune branches in winter.

▨ Take softwood cuttings in either spring or summer.

Fuchsia microphylla, *leaf two-thirds life size*

Fuchsia microphylla
DWARF FUCHSIA
This species is grown for its attractive structure rather than for floral interest. The eight-year-old tree is just 15cm (6in) high. It has been grown from a cutting in root-over-rock style.

Root-over-rock
The styling on rock effectively displays interesting shapes and textures in both trunk and roots.

Tree-like form
Tiny leaves and delicate twigs contribute to a realistic, tree-like appearance, even on this very small scale.

Japanese Tokoname oval container
The simplicity and shallowness of this brown, unglazed dish focuses attention on the attractiveness of the tree.

Gingko biloba *Maidenhair tree*

The gingko is grown as an ornamental tree all over the world. The Japanese plant it on sacred sites, often by Buddhist temples. As the tree matures, its open, upright branches take on a dense, columnar shape. In bonsai, pruning is the only way to encourage this fine 'flame-shaped' tendency. The gingko is one of the few deciduous conifers, and sole survivor of a tree family common in prehistoric times. Botanists long thought the tree extinct in the wild, until it was rediscovered in eastern China in the seventeenth century.

Bonsai suggestions
Informal upright and clump styles, and medium to extra-large sizes are best, because of the large leaves and coarse twigs.

CULTIVATION

⦿ Site in full sun, or slight shade for young trees. Protect from frost, especially the roots.
◌ Water daily throughout growing season: moisten soil thoroughly. Relatively dry in winter; wet roots are easily frost-damaged.
⦙ Feed every two weeks, spring to midsummer.
▦ Repot annually, in early spring, until ten years old; then every second year. Every three years for very mature trees. Use basic soil mix.
▨ Twice during growing season, trim new shoots to two or three leaves, leaving topmost leaf on outside. Prune branches after leaf fall. Avoid large, visible cuts, as they will not grow over. Avoid wiring: bark marks easily.
▧ Stratify seeds in autumn and sow in early spring. Hardwood cuttings in autumn. Air layering in spring.

***Gingko biloba**, leaf one-third life size*

Gingko biloba
MAIDENHAIR TREE
This 20-year-old formal upright tree is 75cm (30in) high.

Autumn foliage
The large, attractively shaped leaves change from green to this pale yellow in autumn.

Heavy trunk
The young tree was planted out for several years to build a sturdy trunk. It has been pot-grown for 12 years.

Unglazed ware
The width and depth of the Japanese Tokoname pot counterbalances the narrow, upright design.

Gleditsia triacanthos *Honey locust*

The honey locust is an elegant tree, with delicate, fern-like leaves that turn a pale yellow in autumn. Its seeds are enclosed in the long, brown pods characteristic of the pea family (*Leguminosae*) to which it belongs, and its branches are covered with distinctive three-pointed thorns. The honey locust originates in the central and eastern United States of America. It tolerates air pollution well, so the full-sized tree is often planted in cities. For the same reason, it also grows well as a bonsai in town gardens.

Bonsai suggestions
Informal upright, slanting, semicascade, cascade, or twin-trunk are suitable styles. The best sizes are small to medium.

CULTIVATION

◉ Position in full sun. Protect from frost in winter to avoid twig die-back.
◌ Water daily throughout growing season; sparingly in winter to keep soil evenly moist.
⊡ Feed every two weeks in growing season.
▣ Repot every other year in spring. Use basic soil mix.
▧ In winter, prune branches hard, or remove them completely back to the trunk: in spring, new shoots will appear readily from old wood. Summer pruning consists of shortening new shoots as they grow.
☒ Sow seeds in spring. Softwood cuttings in summer.

***Gleditsia triacanthos**, leaf two-thirds life size*

Fresh green leaves
The dainty, compound foliage gives a deceptively delicate appearance to the bonsai. The tree has, in fact, a strong, tolerant constitution.

Gleditsia triacanthos
HONEY LOCUST
This tree is six years old, styled as an informal upright, and 25cm (10in) high.

Creating the shape
The trunk was thickened by growing in open ground for four years. The tree has been potted for only a few months, and its shape will be further refined.

German "Schilf" pot
The glazed, round container by Petra Engelke balances the height and radial spread of this bonsai.

Ilex crenata *Japanese evergreen holly*

The hollies are native trees and shrubs of the northern hemisphere. *Ilex crenata* and *I. serrata* (*see opposite*) are both commonly called Japanese holly, although they do not look alike and have different growth habits. *I. crenata* is a slow-growing, evergreen shrub, with tiny white flowers and box-like leaves (*see p. 190*); female plants bear shiny black berries. Its small leaves and neater twigs make *I. crenata* much better for bonsai than *I. aquifolium*, the well-known European or English holly. Useful compact varieties to try growing are *I. c.* 'Convexa' and *I. c.* 'Stokes'.

Bonsai suggestions

Suitable for every style except broom, and extra-small to large sizes. You can feature the interesting roots that sometimes grow.

CULTIVATION

◉ Indifferent to sun or shade: extremely tolerant of shade, so sometimes used for indoor bonsai where low light would not suit other plants. Protect roots of outdoor bonsai from frost, and foliage from freezing winds.

◌ Water daily at least throughout summer, less frequently in winter. Mist-spray daily all summer unless in full sun.

⁙ Feed every two weeks in growing season.

▣ Repot every second spring. Use basic soil mix.

▧ To form a neat shape, clip young specimens constantly as if they were topiary. To train subsequently, remove surplus branches, and trim new shoots back to two or three leaves. Take care if you wire, because the stems are brittle.

▨ Take softwood cuttings in spring or summer; for fruiting trees, use material from female plants.

Ilex crenata 'Convexa'
JAPANESE EVERGREEN HOLLY
This 15-year-old, informal upright is 20cm (8in) high.

Ilex crenata 'Convexa', leaf two-thirds life size

Colour interest
Glossy, evergreen leaves provide year-round interest.

Textural complexity
Heavy, twisted roots, exposed above the soil, add to the interest of the design.

Asymmetrical shape
The long, low branches extending from the main angle of the trunk contribute to a triangular silhouette.

Green, glazed pot
This round pot with subtly shaded hues is by Petra Engelke.

Ilex serrata (I. sieboldii) *Japanese deciduous holly*

The narrow, serrated leaves of *Ilex serrata* look more like the leaves of a cherry or apple tree than those of the European holly, *I. aquifolium*, and make this Japanese native an excellent plant for bonsai. In autumn and winter, the greyish bark contrasts well with bright red berries and colourful leaves. To obtain berries, you must grow a female form, with a male (not necessarily bonsai) nearby for pollination. In Japan, the white-berried *I. s.* 'Leucocarpa' is sometimes used for bonsai; there is also a variety with yellow berries. The hermaphrodite *I. s.* 'Subtilis' ('Koshobai') is an ideal miniature for the smallest bonsai sizes.

Bonsai suggestions

The Japanese deciduous holly can be cultivated in every style of bonsai. It looks well in all sizes.

CULTIVATION

⦿ Position in sun or shade, but sun is best for good autumn colour and early ripening of berries. Protect from frost.

◌ Water daily throughout summer. Always keep soil moist so that fruits do not drop.

⁘ Feed every two weeks in growing season.

▣ Repot annually, in early spring, until tree is ten years old, then every second year. Use basic soil mix.

▧ In early summer, remove all unwanted new shoots while still tender. Trim other shoots to two or three leaves.

☑ Sow stratified seeds in early spring: most seedlings are male, and will not fruit. Softwood cuttings in spring or summer. Air layering in spring.

Ilex serrata,
leaf two-thirds
life size

Striking colours
The delicate, oval leaves turn from light green to shades of red and purple before they fall in autumn.

Ilex serrata
JAPANESE
DECIDUOUS HOLLY
This 15-year-old, informal upright is 45cm (18in) high.

Open-branch structure
The split trunk, attractively aged, supports a head of open branches which is particularly interesting in winter when adorned with bright red berries.

Blue, glazed ware
A Japanese Tokoname, cloud-shaped container balances the design of the tree.

Jasminum nudiflorum *Winter jasmine*

In the depths of winter, the bright yellow flowers of *Jasminum nudiflorum* stand out well against its arching, green, leafless branches. Whether the winter jasmine is grown as the familiar climbing shrub, or trained as a bonsai, its cheerful, star-shaped blossoms are very welcome. In spring and summer, narrow, dark green leaves cover the stems. The scale of both leaves and flowers makes this charming deciduous shrub especially suitable for cultivating as a bonsai.

Bonsai suggestions
Winter jasmine looks well in informal upright, slanting, semicascade, root-over-rock, clasped-to-rock, and clump styles. It can be grown in extra-small to medium sizes.

CULTIVATION

⦿ Site in sunny position, but shaded from full sun in summer. In winter, protect from hard frosts.

▣ Water daily in summer. Keep always moist.

⦿ Feed two or three times a month, from end of flowering until late summer.

▣ Repot annually, at any time of year if treated carefully, but preferably in autumn. Use basic soil mix.

▨ Flowers appear on previous year's wood. In late spring, prune new shoots to one set of leaves; prune branches again in autumn to three or four sets of leaves.

▣ Take softwood cuttings in summer, hardwood cuttings in autumn or winter. Air layering in summer.

Flowers before foliage
In winter, sunshine yellow flowers appear on bare branches and are soon followed by tiny, dark green leaves.

Jasminum nudiflorum, leaf two-thirds life size

Tree-like appearance
No wiring was needed to achieve this configuration of trunk and branches; it has been styled by pruning only.

Jasminum nudiflorum
WINTER JASMINE
This shrubby plant, grown as an informal upright bonsai, is ten years old and 17cm (7in) high.

Tokoname pot
This blue, glazed oval creates a striking colour contrast with the flowers.

Juniperus × media 'Blaauw' *Chinese juniper*

Two junipers, *Juniperus chinensis* and *J. sabina*, from north-east Asia hybridized naturally to form *J. × media*. From this cross, horticulturalists have developed many very different garden varieties. The foliage is often a mixture of juvenile, needle-like and adult, scale-like leaves: a difficult combination for an effective bonsai, so growers mostly use varieties or clones with mainly one or the other leaf type. *J. × m.* 'Blaauw' is a strong-growing conifer, with stems that splay upwards in a fan shape, and scale-like blue-green foliage. The shaggy, purple-brown bark enhances the tree by looking mature while still young.

Bonsai suggestions

Chinese junipers are suitable for every style of bonsai, except broom. The trees can be grown in all sizes.

CULTIVATION

⦿ Position in full light, but in partial shade in summer to protect foliage from scorch. Protect from hard frost.

⬙ Water daily throughout summer, and mist-spray. Keep moist in winter.

⬚ Feed every two weeks from beginning of the growing season until mid autumn.

▣ Repot every second year, preferably in early spring, until ten years old, then up to every five years as necessary (inspect roots annually). Use free-draining soil mix.

⬘ Throughout growing season, finger prune tips of new shoots for compact shape, but not too hard at any one time as this encourages juvenile, needle-like growth. Wire at any time.

⬕ Take softwood cuttings at any time.

Juniperus × media 'Blaauw'
CHINESE JUNIPER
This 20-year-old tree in root-connected, triple-trunk style, which displays many fine characteristics, measures 85cm (34in) in height.

Juniperus × media 'Blaauw', *leaf one-third life size*

Evergreen foliage
Fine, scale-like leaves contribute a rich texture to the design.

Extensive training
The three-trunk style was created from a multi-trunk tree by pruning and wiring to give horizontal branch spread. It has been grown as a bonsai for only four years.

Rectangular pot
The grey, unglazed, Japanese Tokoname ware complements the grey-green of the foliage.

Juniperus rigida *Needle juniper*

This small evergreen tree with graceful arching branches is a popular bonsai plant in its native Japan. The common name derives from its fine, needle-like leaves. If male and female trees are grown together during the flowering season, the female trees will produce green berries that will ripen over two years to purplish-black. Another attractive needle juniper is *J. communis*. It has pale needles, and the many cultivated varieties include prostrate and columnar forms. *J. communis* grows wild across Europe, North America, and Asia.

Bonsai suggestions

Needle junipers are suitable for training into every bonsai style, except broom, and can be grown in all sizes.

CULTIVATION

◉ Position in full sun. Protect from frost, or needles will turn brown.

◌ Throughout summer, water and mist-spray daily. Water sparingly in winter, but keep moist.

▨ Feed every two weeks, from beginning of spring to early autumn.

▣ Repot during growing season (ideally, early to mid spring) every second year until tree is ten years old, then every five years as roots develop. Use free-draining soil mix.

▨ Pinch out tops of new growth throughout growing season. Prune to allow light into lower and inner branches and prevent die-back. Wiring is best done in autumn and winter.

▧ Sow stratified seeds in spring. Softwood cuttings in summer.

Juniperus rigida,
leaf two-thirds life size

Juniperus rigida
NEEDLE JUNIPER
This 30-year-old, informal upright is 51cm (20in) high.

Decorative berries
Purplish-black, ripe berries contrast attractively with the spiky needles. This tree is shown in spring with the previous season's crop of fruit.

Prickly foliage
The full length of each branch is clothed with short, evergreen needles.

Wired shape
To create an open spread of branches, and to redistribute the masses of foliage, this tree has been wired.

Driftwood effect
To achieve this look, the tree was grown in open ground for several years, then severely pruned back and the trunk heavily sculpted.

Japanese Tokoname "drum" pot
The colour contrast of bark and foliage is echoed by a terracotta-coloured, unglazed pot with its design of glazed, green rivets.

Juniperus sargentii *Chinese* or *Sargent's juniper*

In its native Japan, this juniper grows as a semi-prostrate shrub in rocky mountainous and coastal areas. The adult, scale-like foliage is bright green, and the shaggy bark an attractive red-brown. You can bend the very flexible trunk and branches without causing any damage. Many fine bonsai specimens exist in Japan, some several generations old. A few of the finest have been trained from trees collected from the wild, and given a rugged and very ancient appearance by carving and bleaching the existing dead wood.

Bonsai suggestions
This juniper can be trained into every style of bonsai except broom. It is suitable for growing in all sizes.

CULTIVATION

◉ Keep in full sun, slight shade in summer. Protect from hard frosts (which discolour foliage).
◌ Water daily throughout growing season. Mist-spray in summer. Keep moist in winter, as freezing winds can dry out foliage.
⊡ Feed every two weeks, spring to mid autumn.
▣ With care at any time, but preferably in early spring; repot every second year until tree is ten years old, then every five years as roots develop. Use free-draining soil mix.
▨ Pinch back new shoots throughout growing season: over-hard pruning will encourage juvenile, needle-like growth. Wire at any time.
▤ Take softwood cuttings at any time.

Juniperus sargentii,
leaf two-thirds life size

Juniperus sargentii
CHINESE or SARGENT'S
JUNIPER
A 25-year-old tree, styled as an informal upright, gives an impression of massive height; it is really 75cm (30in) tall.

Cloud-like foliage
Repeated finger
pruning is needed to
achieve such masses of
finely textured foliage.

Informal shape
Wiring has been used to
develop the informal,
solid structure on which
the neat pads of foliage
are displayed.

Textural detail
The fluid line of the
trunk is enhanced by
the typical, flaky bark
which gives an aged
appearance.

Complementary pot
The red-brown,
Japanese Tokoname
oval was chosen to
highlight the warm
tones of the bark.

Lagerstroemia indica *Crape myrtle*

I n late summer, the crape myrtle produces a generous display of showy flowers in shades of white, pink, and mauve. This sub-tropical, tree-like shrub is native to China, Japan, and Korea, and a popular ornamental plant in Mediterranean countries and the southern USA. The flowers do not last very long, however, and for bonsai growers the decorative bark is equally attractive all year round. This peels away in strips, leaving a grey trunk patterned with pink and brown. It is at its best in winter when most other flowering bonsai are uninteresting.

Bonsai suggestions
Informal upright, slanting, semicascade, and root-over-rock styles suit crape myrtles, as do medium to extra-large sizes.

Lagerstroemia
indica
CRAPE MYRTLE
This 20-year-old tree is 51cm (20in) tall and has been grown in root-over-rock style.

CULTIVATION

◉ Site outdoors in summer in temperate areas in full sun. Cool but frost-free conditions in winter to allow leaf-drop and dormancy. Keep cool in early spring when daylight hours are short: warm temperatures and low light levels produce sappy, elongated growths.
◌ Water daily from spring to late autumn. Sparingly in winter, but keep moist.
⚬ Feed every two weeks in growing season.
▦ Repot in early spring. Use basic soil mix.
✎ In late spring, trim new growth to two or three leaves. Flowers will appear on the new shoots, so trim again in autumn after flowering.
✣ Sow seeds in spring. Take softwood cuttings in summer.

Lagerstroemia
indica, leaf one-third life size

Canopy of foliage
The spread of bright green leaves balances the depth created in the design by the rock planting.

Growing into shape
The lower trunk and heavy roots integrate well with the angular rock. In time, the upper trunk will thicken into a more subtle taper.

Decorative bark
With age, colourful, mottled patches develop on the bark.

Brown, unglazed pot
This deep, Japanese Tokoname oval provides a solid base, a foil for the imaginative design of the bonsai.

Larix decidua *European larch*

These tough, adaptable trees are highly recommended for beginners in bonsai. Larches grow naturally in the mountains and cooler parts of the northern hemisphere. The slender, upright, conical trees have gracefully drooping branches and foliage. They are among the few deciduous conifers, and their bright green, needle-like leaves turn golden in autumn before being shed. The elegant *Larix decidua*, the European larch native to southern and central parts of the continent, has pale, straw-coloured twigs. In older trees, the greyish bark develops an interesting pattern of cracks and ridges.

Bonsai suggestions
Members of the larch family are suitable for every style of bonsai, except broom. They can be grown in all sizes.

CULTIVATION

⦿ Site in full sun. Keep air cool and dry for compact needles. Protect smaller sizes from frost.
◌ Water daily throughout growing season. Sparingly in winter, but keep soil moist.
Feed every two weeks during growing season.
◼ Repot annually in early spring, before buds show green. Use basic soil mix. May need annual root pruning, as tree resents being pot-bound.
Pinch back new growth from side branches and trunk throughout growing season. In winter refine branches and twigs, prune to shape and wire, as necessary.
Sow seeds in late spring. Cuttings from leading shoots in late summer or early autumn. Layering in late spring or early summer.

Larix decidua,
leaf half life size

Larix decidua
EUROPEAN LARCH
This 24-year-old specimen was grown from seed and styled as a formal upright. It is now 30cm (12in) tall.

Deciduous foliage
In autumn, small, fine, needle-like leaves turn to straw colour before they drop.

Formal style
An even spread of horizontal branches is carried on a straight, gently tapering trunk.

Cracked and ridged bark
The bark's aged appearance has developed naturally over the life of the tree.

Oval container
The shade of the red-brown pot subtly enhances the tree's changing colours over the seasons.

Larix kaempferi (L. leptolepis) *Japanese larch*

This graceful conical tree has drooping branches, and reddish-orange new twigs that darken to almost purple by winter. This colouring is the main way of distinguishing between *Larix kaempferi* and *L. decidua* (*see p. 79*). As its common name suggests, *L. kaempferi* is a native of Japan, although planted extensively around the world. It grows more strongly and quickly than *L. decidua*, and so is often grown as a forestry tree. For the same reason, it is excellent as bonsai. These two trees are the larches most grown in Europe. *L. laricina*, the tamarack, is widely grown in Canada and the northern USA.

(*see p. 79*)

Bonsai suggestions

The Japanese larch can be grown in every bonsai style, except broom. It is suitable for all sizes of bonsai.

CULTIVATION

◉ Keep in full sun. Keep air cool and dry; larches do not grow very well in warmth or humidity. Protect smaller sizes from frost.
◌ Water daily throughout growing season. Sparingly in winter, but keep soil moist.
⚛ Feed every two weeks throughout growing season.
▦ Repot annually in early spring, before buds show green. Use basic soil mix. Larches grow strong roots and resent being pot-bound. Inspect roots every year to see if root pruning is needed.
▧ Pinch back new growth from side branches and trunk throughout growing season. In winter when branches are bare, refine branches and twigs, prune to shape, and wire if needed.
▨ Sow seeds in late spring. Cuttings from leading shoots in late summer or early autumn. Layering in late spring or early summer.

Larix kaempferi,
leaf two-thirds
life size

Larix kaempferi
JAPANESE LARCH
This 20-year-old tree, in slanting style, is 65cm (26in) high. It has been trained as a bonsai for ten years.

Clusters of foliage
Short needles are distributed evenly in dense masses over the spreading branches. In autumn, they fade to pale yellow.

Thickened trunk
This stout trunk and strong root buttress developed over several years in open ground, before being potted.

Unglazed, oval container
The wide, Japanese Tokoname pot balances the spread of the lower branches.

Lonicera *Honeysuckle*

The honeysuckles, natives of the northern hemisphere, display a great variety: deciduous and evergreen species, shrubby and climbing plants, many with fragrant flowers, and all worth trying to grow as bonsai. As long as you achieve a solid trunk, you can successfully train the softer, whippy branches to shape. *Lonicera nitida*, the dwarf shrubby honeysuckle often used in hedges, has tiny evergreen leaves that make it excellent for even the smallest bonsai. You can clip and shape it easily, transforming its floppy growth into dense pads of foliage.

Bonsai suggestions
Grow honeysuckles in every style, except broom, and in all sizes. Dwarf types are especially suitable for small sizes.

CULTIVATION
● Position in full sun, slight shade in summer. Protect small bonsai from frost, as well as those on slabs or in shallow pots.
◻ Water daily throughout growing season. Keep moist at all times, especially evergreens.
⬛ Feed every two weeks during summer.
▮ Repot every second year in late spring. Use basic soil mix.
▧ For dense growth, clip young plants constantly during growing season, almost as if they were topiary. Later, refine design with fine scissors. Carve old trunks in winter. Wire late spring or early summer.
▣ Take softwood or hardwood cuttings in spring or summer. Layering or air layering in summer.

Lonicera nitida,
leaf two-thirds life size

Lonicera nitida
DWARF HONEYSUCKLE
This informal upright is 25 years old and 65cm (26in) tall.

Tapering shape
An old hedging plant, grown as bonsai for five years, has been pruned and trained to create a tree with a clean, tapering trunk line.

Densely packed foliage
Tiny, evergreen leaves form attractive, massed foliage pads.

Glazed, oval pot by Gordon Duffet
The curving sides, subtle colour variations, and crackle glaze enhance the textural quality of this bonsai.

Malus *Crab apple*

Crab apples make delightful shrubs and small trees. Their spectacular spring blossom and colourful autumn fruits (mostly inedible) make them as popular with gardeners as with bonsai enthusiasts. Hall's crab apple, *Malus halliana*, has glossy green foliage. Its charming pink flowers give way to small, scattered, purple fruits. The lavish display of yellow crab apples on *M*. 'Golden Hornet' hang on the tree long after the leaves have fallen.

Many *Malus* varieties are very suited to bonsai. *M. cerasifera*, the Nagasaki crab apple, is very popular with bonsai growers because it bears flowers and fruits in profusion. The flower buds are pink, opening to white blossoms, and are followed by a mass of crimson, cherry-like fruits. The weeping cultivar *M*. 'Red Jade' is particularly beautiful, and *M*. 'Profusion' has attractive purple leaves, wine-red flowers, and deep red crab apples.

**Malus
cerasifera,**
*leaf one-third
life size*

Malus cerasifera
NAGASAKI CRAB
APPLE
This beautiful example
of an informal upright
was grown from a
graft. It is 12 years old
and 30cm (12in) high.

Bonsai suggestions
Informal upright, slanting, semicascade, twin-trunk, and clump are all good styles. Every size is suitable; for small bonsai, choose varieties with the smallest fruits.

Spring colour
*The fresh green foliage
of late spring sets off the
white flowers.*

Scented blossom
*Fragrant, white flowers
with prominent stamens
unfold from small, tight
pink buds.*

Rugged trunk
*Growing in open ground for some years
results in a weighty trunk. The shape
of the bonsai was formed by pruning.*

Large container
*A deep, unglazed pot holds
the reservoir of moisture
needed to encourage the
bonsai to fruit.*

CULTIVATION

◉ Keep in full sun all year. If grown in a shallow container, protect roots from frost.
◌ Water daily in growing season. Be very careful to keep moist when in fruit, or apples will shrivel and drop. Spray regularly against mildew.
⊞ Feed weekly from early spring until flowering. Resume feeding when fruits are well developed and continue until autumn.
▣ Repot annually in early spring, before bud burst. Use basic soil mix.
◩ Finger prune new shoots to one or two leaves in spring. Trim long shoots in autumn.
◪ Grafting is most common means of propagation. Seeds in late autumn. Layering in spring or early autumn.

Autumn interest
Leaves take on red tints in autumn and, as they fall, the main focus of interest becomes the bright fruits.

Malus halliana
HALL'S CRAB APPLE
This small, informal upright is six years old and just 12cm (5in) tall. Lichens and mosses give the bark a look of age. It has neat, oval leaves, tinted purple on their undersides, and deep pink buds that open to brighter pink flowers.

Twiggy structure
To maximize the production of flowers and fruit, a mass of twiggy branches was retained after pruning.

Malus cerasifera
NAGASAKI CRAB APPLE
An informal upright, 25 years old and 85cm (34in) high, demonstrates the autumn display of *M. cerasifera*. Comparison with the bonsai in full bloom (*opposite*) shows the range of seasonal attractions in this species.

Deep container
The depth of the pot allows enough moisture to be retained and swell the crop of berries.

Morus *Mulberry*

In nature, mulberries are small or medium trees that grow in twisted, picturesque shapes. The rough bark, heavy trunk, and serrated leaves offer bonsai growers a good combination of texture and shape. The flowers are not very noticeable, but the small edible fruits ripen from white to reddish-pink. The colour "mulberry" is named after their purple juice. For thousands of years the Chinese have grown mulberry trees for their leaves, which form the staple diet of silkworms. The Romans originally took the trees from their native Asia to Europe for the same purpose. Since then, mulberries have been widely grown as ornamental trees in parks and gardens.

Bonsai suggestions
Informal upright, slanting, semicascade, cascade, root-over-rock, twin-trunk, and clump styles, and all sizes are suitable.

Morus alba
WHITE MULBERRY
This 30-year-old, informal upright, which gives an impressive effect of age, stands 51cm (20in) high.

Decorative foliage
The mass of bright green, toothed leaves provides an attractive contrast to the gnarled bark.

Weighty base
A grey, unglazed, oval Japanese Tokoname pot forms a suitably strong base for the heavy trunk of the bonsai.

<table>
<tr><th colspan="2">CULTIVATION</th></tr>
</table>

◉ Position in full sun. Provide some frost protection in winter.

◿ Water daily throughout growing season. Keep soil damp all year: *Morus* love moisture.

⚬ Feed every two weeks from spring to summer. Change to high-potash fertilizer in late summer and continue to feed until autumn.

▣ Repot every second year in early spring. Use free-draining soil mix.

◩ Trim back new growth to two leaves. Remove large leaves as they appear. Prune heavy branches in winter or early spring before bud burst.

◪ Sow stratified seeds in spring. Cuttings in spring. Layering or air layering in summer.

***Morus alba**, leaf one fifth life size*

Movement in design
The excellent, tapering trunk creates a sense of movement and is anchored by the powerful root spread.

Murraya paniculata *Jasmine orange* or *Satinwood tree*

The first part of this tropical evergreen shrub's common name refers to its strongly fragrant, white, bell-shaped flowers, reminiscent of those of Jasmine (*see p. 198*). The rest of the name refers to its small, colourful berries, which look like tiny oranges. Jasmine orange is also sometimes called the satinwood tree, after the texture of its trunk. It is often grown as a bonsai in its native India and southern China, but because it needs warmth, you can grow it in temperate climates only as an indoor bonsai.

Bonsai suggestions
Informal upright, slanting, semicascade, cascade, twin-trunk, clump, and group styles, and all bonsai sizes are suitable.

Murraya paniculata
JASMINE ORANGE
An informal, upright specimen which, at 20 years old, has reached a height of 85cm (34in).

Satinwood tree
The pale, smooth bark, a feature of the species, is the origin of one of its common names.

Chinese container
The elegance of the tree is matched by that of the softly curving pot.

CULTIVATION

◉ Position in full sun, slight shade in hot summer sun. Indoors in temperate climates. Minimum temperature 17°C (63°F).
◌ Water daily during growing season. Keep slightly moist and humid at all times.
◈ Feed every two weeks from mid spring to early autumn, every four to six weeks all winter.
▬ Repot every second year in spring. Use basic soil mix.
✎ During growing season, trim new shoots to two leaves at any time after five or six leaves have been produced.
✂ Sow seeds in autumn. Softwood cuttings in spring or summer.

Murraya paniculata,
leaf one-sixth life size

Dainty leaves
The small leaflets of the evergreen, pinnate foliage give a delicate look to the bonsai.

Structural contrast
Strong roots form flowing ridges and hollows at the base, and highlight the upright line and clean taper of the trunk.

Picea *Spruce*

Members of the spruce family originate in the northern hemisphere. They are evergreen conifers and grow extremely fast. Japanese bonsai growers prefer *Picea glehnii*, the Sakhalin spruce, but it cannot be exported because of plant health regulations. *P. abies*, the common or Norway spruce from northern Europe, is used widely as a Christmas tree. It is conical in shape, the bark is red-brown, and the needles dark green. The dwarf *P. a.* 'Little Gem' is a very good subject for small bonsai and in rock plantings. Another dwarf spruce, *P. glehnii* 'Yatsubusa', is used in the same way in Japan, and is almost indistinguishable. *P. glauca albertiana* 'Conica', is native to the Rocky Mountains of Canada and is often cultivated in group plantings.

Bonsai suggestions

Spruces are suitable for every style, except broom. Dwarf cultivars are best grown in small sizes, others in medium to large sizes.

CULTIVATION

◉ Position in full sun. Protect small bonsai from frost.

◌ Water daily in summer, and mist-spray. Sparingly in winter; do not let soil dry out.

⁙ Feed fortnightly early spring to mid autumn.

▣ Repot every second year early to mid spring, before bud break, or in autumn; every five years once trees are more than ten years old. Use free-draining soil mix.

▧ During spring and summer, finger prune growth shoots 2.5cm (1in) long to two-thirds their length. Prune and wire branches in late autumn to winter.

▣ Sow stratified seeds in winter or early spring. Cuttings of current season's growth in late autumn or early spring.

Picea abies 'Little Gem'
DWARF SPRUCE

Tiny, ten-year-old trees, planted on rock, create a dramatic landscape. The tallest tree is 8cm (3in).

Picea abies,
'Little Gem',
*leaf two-thirds
life size*

Tree-like silhouettes
Thinning out the tight green "buns" of small needles has resulted in authentic-looking trees.

Rock shape
Arranging the trunks of the small trees to lead the eye through the design accentuates the striking profile of the overhanging rock.

Watery landscape
A grey-green suiban *(water tray) forms the pool surrounding a rugged piece of Ibigawa rock.*

Pinus mugo *Mountain pine*

In poor or harsh locations resembling its native Central European mountains, the tough mountain pine grows as a semi-prostrate, twisted, shrubby tree. Many gnarled old trees collected from the mountains of Switzerland and Austria have with time become superb bonsai. In better conditions, however, the mountain pine grows into a bushy small tree or large shrub. From this natural variety, horticulturalists have developed many dwarf and slow-growing clones. 'Gnom', a small, tight sphere of short, dark green needles, is popular. 'Mops' is similar in appearance, but slower-growing and more dwarf in size.

Bonsai suggestions
Pinus mugo is suitable for every style, except broom, and for all sizes. Grow dwarf forms in smaller sizes. They look very good in clasped-to-rock style.

Pinus mugo, leaf two-thirds life size

CULTIVATION

◉ Position in full sun. Protect from severe frost and freezing winds.

◌ Water daily throughout summer, unless soil is already moist. Mist-spray. Water sparingly in winter. Keep fairly dry.

⬚ Feed every three to four weeks, from spring to early winter.

▣ Repot every three to five years, early to mid spring or late summer. Use free-draining soil mix.

▨ Finger prune overgrown new shoots. Remove long primary shoots during growing season. Thin or remove old or crowded twigs and foliage in autumn or winter. A very flexible tree for wiring.

▣ For easy germination, in mid to late winter, soak fresh seed in water overnight; expose to frost after sowing. Graft dwarf forms.

Pairs of needles
The firm, upright needles, growing in pairs, give the bonsai its vigorous character.

Pinus mugo
MOUNTAIN PINE
The tree is 21 years old and 63 cm (25in) tall. It has been grown in slanting style.

Creating the shape
The stout trunk was developed over 14 years in open ground. Then the shape of the bonsai was formed by pruning and wiring in just five years.

Unglazed, rectangular pot
The shape of the pot balances the slanting line of the trunk.

Pinus parviflora (P. pentaphylla) *Japanese white pine*

The Japanese white pine is native to Japan, and often cultivated there both in gardens and as bonsai. It is also called the Japanese five-needled pine, because its twisted, bluish needles grow in bundles of five.

This medium-sized tree is conical when young, but as it grows older it becomes irregular in shape with a flat top. The bark is smooth and grey. In spring, the tree produces the clusters of little flowers suggested by its Latin name, which translates as "small-flowered pine". If the flowers are fertilized, they will develop into dark-brown cones that may hang on the tree for several years. However, bonsai growers usually remove the cones so that the tree does not expend all its energy in setting seed. Another reason is that cones spoil the visual effect of a bonsai since they are too large for the tree's small scale.

There are many cultivars, those most often seen being dwarf forms such as *P. p.* 'Kokonoe' and *P. p.* 'Nasamasume'. *P. parviflora* is often grafted on to the stronger rootstock of *P. thunbergii* (see p. 91).

Bonsai suggestions
Pinus parviflora is suitable for every style of bonsai, except broom, and for all sizes. Smaller sizes and clasped-to-rock style are particularly good for dwarf forms.

***Pinus parviflora**, leaf one-third life size*

Striped foliage
The needles grow in bunches of five and have white stripes on the undersides.

Pinus parviflora
JAPANESE WHITE PINE
This informal upright, 50 years old and 75cm (30in) tall, was field-grown for some years to thicken the trunk.

Rugged bark
This bonsai was grafted on a lower trunk of Japanese black pine (P. thunbergii) to provide rugged bark and strong roots.

Rectangular container
The unglazed, Japanese Tokoname pot complements the pleasing symmetry of the tree's silhouette.

CULTIVATION

⦿ Position in full sun. Protect from frost and cold winds.

◌ Water daily, and mist-spray, during summer, unless soil is already moist. Sparingly in winter. Keep almost dry.

⦿ Feed every three or four weeks, from spring to early winter.

▣ Repot every two to five years, in early to mid spring, depending on age and root development. Use free-draining soil mix.

◪ Pinch off one-third to half of new shoots each spring. Every other year, prune branch tips in early autumn. To allow light into tree, remove old needles in late summer or early autumn.

◪ Germination is reliable if seeds are fresh. In winter, soak seeds overnight in water, discard any that float, and sow the rest. Expose outside to frosts, but protect from rodents or birds. Graft late winter or early spring.

Pinus parviflora **'Kokonoe'** DWARF JAPANESE WHITE PINE Close-growing, tiny needles make this form suitable for a smaller bonsai. It will take several more seasons for the foliage masses to fill out in this 12-year-old, 35cm (14in) high tree.

Pinus parviflora **'Miyajima'** DWARF JAPANESE WHITE PINE The dwarf cultivars are perfectly suited to growing on rock. The four-year-old trees in this planting are just 8cm (3in).

Integrated design
A certain amount of wire training on the small trees encourages them to follow the natural lines of the rock.

Water tray
The bonsai material is planted on Ibigawa rock, displayed in a grey-green, unglazed, Japanese Tokoname suiban, or tray.

Pinus sylvestris *Scots pine*

In the wild, a Scots pine matures naturally into the same style as a bonsai literati, with branches spreading horizontally below its flattened apex. The tree was not used as often in bonsai as Japanese pines (*see pp. 88–9 and opposite*) in the past, perhaps because its conical shape when young is not inspiring. British growers have recently found that Scots pines, especially the many dwarf forms with smaller needles, make fine bonsai.

Bonsai suggestions

Scots pines grow well in every style except broom, although they are exceptionally fine as literati. All sizes are good, but smaller sizes are most suitable for dwarf forms.

***Pinus sylvestris* 'Beuvronensis',** *leaf one-third life size*

***Pinus sylvestris* 'Beuvronensis'** DWARF SCOTS PINE This tree, which is 28 years old and measures 99cm (39in) high, has been grown in literati style.

Sturdy base
The brown, unglazed, incurved, round pot directs the eye to the vertical trunk.

Compact masses
Neat clusters of short, blue-green needles make this tree an excellent subject for bonsai.

Wired branches
The tree has been in bonsai training for one year and, to redirect previously upward growth, the branches have been extensively wired.

Sinuous line
The naturally graceful line of the trunk lends itself to literati style. Flaking orange bark clothes the branches and upper trunk.

Pinus thunbergii *Japanese black pine*

Growing wild in its native Japan, the black pine is able to survive on poor, stony soil. This tolerance, and its craggy appearance, is the reason why its rootstock is often used when grafting the softer-looking *Pinus parviflora*, the Japanese white pine (*see pp. 88–9*). Pines are among the favourite plants of bonsai growers, and the Japanese black and white pines are some of the most popular. *P. thunbergii* is a popular ornamental in parks and gardens, where this impressive tree is still pruned and groomed like a bonsai.

Bonsai suggestions
Literati style emphasizes the rugged bark, but every style except broom is suitable. Black pines can be grown in all sizes. Use dwarf forms for small rock plantings.

CULTIVATION

◉ Position in full sun. Protect from frost and cold winds.

◌ Check daily: water only if soil is drying out, freely if free-draining. Very sparingly in winter.

⚬ Feed every three to four weeks, from spring to early winter.

▣ Repot every two to five years, in early to mid spring, as needed. Use free-draining soil mix.

▨ As needles appear, pinch back overgrown shoots. In growing season, remove long main shoots, trim one-third to half of new candles on smaller shoots. Prune branch tips every other year. In late summer or early autumn, remove old needles and crowded twigs to let in light.

▣ In winter, soak fresh seeds overnight; sow only those that sink – leave exposed to frosts, protect from rodents and birds. Graft cultivars in late winter or early spring.

Pinus thunbergii,
leaf one-third life size

Vigorous character
The stiff, upright growth of the bright green needles grouped in pairs contributes to the tree's strong design.

Pinus thunbergii
JAPANESE BLACK PINE
This tree, grown in literati style, is 35 years old and stands 70cm (28in) high.

Trunk interest
Literati styling reinforces the sense of movement in the trunk and draws attention to the rugged texture of its bark.

Unglazed, red-brown pot
The shape of this container by Gordon Duffet echoes the curves of the trunk.

Prunus mume *Japanese flowering apricot*

Most of the extensive *Prunus* family are natives of Japan and the Far East, but some grow in temperate countries right across the northern hemisphere. Many of these trees and shrubs produce luscious stoned fruit (plums, peaches, apricots, and cherries), but their delicate blossoms are overshadowed by the spectacular blooms of the huge range of ornamental species. For hundreds of years, the Japanese have grown *Prunus mume* for the wonderfully fragrant flowers which clothe its bare branches in late winter. Few of its many cultivars, however, are seen in the West. A common European hedgerow plant, *P. spinosa*, the blackthorn or sloe, with delicate white blossoms, is a good alternative to *P. mume*.

Bonsai suggestions
Prunus trees and shrubs are suitable for every style of bonsai, except formal upright or broom. You can grow them in all sizes.

Prunus mume,
leaf one-third life size

Prunus mume
JAPANESE
FLOWERING
APRICOT
This unusually dramatic, 30-year-old tree is 40cm (16in) tall.

CULTIVATION

◉ Position in full sun. Protect from frost to avoid twig die-back and damage to flowers.
◌ Water daily throughout growing season. To avoid bud and flower drop, keep moist from the time flower buds begin to swell. Water sparingly in winter.
⊞ Feed at least every two weeks in summer, increasing amount and frequency if needed: heavy summer feeding makes more flowers in winter. Amount of feed depends on soil type and amount of water.
▣ Repot annually in late winter, as soon as flowering has ceased. Use basic soil mix.
▧ Trim back hard after flowering. Allow rampant growth in summer; trim resulting shoots back again in autumn.
▣ Take hardwood cuttings in late winter. Layer in summer. Graft in winter or spring.

Fragrant flowers
In late winter, the bare branches carry scented pink and white blossoms.

Sculpted form
A gnarled trunk, shaped by carving into a look of clasped-to-rock style, forms a solid base for the low branch trained as a semicascade.

Brown, unglazed pot
The clean, rectangular lines of the pot offset the complex textures of the bonsai.

Prunus spinosa
SLOE

The sloe is much appreciated in bonsai for its fine twigs, small leaves, and delicate, white, spring flowers. It is similar in character to *P. mume* and can be grown as an alternative where it is more readily available. This specimen is ten years old, has been styled over one year by carving and pruning, and stands 53cm (21in) tall.

Flowers before leaves
*Red blossoms appear
before the leaf buds.
Their fragrance
will fill a room.*

Prunus mume
JAPANESE FLOWERING APRICOT

This slender tree has a very different mood from that of the carved specimen (*opposite*). It has been styled as an informal upright, is 30 years old, and 75cm (30in) tall.

Delicate branches
*This grafted plant was grown
in the ground for a number
of years to thicken the trunk.
Because the branches are
brittle, they have been carefully
wired to avoid cracking.*

Simple, round container
*The solid, brown, unglazed,
Japanese Tokoname pot has
a clean elegance.*

Prunus serrulata *Flowering cherry*

Flowering cherries are some of the loveliest ornamental trees when massed with spectacular blossoms in white or shades of pink and carmine. Sadly, this magnificent display is compressed into only a few spring days; for the rest of the year, most of the hundreds of hybrids offer little to tempt the bonsai grower, except, occasionally, some coloured autumn foliage. A few, however, such as *P. serrulata* 'Kanzan', produce such glorious flowers that they are worth growing despite their coarse twigs and leaves. *P. subhirtella* 'Autumnalis' is another exception. It has delicate twigs, its small leaves colour well in autumn and, during frost-free periods in winter, clusters of white or pale pink flowers appear on the bare branches.

CULTIVATION

◉ Site in full sun. Protect from frost. From late winter to early spring, protect swelling flower buds from birds. Shield open flowers from heavy rain which can spoil them.

◌ Water daily in growing season: do not drop water on to open flowers, as it spoils the petals. Sparingly in winter, but do not allow to dry out.

⦂ Feed every two weeks, from end of flowering until late summer.

▣ Repot annually, in late spring before bud burst, or in late autumn. Use basic soil mix.

▧ Trim back after flowering. Prune tips of new shoots as they grow in summer. Prune branches in winter where necessary.

⌇ Propagate by grafting in early spring.

Bonsai suggestions
Flowering cherries can be grown in every style of bonsai, except broom, and in all sizes.

Prunus serrulata
'Kiku-shidare Sakura'
JAPANESE FLOWERING CHERRY
This young tree, propagated by air layering, is just 10cm (4in) high, but the semicascade style shows how effective this species can be as a bonsai.

Simple structure
The clean line of the single trunk is the perfect foil for showing off the heavy clusters of flowers.

Early blossom
The double, pink flowers appear in early spring before the leaves, and completely clothe the bare branches.

Biscuit-coloured pot
The square, glazed, Japanese Tokoname pot has the weight and depth needed to offset the sharp angle of the semicascade.

Prunus serrulata
'Kiku-shidare Sakura',
leaf one-third life size

Punica granatum *Pomegranate*

The pomegranate is happiest growing in warmth similar to that in its native Asia and the Mediterranean. In temperate climates, it seldom produces fruit, except in abnormally hot summers. The round, edible fruits are yellow flushed red, with a leathery outside, succulent pulp, and black seeds. This broad-leaved, deciduous tree is also grown for its single or double flowers, which are usually a brilliant scarlet, although some varieties produce white, pink, or yellow blooms.

Bonsai suggestions

Train pomegranates into any style, except formal upright and broom. Sizes range from small to extra-large; extra-small and small sizes are best for dwarf forms.

Punica granatum,
leaf one-third life size

Punica granatum
POMEGRANATE
This handsome specimen, grown as an informal upright, is 30 years old and 53cm (21in) tall.

CULTIVATION
● Position in full sun. Protect from low temperatures and frost: tree is not fully hardy.
◌ Water daily during growing season; generously after flowering to help fruits to swell. Keep moist during winter.
⣀ Feed weekly from start of growing season until flowering begins.
▣ Repot every second year, in early spring until ten years old, then as needed. Use basic soil mix.
⬚ During growing season, trim back new shoots to two sets of leaves when three to four sets have grown. Do not trim shorter, round-tipped shoots, as they will carry flowers. Thin unwanted bushy growth during growing season.
⬚ Sow stratified seeds in spring. Softwood cuttings in midsummer.

Attractive foliage
Glossy, bright green leaves, carried on reddish stalks, create an interesting display during the growing season.

Slender branches
A twisted trunk, thickened by some years' growth in open ground, supports an elegant spread of branches.

Colour interest
A blue, glazed, Japanese Tokoname, cloud-shaped pot brings additional colour to the design.

Pyracantha *Pyracantha or Firethorn*

The common name of firethorn aptly describes the dense clusters of brilliant red, orange or yellow berries borne in autumn on the pyracantha's wickedly spiky stems. Masses of tiny white flowers, and evergreen, oval leaves make this popular shrub as decorative as a bonsai as in the garden. Pyracantha makes a good starter bonsai: its naturally shrubby nature can easily be styled into a single trunk. *Pyracantha angustifolia*, *P. coccinea*, and their many cultivars and hybrids are often used. A valuable dwarf is *P. c.* 'Teton', with yellow-orange berries and small, vivid green leaves.

Bonsai suggestions
Informal upright, slanting, semicascade, cascade, root-over-rock, clasped-to-rock, twin-trunk, and clump are good styles. All sizes are suitable, except extra-large.

CULTIVATION

● Position in full light or partial shade. Protect from frost and freezing winds, especially tropical species imported into temperate areas.

◊ Water daily during growing season. Keep moist at all times.

⁂ Feed weekly in early spring until flowering. When the fruit has developed, feed every two weeks to mid autumn.

▣ Repot every second year in early spring. Use basic soil mix.

◨ In late spring, trim new shoots to two sets of leaves; prune older wood in early spring or late summer. Remove large leaves during growing season. Wire carefully: old woody branches are very brittle.

☒ Sow seeds in autumn or winter. Cuttings of current season's growth at any time. Air layering or layering from spring to early summer.

Pyracantha angustifolia
PYRACANTHA or FIRETHORN
This specimen is eight years old and 25cm (10in) tall. It is grown in semicascade style.

Pyracantha angustifolia, *leaf one-third life size*

Seasonal interest
Bright green, oval leaves act as a foil for the decorative spring flowers and autumn fruit.

Tall container
The greyish, unglazed, Japanese Tokoname, semicascade pot has the necessary height to allow for the full sweep of the lower branch.

Early training
While it was still young and supple, the plant was pot-grown and wired to shape.

Quercus robur *English oak*

The traditional old oak tree of England can live for many centuries, some reaching 800 years old or even more. As the tree matures, its trunk thickens to an impressive girth, the heavy branches splay out, and the crown broadens. Bonsai should also display this same structure. The lobed, deciduous leaves gradually change colour, from a fresh light green in spring, through the darker greens of summer, to a rich bronze-gold in autumn. The seeds are the familiar acorns. This broad-leaved tree is the more common of the two native British oaks. It grows also in Europe, North Africa, and south-west Asia.

Bonsai suggestions
Grow English oaks in informal upright, slanting, broom, twin-trunk, clump, straight line, sinuous, or group styles, and in medium to extra-large sizes.

CULTIVATION

◉ Position in full sun. Protect from frost.
◯ Water daily during growing season. Sparingly in winter, but keep moist. Spray regularly against mildew: oaks are very vulnerable to the disease.
⦿ Feed every two weeks throughout summer and autumn.
▣ Repot annually until tree is ten years old; then every two to three years, in early spring before bud break. Use basic soil mix.
▧ Trim new shoots continually to one or two pairs of leaves.
⛏ Sow fresh acorns in autumn; if you protect them from attack by rodents, one hundred per cent should germinate successfully in spring. Air layering in summer.

Quercus robur,
leaf one-third life size

Small-sized foliage
Due to careful pruning and cultivation, the typical, lobed, bright green leaves have reduced in size.

Quercus robur
ENGLISH OAK
This impressive, award-winning, informal upright has been trained as a bonsai for a mere five years. It is 60 years old and measures 70cm (28in) high.

Natural look
The rugged solidity of this bonsai creates an impression of a majestic oak in nature.

Unglazed pot
This simple Japanese Tokoname rectangle with rounded corners gives weight to the design.

Rhododendron *Azalea*

Members of the huge *Rhododendron* family are the most flamboyant of flowering shrubs, producing masses of bright flowers in late spring. Many originate from Japan, where these plants have been propagated and hybridized since the 1600s. The hundreds of species and thousands of cultivars are usually classified as either evergreen rhododendrons, or azaleas (which can be deciduous or evergreen); botanically, however, azaleas and rhododendrons are the same. The second most popular group for bonsai are the Kurume azaleas, most deriving from *Rhododendron kiusianum*. Most popular of all as bonsai are the evergreen Satsuki azaleas: many Japanese enthusiasts grow nothing else. Unusually, Satsuki azaleas flower in midsummer.

CULTIVATION

◉ Position in partial shade. Protect from frost, and from heavy rain when in flower.
◌ Water at least once a day in growing season, and mist-spray. Use lime-free water: rainwater is ideal. Keep soil moist at all times: the fine, fibrous roots soon become desiccated in dry soil.
⊡ Feed every two weeks from early spring until flowering; monthly from end of flowering until early autumn. Use ericaceous fertilizer.
▣ After flowers have withered, repot annually or as necessary when roots fill pot. Use lime-free soil mix: all rhododendrons need acid soil.
▧ Remove flowers as soon as they fade. Remove all new shoots after flowering. Prune secondary shoots more lightly until midsummer.
▨ Take softwood cuttings in early summer. Air layering in early summer.

Bonsai suggestions

All styles, except broom; all sizes are suitable, although small-leaved and small-flowered varieties are better in smaller sizes.

Brilliant pink flowers
The colourful blooms are massed on the branches, obscuring the sparser growth of foliage.

Rhododendron obtusum
JAPANESE KURUME AZALEA
This multiple-trunk specimen represents the range of visual interest offered by Kurume azaleas very well. It is 30 years old and 40cm (16in) in height.

Creating the design
A shrub's discarded stump grew freely for two years, was potted, and its new growth pruned and wired to shape.

Compact base
A smooth, grey, unglazed container draws the eye towards the complex root system.

Rhododendron indicum 'Hakurei'

SATSUKI AZALEA 'HAKUREI'
The cascade style of this 20-year-old, evergreen azalea, which is 25cm (10in) high with a spread of 90cm (36in), perfectly displays the delicacy of the creamy buds, white, starry flowers, and slender, dark green leaves.'

Evergreen leaves
In midsummer, the oval leaves are almost obscured by the spectacular flowers.

Large blooms
The individual blossoms are comparatively large for bonsai, but the effect depends on the mass of so many flowers.

Rhododendron indicum 'Kaho'

SATSUKI AZALEA 'KAHO'
This informal upright is 25 years old and 50cm (20in) tall. It is shown in its spectacular phase when flowers cover the branches.

***Rhododendron indicum* 'Kaho',**
leaf two-thirds life size

Wide silhouette
The low, spreading canopy of branches is supported by a sturdy trunk.

Grey, unglazed oval
The simple container acts as a foil for the showy bonsai.

Sageretia theezans *Sageretia*

Sageretias must have warmth, so in cooler temperate countries they are grown as indoor bonsai. These tender shrubs originate in the warmer parts of North America, as well as central and southern Asia. The species most usually trained as bonsai is *Sageretia theezans* from southern China. Its trunk is adorned with a fascinating patchy effect, like that of an old trident maple or a plane tree, which is caused by the peeling of its rough, brown bark. The branches are slender and occasionally thorny, the leaves small, evergreen, and shiny. In the summer, the plant produces small, white flowers, and these give way to blue berries.

Bonsai suggestions
Sageretias are popular indoor bonsai suitable for growing in all styles. They also look good in every size.

CULTIVATION

◉ Position in full sun, slight shade in summer. Minimum temperature in summer 18°C (65°F), in winter 12°C (54°F), with high humidity. Indoor bonsai need to be well lit all year, but shaded from scorching summer sun.

◯ Water daily throughout summer. Keep soil continually moist: check indoor bonsai daily. High humidity is essential.

⚎ Feed every two weeks throughout summer, monthly in winter.

▣ Repot every second year in spring. Use basic soil mix.

◩ Trim new shoots to one or two pairs of leaves during growing season.

▤ Propagate from softwood cuttings in spring or in summer.

Sageretia theezans, leaf one-third life size

Sageretia theezans
SAGERETIA
This species is popular as an indoor bonsai for its attractive bark and foliage. This tree, grown in slanting style, is 35 years old and 63cm (25in) high.

Mid green foliage
The rounded masses of glossy, oval leaves have been formed by regular clipping of the tree.

Textured trunk
Peeling bark provides a range of colour along the beautifully patterned trunk.

Chinese container
This rectangular, blue, glazed pot adds subtle colour and shape to the design.

Salix *Willow*

The graceful shrubs and small trees in the large willow family may be upright or twisted, or pendent like the popular *Salix babylonica*, the weeping willow. This strikingly lovely tree from China often grows by water, over which its narrow leaves droop and sway on an elegant curtain of branches: like all willows, it loves moisture. Several varieties bear smaller leaves, and one has golden foliage. All are very good as bonsai. Willows grow in cool and temperate parts of the world. The colours of their foliage and bark vary, and in spring they produce beautiful catkins. Many grow very vigorously.

Bonsai suggestions
Willows are suitable for informal upright, slanting, semicascade, cascade, twin-trunk, root-over-rock, and saikei styles. Grow them in medium to extra-large sizes.

CULTIVATION

◉ Site in full sun, slight shade in hot sun. Protect from severe frost to avoid twig die-back.
◔ Water daily throughout growing season, more often in hot weather as needed. This is one of the few bonsai that benefits from standing in shallow water in midsummer. Reduce rate of watering in winter, but do not allow soil to dry out at any time.
◖◗ Feed every two weeks from early spring to late summer.
▣ Repotting twice a year, in early spring and at midsummer, may be necessary for this fast-growing tree. Use basic soil mix.
▨ Trim previous year's growth to one or two buds in early spring after repotting.
▣ Take softwood or hardwood cuttings at any time: even wrist-thick branches will root easily in moist sand.

Salix babylonica, leaf one-sixth life size

Salix babylonica
WEEPING WILLOW
This graceful species lends itself to an atmospheric design, demonstrated here by a pair of trees grown over water in slanting style. They are 15 years old and the larger is 35cm (14in) high.

Attractive canopy
The fine, strap-like, fresh green foliage is borne on golden shoots.

Weeping habit
Twice a year, branches are cut back to encourage a refined, weeping habit and delicate shoots.

"Saikei style" ware
A brown, unglazed pot, with glazed reservoir, provides a naturalistic setting for the bonsai.

Sequoiadendron giganteum *Wellingtonia*

The world's largest living thing is a Wellingtonia, or "big tree", in California. Called General Sherman, this famous tree is 83 metres (272ft) tall and 24 metres (79ft) around the trunk. The oldest known tree of this species was 3,200 years old when felled. With all these superlatives, this monumental evergreen conifer is a real challenge to a bonsai grower, although there are always some prepared to try. The Wellingtonia grows very fast, so needs constant finger pruning. Wiring is essential to maintain a bonsai in a good shape.

Bonsai suggestions

Wellingtonias can be grown in formal upright, twin-trunk, or group styles. They are suitable for medium to extra-large sizes.

Sequoiadendron giganteum, leaf two-fifths life size

Sequoiadendron giganteum
WELLINGTONIA
This 20-year-old specimen is 90cm (36in) tall and styled as a formal upright.

Graceful shape
The evergreen, scale-like foliage fills out an elegant, conical outline.

Upright style
The tall, straight trunk and even spread of branches mirror perfectly the way the tree grows in nature.

Rectangular container
This blue, unglazed pot is Japanese Tokoname ware.

Serissa foetida *Tree of a thousand stars*

The masses of white, star-like flowers, which bloom in summer, give this evergreen shrub its common name, while the unpleasant odour of its roots and bark amply justify its botanical name of *Serissa foetida*. Native to sub-tropical areas of India, China, and Japan, the plant can be grown as an indoor bonsai in temperate areas of the world. It produces small, smooth, green leaves, and the white flowers can be either single or double. There is a form with purple flowers, as well as one with variegated leaves.

Bonsai suggestions
Serissa foetida is suitable for every bonsai style, except formal upright and broom. Grow it in extra-small to medium sizes.

Variegated foliage
The green and pale yellow variegation of the small, oval leaves lightens the dense canopy of foliage.

Serissa foetida 'Variegata', *leaf two-thirds life size*

Serissa foetida 'Variegata'
TREE OF A THOUSAND STARS
This delightful specimen is six years old and 15cm (6in) high, and grown as an informal upright.

Clipped to shape
This tree has an interesting natural growth pattern, so the only training necessary is clipping, to create a pleasing shape and to encourage it to flower.

Brown, glazed pot
The deep, rectangular shape gives drama to this little tree.

Sorbus aucuparia *Rowan* or *Mountain ash*

The mountain ash is an excellent decorative tree for the garden all year round. In spring, it is covered with masses of small, creamy flowers. The delicate compound leaves are a lovely fresh green throughout the growing season. In autumn, these turn brilliant shades of orange and gold, making a striking backdrop to the clusters of bright red berries. This popular small tree is probably the most familiar of the *Sorbus* family, which includes a number of deciduous trees and shrubs that are extremely attractive. Their graceful pinnate leaves and slender, upright shapes make them particularly good as bonsai.

Bonsai suggestions

Sorbus trees are suitable for every style of bonsai, except formal upright and broom, and for all sizes.

CULTIVATION

◉ Position in full sun. The tree is particularly hardy and frost-resistant, so no winter protection should be necessary.

◔ Water daily throughout growing season. In winter, water only sparingly but do not allow soil to dry out.

⠿ Feed every two weeks in growing season.

▣ Repot annually or every second year, in spring before bud burst. Use basic soil mix.

◩ Trim new shoots to one or two leaves continually to create and maintain shape, except where extension growth is needed to develop the overall shape.

◪ Stratify seeds and sow them in late winter or in early spring. Graft named cultivars on to common stock.

Graceful foliage

The compound leaves of serrated leaflets adapt well to the scale of a bonsai tree.

Sorbus aucuparia, leaf one-fifth life size

Sorbus aucuparia
ROWAN or
MOUNTAIN ASH
This eight-year-old tree, which has been styled as an informal upright, is 25cm (10in) tall.

Elegant contrast

The structure of fine twigs contrasts attractively with a sturdy trunk, developed during six years' growth in open ground.

Drum-shaped container

The bonsai's spreading crown is balanced by the sturdiness of the round, Japanese Tokoname pot.

Stewartia *Stewartia*

The small family of deciduous *Stewartia* shrubs are close relatives of camellias and have the same need for acid, lime-free soil. Stewartias are natives of Japan. Over the past few years, they have been increasingly used for bonsai, partly because of the delicate, small twigs and the shiny, copper bark that make the shrubs attractive even when leafless in winter. Their other main attraction as bonsai is the spectacular scarlet and purple of their autumn leaves. The two species usually chosen for bonsai are *Stewartia pseudocamellia* and the compact dwarf *S. monodelpha*.

Bonsai suggestions
Stewartias can be grown in formal upright or group styles. They are suitable for small to medium sizes.

CULTIVATION

⬤ Position in full sun in autumn to enhance leaf colour, place in partial shade in summer. Protect from frost.

◌ Water daily during growing season, using lime-free (soft) water: rain water is ideal. Do not allow soil to dry out: Stewartias resent drying out, like other thin-leaved plants, and lack of moisture causes leaves to shrivel.

⦙ Feed every two weeks during growing season. Use only ericaceous fertilizer.

▣ Repot every second year in early spring. Use lime-free soil mix.

▧ Trim new growth to one or two leaves continually to create and maintain shape, except where extension growth is needed to develop overall shape. Wire with great care: the soft bark is easily marked.

▣ Sow seeds in winter or spring. Softwood cuttings in summer.

Stewartia monodelpha
STEWARTIA
These trees are ten years old and have been grown together for two years. The overall height is 50cm (20in).

Foliage colour
In autumn, the fresh green leaves turn red and purple.

Winter interest
The coppery bark of the numerous, slender trunks and fine twigs make an attractive feature after the leaves have fallen.

Naturalistic base
A handmade, unglazed, ceramic slab, by Petra Engelke, adds to the illusion of a natural, open landscape.

Stewartia monodelpha, *leaf one-fifth life size*

Tamarix *Tamarisk*

Tamarisks grow wild from western Europe to China, but the Mediterranean countries are home to most of the cultivated varieties. Despite their apparent fragility, these shrubs are extremely tough and wind-resistant, and are often planted on the coast as shelter belts and hedges. They are excellent for bonsai: the deciduous leaves are small and scale-like, the branches slim and feathery, and the dainty pinkish-brown or purple flowers appear in great profusion in spring and summer.

Bonsai suggestions

Grow tamarisks in informal upright, slanting, semicascade, cascade, twin-trunk, clump, root-over-rock, or clasped-to-rock styles. They are suitable for small to large sizes.

Tamarix juniperina
TAMARISK
This tree, a dramatic, informal upright, is 40 years old and 85cm (34in) tall.

Tamarix juniperina, *leaf one-fifth life size*

Sculpted shape
This bonsai was created from an old, sawn-off stump. It was skilfully carved and styled to develop the striking form and colour of the aged trunk.

Creating a weeping habit
The feathery foliage grows upwards in nature, so this weeping effect is achieved by careful wiring.

Brown, glazed pot
The Japanese Tokoname, curving, round pot closely encloses the broad base of the bonsai.

Taxus baccata *Common yew*

Yews are attractive, slow-growing, evergreen conifers that may live for hundreds, even thousands of years. The spreading branches of the common yew are clothed with dark green, needle-like leaves. Sometimes the grey-brown bark strips away to show a russet layer underneath. Small green flowers appear in spring. Both leaves and red berries are poisonous, so yews must be grown well away from children, pets, and grazing animals; in the past, the best place was the churchyard, the only area fenced off from the common grazing land. In medieval times, longbows were made from the flexible wood; today it is as easily shaped into bonsai.

Bonsai suggestions
Taxus baccata, the common yew, is suitable for every style of bonsai, except broom. It can be grown in all sizes.

CULTIVATION

◉ Yews tolerate some sun, but partial shade is better; they will grow even in dense shade.
▣ Water daily in growing season, and mist-spray. Sparingly in winter, but keep soil moist.
▣ Feed twice a month during growing season.
▣ Repot every three or four years, in spring. Use free-draining soil mix.
▣ Finger pinch new shoots during growing season to encourage branching: wait until flowering is over if you want the tree to fruit. Wire at any time, although the autumn season is the best.
▣ Take cuttings of current season's growth in autumn: given winter protection, they should root successfully by spring. Layering or air layering in summer.

Taxus baccata, leaf
one-third life size

Needle-like foliage
The dark green leaves have a flattened, needle-like look. Further refining and training of the foliage masses will fill out the design.

Balanced design
The arrangement of branches, which contrasts leafy twigs with starkly cut jins, or stumps, highlights the good trunk line.

Taxus baccata
COMMON YEW
This 20-year-old, informal upright was trained from normal nursery stock. It measures 45cm (18in) in height.

Echoing the trunk colour
The dark shade of the trunk is complemented by the brown, unglazed, oval container.

Taxus cuspidata *Japanese yew*

As its common name suggests, *Taxus cuspidata* originates from Japan. This evergreen tree is small to medium in size, and looks like *T. baccata*, the common yew, except that its needle-like leaves are dark green above and cream underneath. The flowers are small and green: for a female tree to produce the deep pink fruits, it must be pollinated by a male form grown nearby. You can easily bend and wire the flexible wood into an excellent bonsai. The finely grained wood also happily accepts carving into the jin or driftwood elements of a design. A more compact dwarf form, *T. c.* 'Nana', is a better choice for the smaller bonsai sizes.

Bonsai suggestions
Japanese yews can be cultivated in every style of bonsai, except broom. They look very pleasing in all sizes.

CULTIVATION

⦿ Yews tolerate some sun, but prefer at least partial shade, and will even grow in dense shade.
◌ Water daily during growing season, and mist-spray. Water less in winter, but keep soil evenly moist.
⁜ Feed twice a month during growing season.
▥ Repot every three or four years, in spring. Use free-draining soil mix.
▧ Finger pinch new shoots during growing season to encourage branching; wait until after flowering if fruits are wanted. Prune branches in autumn. Wire with care at any time, but the autumn season is best.
☑ Take cuttings in autumn: given winter protection, they should root by spring. Layering or air layering in summer.

Taxus cuspidata,
leaf one-third life size

Sparse foliage
The flattened, needle-like leaves are thinned out to focus attention on the lines of the trunk and branches.

Taxus cuspidata
JAPANESE YEW
This 20-year-old informal upright, with a wide spread of branches, is 30cm (12in) high.

Wired to shape
The trunk was heavily wired to create the strong curves. It was then thickened by a period of growth in open ground.

Making a solid base
The fluid movement of the design has a visual anchor in the brown, unglazed, Japanese Tokoname pot, with its round shape.

Tsuga heterophylla *Western hemlock*

The tall, elegant hemlocks are pyramidal in shape, their branch tips drooping gracefully downwards to look like a waterfall. This family of evergreen conifers grows wild in Japan, China, and North America. The western hemlock is often grown as an ornamental tree. As its common name partly implies, *Tsuga heterophylla* originates from the western areas of North America. When young, the soft, short, needle-like leaves are a lovely light green, but mature to dark green.

Bonsai suggestions
Hemlocks can be cultivated in every style of bonsai, except broom, and look well in sizes from small to extra-large.

CULTIVATION

● Position in partial shade. Tree is very hardy, but protect it from freezing winds that will dry out the foliage.

◌ Water daily during growing season, and mist-spray in summer. Reduce watering in winter, but do not allow soil to dry out.

⊡ Feed twice a month during growing season.

▦ Repot every second year in spring, until about ten years old, then every three to four years as necessary. Use free-draining soil mix.

▨ Finger pinch new shoots during growing season just before they harden, leaving only a few needles. Wire at any time, but preferably not in spring, to avoid damaging new shoots.

▣ Sow seeds in winter or early spring. Softwood cuttings in summer and autumn.

Tsuga heterophylla,
leaf two-fifths life size

Short, soft leaves
The delicate, needle-like leaves are a fresh green.

Open shape
The airy, spreading effect is a result of careful, detailed wiring of the branches.

Tsuga heterophylla
WESTERN HEMLOCK
This six-year-old tree, trained as an informal upright for two years, is 23cm (9in) tall.

Wide, shallow dish
The brown, unglazed container is Japanese Tokoname ware.

Ulmus parvifolia *Chinese elm*

Among bonsai growers, the Chinese elm is arguably the most popular species of elm. As well as in China, this small, rounded tree grows wild in Japan, Korea, and Taiwan. The delicate twigs make this one of the few species which can be grown successfully in broom style, and the stout, long, flexible roots are ideal for clasped-to-rock style. As the botanical name *parvifolia* suggests, the leaves are very small. They are usually deciduous, although often reluctant to fall. In warmer climates such as California, they do not drop at all and the plant is evergreen. A popular variegated form is *Ulmus parvifolia* 'Variegata'.

Bonsai suggestions

Chinese elms are suitable for training into every style of bonsai, and for cultivating in all sizes.

CULTIVATION

◉ Position in full light and sun. Protect roots from frost, as they are vulnerable to damage.

◌ Water daily during growing season, more often in very hot weather, if necessary. More sparingly in winter, but keep moist at all times.

⁂ Feed weekly for first month after leaf buds open, then every two weeks until late summer.

▣ Repot annually, in early spring, until about ten years old, then as necessary. Use free-draining soil mix.

◸ Trim back all new shoots to one or two sets of leaves in spring. All elms respond well to leaf cutting in midsummer, but for small-leaved forms such as *U. parvifolia* leaf cutting is not usually necessary.

◪ Take softwood or hardwood cuttings in early summer. Root cuttings in winter do well.

Ulmus parvifolia,
leaf two-thirds life size

Ulmus parvifolia
CHINESE ELM
This tree, grown in root-over-rock style, is ten years old and 17cm (7in) high.

Year-round interest
This bonsai, with its small, serrated, oval leaves and delicate twigs, is attractive at all seasons of the year.

Balanced design
The triangular silhouette of the branches is well-balanced on the slight curve of the bare trunk, which rises naturally above the rock.

Open setting
The rose-brown, unglazed, wide oval provides a sense of space around the rocky base.

Ulmus procera *English elm*

In nature, the English elm grows like an inverted figure eight, although the ravages of Dutch elm disease have made these trees no longer the common sight they once were. They make, however, excellent bonsai, as the leaves of a pot-grown specimen are much smaller, especially if leaf-cut in midsummer. In autumn, the foliage turns a beautiful bright yellow. The grey-brown bark develops fissures as it ages. Dutch elm disease is not much of a problem with bonsai, partly because there is less bark to be infected, partly because such a small plant is easily treated with systemic insecticide and fungicide.

Bonsai suggestions
English elms can be cultivated in every style of bonsai. They can also be grown in all sizes.

CULTIVATION

⬤ Position in full light and sun. Protect smaller sizes from frost.

◌ Water daily during growing season, more frequently in very hot weather, if necessary. Water less often in winter, but do not allow soil to dry out.

⚬ Feed weekly for a month after leaf buds open in spring, then every two weeks to late summer.

▥ Repot annually, in early spring, until about ten years old; then inspect root development annually and repot as necessary when roots fill pot. Use free-draining soil mix.

▧ Trim new shoots to one or two sets of leaves in spring. English elms respond well to leaf cutting in midsummer.

▨ Take softwood or hardwood cuttings in early summer. Root cuttings in winter do exceptionally well. Propagating suckers is also possible.

Ulmus procera
ENGLISH ELM
This tree was collected from the wild and then trained as a formal upright. It is 30 years old and 105cm (42in) high.

Bonsai foliage
Small, serrated leaves, which turn from mid green to clear yellow in autumn, are well suited to the overall scale of the bonsai.

Typical shape
The characteristic silhouette of the English elm in nature, with its tall, straight trunk forming the central axis of the design, is created by careful training.

Ulmus procera*, leaf one-third life size*

Light green, glazed pot
The colour of this oval pot complements that of the summer and autumn foliage.

Wisteria *Wisteria*

In late spring or early summer, the wisteria's drooping racemes of blue, mauve, or white flowers make a spectacular sight in the garden. The shrub is as impressive as a bonsai: growers usually feature its sweet-smelling flowers rather than the fresh green leaves. Two popular species are *Wisteria floribunda*, the Japanese wisteria, and the Chinese *W. sinensis*, a stronger grower, with shorter, more fragrant racemes.

Bonsai suggestions

Wisterias look good in informal upright, slanting, semicascade, cascade, and root-over-rock styles, and medium to extra-large sizes.

Wisteria floribunda,
leaf one-tenth life size

Wisteria floribunda
JAPANESE WISTERIA
This 12-year-old, informal upright measures 35cm (14in) in height.

Weeping "branches"
The graceful flower racemes are treated as pendent branches, creating an elegant weeping effect to the overall design.

Slanting, upright shape
The grafted trunk has been grown tall enough to accommodate the cascading, pea-type flowers.

Deep, oval pot
The grey-brown, unglazed pot provides a solid base for the dainty tree.

Zelkova serrata *Japanese elm*

The Japanese elm is ideal for bonsai on several counts. It is a strong growing, deciduous tree, with long, erect branches rising out of a short, straight trunk. It is the classic tree for growing in broom style because of its dense mass of delicate twigs. For the same reason, it looks good in multiple-trunk style. In autumn, the foliage gives an attractive display with gradations of crimson, bronze, orange, and yellow. It is one of the best bonsai for winter, when its fascinating arrangement of fine twigs is not hidden by leaves. *Zelkova serrata* belongs to a family of fine trees from Japan, China, and the Caucasus, and is closely related to the native European elms.

Bonsai suggestions
Japanese elms are suitable for every style, except literati, but especially good in broom and group styles. Grow them in all sizes.

CULTIVATION

◉ Position in full sun for most of the year, slight shade in hot summer sun. Protect from frost to avoid twig die-back.

◻ Water daily during summer, moderately at other times, but do not allow soil to dry out between waterings.

⬚ Feed weekly for a month after leaf buds open in spring, then every two weeks in summer.

▣ Repot annually, in early spring until about ten years old; then as necessary depending on root development. Use basic soil mix.

▧ Trim new shoots back to one or two sets of leaves. Remove large leaves during growing season. Leaf cut strong, established trees in midsummer if necessary.

▨ Sow seeds in late winter or early spring. Cuttings in summer. Air layering in summer.

Zelkova serrata,
leaf two-thirds
life size

Zelkova serrata
JAPANESE ELM
These 15- to 20-year-old trees, with an overall height of 38cm (15in), were planted as a group ten years ago.

Colourful foliage
In autumn, the small, serrated leaves turn orange and yellow.

Landscape effect
The trees have been arranged so that they create the spacious perspective found in an open landscape.

Shallow oval
The unglazed dish affords a low, understated base for the broad, spreading design.

Chapter Three

Creating a Bonsai

As a bonsai grower, you aim to deploy your creative skill and judgment, and to adapt the character of the original plant into a uniquely special bonsai. The following pages offer clear step-by-step examples of how to shape and train a bonsai. The fifteen principal bonsai styles are explained and illustrated; so too are methods of creating the impression of a woodland or landscape planting, and of enhancing your design with rocks and other plants. Another section discusses the different kinds of bonsai container, and the factors that will govern your choice of one for a particular bonsai. The basic tools are explained, as well as hints on how to use them. You will see how the technique of pruning to shape can turn a garden centre plant into a bonsai in minutes. Alternatively, you can learn how to grow on a plant that you have propagated from seed or a cutting until it reaches a stage at which you can train it into a bonsai. More advanced techniques of clipping and wiring are also shown, so that you can steadily improve and refine your bonsai as it grows and matures.

Grooming established bonsai
A session of clipping and wiring is best performed with the bonsai specimen placed at eye level, and with all the necessary tools and grades of wire readily to hand.

Directory of bonsai styles

Over the years, bonsai enthusiasts have frequently tried to reclassify the styles, and their many sub-divisions, into which plants can be trained. Within the broader classification of single trunk, multiple-trunk or group plantings, the fifteen styles described on the following pages are now generally accepted. Once you understand the principles behind these styles, you will have a reference point from which to assess a tree's bonsai potential, and to decide what style suits it.

If you study very carefully the way trees grow in nature, it is possible to design a realistic bonsai without knowing the names of these styles. The names are, however, useful for understanding references in books and magazines, and for describing a bonsai to other enthusiasts. You do not need to learn their Japanese names or origins. Nor do you need to stick slavishly to the precise rules of your chosen style: adapt them to suit a plant's natural habit.

What style to select
When you start a bonsai, always remember you are working with a living plant. Look very carefully at its natural characteristics, and you may discern within them a suitable style or styles. Often, you can train a plant into several styles, even if it is basically upright like a beech, or elegantly slender like a maple. If only one style suits a particular plant, you can still interpret it in several different ways.

Shrubs like azaleas that are not tree-like in nature have fewer restrictions in the style you choose, but, generally, it is best to base any design on the way a tree grows in nature. Beginners should not try to train a bonsai into a style totally unlike a tree's natural growth pattern, although this is possible as you gain more experience.

Once you have chosen your style, follow the techniques described on pp. 130–61, and you should be able to shape the tree into a satisfactory bonsai.

Basic bonsai styles

Depending on the angle of the trunk, the five basic bonsai styles are formal upright, informal upright, slanting, semicascade, and cascade. In a formal upright, the trunk is straight and vertical; an informal upright has a more sinuous, curving, upright trunk; the entire trunk of a slanting bonsai leans, as much as 45 degrees from the vertical; a semi-cascade bonsai leans still further, finishing at or just below the pot rim; and a cascade falls below the horizontal, often ending beneath the level of the bottom of the pot.

Betula pendula
SILVER BIRCH

An informal upright bonsai
In nature, such trees bend or alter their direction away from wind or shade, other trees or buildings. In a bonsai, the trunk should be essentially upright, or lean less than 15 degrees. The bend should be to the right or left, not leaning towards the viewer. Most species are recommended for this style.

Larix kaempferi
JAPANESE LARCH

Pinus mugo
MOUNTAIN PINE

A slanting bonsai
Such trees lean away from buffeting winds or deep shade. Whether curved or straight, the whole trunk leans at a definite angle. The stronger roots grow out on the side away from the angle of the trunk lean, to support the weight. Most species are suitable.

A formal upright bonsai
In nature, such a tree grows in the open under perfect conditions. A bonsai trunk should taper evenly from base to apex. The branches should be well balanced, but not strictly symmetrical. Larches, junipers, pines, and spruces are suitable species, but not fruiting or naturally informal trees.

Pyracantha angustifolia
PYRACANTHA
or FIRETHORN

Prunus serrulata
'Kiku-Shidare Sakura'
JAPANESE FLOWERING CHERRY

A semicascade bonsai
This style occurs when trees grow on cliffs or overhang water. The angle of the trunk in a bonsai is not precise, as long as the effect is strongly horizontal, even if the plant grows well below the level of the pot rim. Any exposed roots should balance the trunk. Many species are suitable, except strongly upright ones.

A cascade bonsai
The trunk of a tree clinging to a cliff or mountainside often grows downwards. A bonsai with a very definite downward growth may be called a cascade, even if the trunk does not end below the pot base. Many species are suitable, if they are not strongly upright.

The literati or *bunjin* style

It is not easy to define the literati style, as it breaks many bonsai rules, but trees trained in this style look as slender and graceful as those in Chinese paintings that inspired the name.

The word literati has a somewhat convoluted origin. The Chinese word *wenjen* means "scholars practised in the arts". Japanese bonsai growers translated this as *bunjin* and applied it to this elegant style of tree. *Bunjin* has no English equivalent, so some growers use the name literati, which derives from the Latin word for "literate" or "educated people".

The trunk of a literati usually twists and curves several times. In nature, such trees often grow on the coast, or in places where they have struggled up to the sunlight through other trees that have since been felled or died. Some Scots pines grow naturally into this style in old age. In bonsai, you can style most conifers as literati.

Pinus thunbergii
JAPANESE BLACK PINE

A literati bonsai
Most conifers, and rugged deciduous trees like hawthorn, are good in literati style.

A broom-style bonsai

An upturned Japanese broom inspired the shape of a broom-style bonsai. This design has an evenly balanced, domed head of twiggy branches rising out of a straight trunk. Deciduous trees grown in broom style look their best in winter when the delicate branches are leafless.

In an ideal situation in the wild, a conifer might grow into a formal upright tree, but maples, elms and many other finely branched deciduous species will probably become broom-style trees. This restrained, classic style is possibly the most difficult to achieve in bonsai. If you want to attempt it, your best chance of success is to use a finely branched tree like a maple.

Zelkova serrata
JAPANESE ELM

A broom-style bonsai
Finely branched trees are good, but not evergreens or coarse-branched trees.

Styling on rock

Single bonsai trees, groups, or landscape plantings may be grown on rock. There are two main types of rock planting. In root-over-rock style, the tree's roots snake over the rock and down into the soil. In clasped-to-rock style, the tree is actually planted on the rock. Style the tree in whichever design seems best suited to the rock. See pp. 148–55 for more details.

Pinus parviflora 'Kokonoe', DWARF JAPANESE WHITE PINE

Acer buergerianum TRIDENT MAPLE

A root-over-rock bonsai
This style gives a "close-up" of the tree growing on the rock, featuring the web of exposed roots. Choose a tree with naturally strong roots, also one that grows naturally on rock.

A clasped-to-rock bonsai
In this style, trees can be made to seem "near" or "distant". An upright rock can be placed in a shallow tray (*suiban*) of sand or water, or a flat piece of rock or slate used as a pot.

Saikei style

A saikei or "tray landscape" uses rocks and living plants to depict a landscape in miniature. A saikei planting is usually permanent, but can also be a short-term composition: you can dismantle it and re-use the materials in another saikei, or "promote" the maturing trees to become individual bonsai. A tray landscape called "bonkei" may include artificial plants or no plants at all.

Chamaecyparis obtusa 'Yatsubusa' DWARF HINOKI CYPRESS

A saikei bonsai
Materials such as rocks, grasses, mosses, and sands, and careful attention to scale and proportion, have literally recreated in miniature the natural variations of a landscape.

Root-connected and multiple-trunk styles

In these styles, several trunks emerge from a single root system. Root-connected bonsai may look like a group planting, but are not separate trees; their trunks arise from a common root. A root-connected bonsai has the advantage over a group planting in that, coming from a common rootstock, its leaf shapes, colour, and texture are all similar.

In nature, a twin-trunk style often occurs when the base of a tree splits into two trunks. The expression "multiple-trunk" is used to describe root-connected styles with three or more trunks, growing in clump, straight-line, and sinuous styles. In clump style, several trunks grow up from the same root. Straight-line style occurs when branches of a fallen tree continue to grow vertically. A sinuous style occurs when suckers emerge from surface roots, or a low branch roots into the ground and grows more trunks. In bonsai, the ground-level pattern of sinuous style trunks is randomly curved; that of straight-line style follows the original trunk line.

Acer palmatum **'Deshojo'**, JAPANESE RED MAPLE

A twin-trunk bonsai
In nature, one trunk is usually smaller than the other. Oriental growers call this "father-and-son" or "mother-and-daughter" style. Aim for this effect to avoid the bonsai resembling a catapult. Often you can train a low branch into a second trunk. The same rules cover three or more trunks.

Rhododendron obtusum
JAPANESE KURUME AZALEA

A clump-style bonsai
Some trees grow naturally in clump formation, each trunk reaching out for its own light. Many clumps exist in old English woodlands where trees were coppiced (sawn off at the ground to grow straight poles for fencing and other construction work).

***Chaenomeles japonica*
'Chojubai',**
DWARF FLOWERING
QUINCE

Ilex serrata
JAPANESE
DECIDUOUS
HOLLY

**A sinuous-style
bonsai (above)**
Species with pliable
branches and trunks, like
yew and pine, are best
for creating a sinuous
style bonsai. Also try
others, like elm, that tend
to throw up suckers from
exposed roots.

**A straight-line style
bonsai (right)**
A tree with lop-sided
branches, that is
unsatisfactory material
for a single bonsai, can
provide material for an
interesting straight-
line design. This is
also called raft style.

Group-planting style

The aim of a group planting in bonsai is to
mimic the effect of a woodland, forest, or
grove, or simply several trees growing
together. You can use most species for this
style, as long as they are ones that would
grow together naturally. A group of
beeches planted to create the effect
of a woodland is very impressive,
but a forest of wisteria trees
would look ludicrous.

A group planting should look
uncontrived. You can more
easily achieve a natural effect
with an odd number of trees –
seven, five, or the minimum of
three. It is important to mass
together a sufficiently large number
of trees to make it difficult to count
the trunks. Never create a group of
four trees, but you could use fourteen,
and forty would look like a real forest.

A group planting
Crossing trunks of more than
20 trees set in a low container
create the natural effect
of a grove or
spinney.

***Acer palmatum*
'Ukon',**
UKON MAPLE

Containers for bonsai

The container is as important as the tree in a bonsai design. Usually, growers select the pot after styling the tree, so the two harmonize in size, shape, colour, and texture. Practical and aesthetic factors affect the choice of pot.

Practical points
The pot must hold enough soil for the roots to develop over a year or two. It should be frost-proof, with enough drainage holes. Bonsai containers are usually shallow, but sometimes you may use a deeper one to hold, say, a fruiting tree that needs plenty of water to swell its fruits. Never save on watering time by using a pot too large for the tree, as the roots may become waterlogged and rot.

Aesthetic factors
In design terms, the pot must balance the tree's height and spread, so a dense evergreen needs a deeper pot than a delicate maple. See p. 125 for guidelines on size. Also, the position of the tree in a pot should emphasize the relationship between the two. In oval or rectangular pots, the tree looks most natural off centre, set nearer to one side of the pot than the other in a ratio of 1:2. It can be roughly centred between the back and front of the pot. For balance, a tree with an extended lower branch on its left side is set towards the side of the pot; a tree with a slanted trunk needs its trunk base set to one side of the pot, so the tree's apex is above the pot's centre.

The interior of a bonsai pot is not glazed, but the outside may be glazed or unglazed (the colour of the latter being that of the clay after firing). Earthy colours and an unglazed finish usually look better than lighter or brightly coloured pots, though sometimes a skilfully selected colour enhances a tree with brilliant flowers or autumn foliage. Some subtle ceramic glazes, discreetly lustrous effects, and speckling and crackle-glaze suit some bonsai.

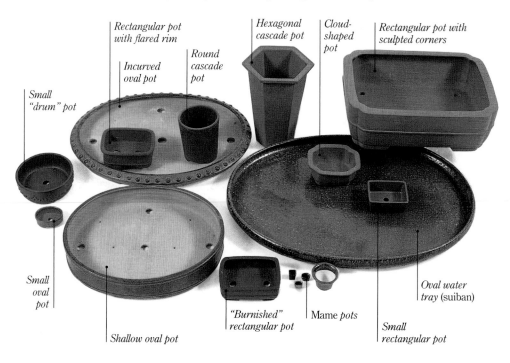

Rectangular pot with flared rim

Incurved oval pot

Round cascade pot

Hexagonal cascade pot

Cloud-shaped pot

Rectangular pot with sculpted corners

Small "drum" pot

Small oval pot

Small oval pot

Shallow oval pot

"Burnished" rectangular pot

Mame pots

Small rectangular pot

Oval water tray (suiban)

Styles of container

Any specialist supplier should offer a good range of pots, mostly from the Tokoname region of Japan. Designers around the world produce interesting hand-made pots. These pages and the next two show some of the many pot styles. The basic shapes are round, oval, and rectangular: usually, a rectangular pot is more formal than an oval. A pot with painted decoration would not suit a forest tree, which demands an unfussy, earthy pot.

Mame pots
These tiny containers vary in size from 1.2cm (½in) to 4cm (1½in). *Mame* pots are notable for their interesting colours and finishes which are designed to make them more eye-catching.

Oval, matt-glazed container
The bold colour and understated lines of this pot by Petra Engelke would dramatically offset a tree with brilliant autumn foliage, or a flowering specimen.

Oval, unglazed, grey Japanese Tokoname pot
This versatile pot, with its formal, elegant lines, would work well with a whole range of different species of tree, from an informal upright pine to a heavy-trunked maple.

Oval, "Schilf"-glazed pot
The subtle colouring of this container by Petra Engelke complements the strong lines and green summer leaves of forest trees such as hawthorn, beech, and hornbeam.

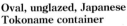

Oval, unglazed, Japanese Tokoname container
Designed for group or saikei plantings, this shallow shape is perfect for creating the feeling of space necessary for landscape effects.

Oval, unglazed, red-brown Japanese Tokoname pot
This fairly formal container has crisp lines and horizontal detailing which visually reduces its depth. It would make a good choice for a Chinese juniper as its colour echoes that of the bark.

Round, glazed, green Japanese Tokoname ware
Pots of this shape are especially suited to upright, slender trees.

Oval, glazed, green Tokoname pot
Because they complement most styles and species, oval containers are very commonly used in bonsai, especially on the trees with rounded outlines. The colour and glazing of this pot act as a foil for autumn foliage.

"Drum"-style, unglazed, red Japanese Tokoname pot
This masculine style of pot is ideal for rugged bonsai, such as a tree trained in literati style.

Rectangular, matt-glazed, grey pot (left)
A satisfyingly weighty-looking, shallow container by Brian Albright, which would create a stable base for a rugged group planting.

Rectangular, glazed, brown pot (right)
This fairly deep container, with something of the look of old Chinese wares, would work well with a heavy-trunked tree such as hornbeam, crab apple or hawthorn.

Rectangular, matt-glazed, brown pot (left)
An unassuming container, by Bryan Albright, that would not detract from the charm of a gentle, formal bonsai design.

Unglazed, brown, Tokoname cascade container (above)
The height of the pot is all-important in cascade-style bonsai as it has to accommodate the cascading fall of the tree.

Rectangular, unglazed, Tokoname pot (right)
Formal pots such as this are becoming less popular due to the current taste for informal bonsai.

Rectangular, unglazed, grey Japanese Tokoname pot (left)
This restrained and imposing design would provide the ideal setting for a dignified old pine.

Unglazed, grey, Tokoname rectangular pot (left)
This pot would be suitable for an informal tree, but one with a thick trunk and a bold silhouette.

Unglazed, brown Japanese Tokoname rectanglar pot (above)
A deepish, formal pot; a good choice for a tree which has a strong visual mass.

Rectangular, grey, unglazed Japanese Tokoname pot (above)
This is similar to the one above left but, less deep, so it needs a tree of less weight and mass.

Unglazed, brown, Tokoname semi-cascade pot (above)
It is essential, when growing a semicascade bonsai, to choose a pot which will accommodate the downward spread of the tree. This example has a clean, strong shape and plain finish.

Container sizes

Keep the container in scale with the tree: an individual tree should not look lost in a large pot, nor overwhelm a tiny one. As a guideline, a mainly vertical tree needs a pot with a length between two-thirds to three-quarters of the tree's height. The pot's length should be two-thirds and three-quarters of the overall width of a strongly horizontal tree. When potting a newly styled deciduous tree, allow for the larger mass and spread when it produces leaves. As a reservoir for soil and water, a smaller pot needs more depth in proportion to its width than a larger pot does. Certain types and styles of tree demand deeper pots.

Visual interest
Larger pots are usually subdued in colour and texture, so that they do not dominate the tree. A smaller pot can be brighter.

How to prepare a pot

You must cover the drainage holes in the bottom of a container, so that watering does not wash away the soil. The traditional gardener's method of inserting broken crocks would take up too much room in a shallow bonsai container. It is better to fix small squares of vinyl mesh over the holes with twists of wire. Secure the wire on each side of a round hole, but diagonally across a rectangular one. Do not try to cover the whole base of the pot with a single, large piece of mesh as it will tangle in the roots and cause problems when you are repotting the tree.

It is wise to anchor the tree securely in the pot, especially if it is a young specimen that has not yet established a vigorous rootball, or an evergreen with dense foliage masses that are easily rocked by the wind. Run a single wire underneath the pot base and up through the drainage holes. After you have set the rootball in the pot, twist the ends of the wire together over the rootball. You will need more wires for a bonsai in a larger container.

HOW TO PREPARE A POT

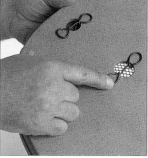

1 Cut a length of wire. Make a loop with a short tail at each end, with the space between the loops equalling the hole's diameter.

2 Place small rectangles of mesh inside each hole. Invert the pot. Push ends of wire twists through each hole. Open out on the inside.

3 Insert a long piece of wire through drainage hole at one side of the pot, take under base, and up through a hole on the other side.

Bonsai tools

The Japanese produce many tools especially for bonsai work, and these can be easily purchased in most parts of the world. You can buy domestic equivalents for some of these specialized tools. Remember that you will get what you pay for: cheaper, poor-quality tools are a false economy.

The enormous selection of tools available may overwhelm a beginner. These pages show the main items. Many are designed for specific functions, so you may not need them all, but it is useful to know their names and uses.

What tools you need will depend on what sort of bonsai work you plan to do. You will need far fewer tools to groom and repot an existing tree than, say, to saw and sculpt a large bonsai from a trunk lifted from the ground. Tools are usually sold separately, but you can sometimes buy a few in a set. A first tool set might include a wire cutter, trimming shears, and concave branch cutter. You can buy a more extensive set for advanced bonsai, but many growers prefer to fill an empty tool case with their preferred items.

Occasionally, you might need heavy-duty power tools, such as a die grinder for carving, a reciprocating saw for cutting through tough roots and branches, or a rotary tool with flexible drive for refining the carving or for working on small trees.

Tools for pruning and cutting
Here are some tools for cutting and pruning. Before you buy any of them, consider the kind of bonsai you intend to create. If it is to be a large tree, you will need heavy-duty tools; more delicate tools are required for precision work on an extra-small bonsai. Information on the basic tools and how to use them is given on pp. 128–9.

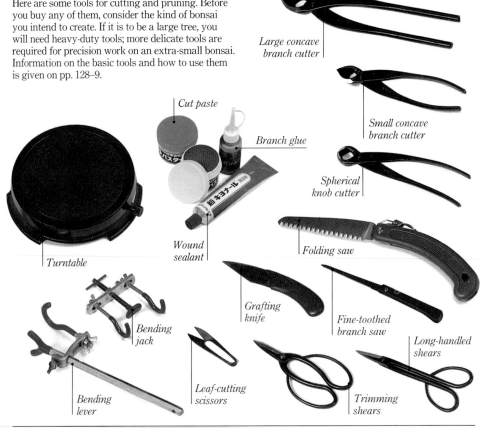

Large concave branch cutter

Cut paste

Branch glue

Small concave branch cutter

Spherical knob cutter

Wound sealant

Folding saw

Turntable

Bending jack

Grafting knife

Fine-toothed branch saw

Long-handled shears

Bending lever

Leaf-cutting scissors

Trimming shears

Tools and equipment for potting

You will need these tools when you first pot a tree as
a bonsai, and then for the regular repotting you will
have to do as an essential part of routine
maintenance *(see pp. 176–7).*

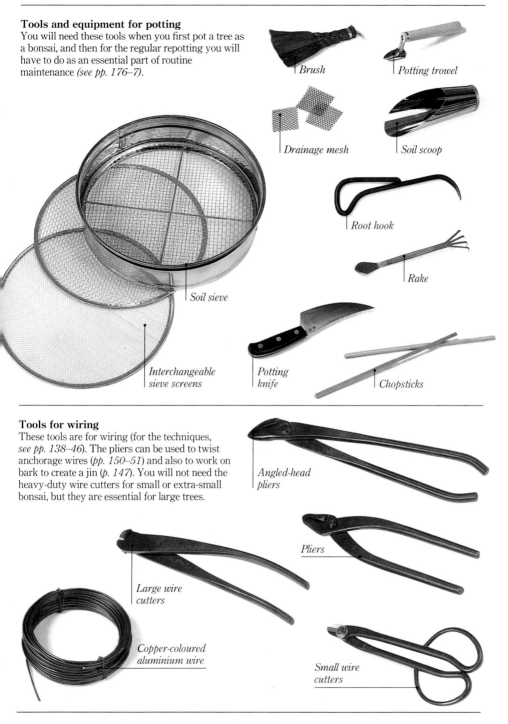

Brush

Potting trowel

Drainage mesh

Soil scoop

Root hook

Rake

Soil sieve

*Interchangeable
sieve screens*

*Potting
knife*

Chopsticks

Tools for wiring

These tools are for wiring (for the techniques,
see pp. 138–46). The pliers can be used to twist
anchorage wires *(pp. 150–51)* and also to work on
bark to create a jin *(p. 147).* You will not need the
heavy-duty wire cutters for small or extra-small
bonsai, but they are essential for large trees.

*Angled-head
pliers*

Pliers

*Large wire
cutters*

*Copper-coloured
aluminium wire*

*Small wire
cutters*

Using bonsai equipment

When you begin to work in bonsai, you will find the six tools shown here the most useful. They are trimming shears, a concave branch cutter, a spherical knob cutter, bud-trimming shears, wire cutters, and a root hook. Between them, you can prune branches and roots, as well as wiring the bonsai if you feel it necessary. As with any craft, you should start quite simply and inexpensively with the most essential items, only buying others as you increase in skill and experience.

The most important of the six bonsai tools, and the first that you should purchase, are the trimming shears and the concave branch cutter. With these two tools alone, you will be able to create and maintain a bonsai. You can add wire cutters if you want to use wiring as part of the bonsai training.

Trimming shears

For trimming roots, twigs, and branches easily and precisely, this is the essential cutting tool. The handles are big enough to accommodate all your fingers, and also to allow you to pick off prunings without putting the shears down.

The rivet should be loose enough for the handles to fall open easily, and not have to be pulled apart. The blades should be sharpened to a fine knife-edge, rather than a scissor-edge, so that you can cut a stem cleanly without crushing it. Use the blade tips for trimming delicate twigs. Cut heavier branches, up to 6mm (¼in) in diameter, closer to the rivet. When you trim roots, make sure that potting soil grit does not chip the blades.

Cutting shoots
Insert the blades so that you cut only the stem, not foliage. Make a clean cut in a single motion, leaving no ragged edges. A clean cut helps healing.

Concave branch cutter

Use this cutter to remove a whole branch at the trunk, leaving a concave cut. As the wound heals, the edges will roll over to fill the hollow and heal flush with the trunk. Shears would cut the branch flush with the trunk, but leave an unsightly bump as the wound heals.

Try to make the cut run vertically up the trunk: rising sap will heal such a cut more quickly than a transverse cut. You may need to cut heavy branches in two stages to control the angle better.

Whichever size of cutter you buy, do not use it on branches with a diameter greater than half the width of the blades.

Cutting out a branch
Approach the branch at an angle that gives a vertical concave cut, rather than one made across the trunk line. A vertical cut will heal better.

Spherical knob cutter

This is a newer tool than the concave cutter, and leaves a circular cut that will heal flush. Surrounding branches, however, sometimes prevent you from holding this tool at the necessary right angle to the trunk. Also called a wen cutter, it can also be used for initial rough carving of dead wood and jins (*see p. 147*), and whittling away at stubs too large for one cut.

Pruning at a right angle
Remove most of the branch before using this tool.

Bud-trimming shears

The long reach on these shears makes them ideal for trimming buds on needle junipers and pines, and also for lightly training trees with delicate twigs. They are the best shears for small bonsai sizes. You will spoil the blades if you use them on branches or twigs that are too thick for them. The golden rule is: if the tool will not cut the item easily, do not use it.

Accurate cutting
Sharp, elongated blades give easy access.

Wire cutters

The Japanese make wire cutters especially for bonsai work. Always check the maximum diameter of wire a tool can cut, however good its quality: it may cut aluminium wire 5mm in diameter, but only 3mm copper wire. Cheaper domestic wire cutters can cut bonsai wires to length, but are seldom strong or accurate enough for cutting wire from the tree without spoiling the bark.

Using snub-nose cutters
Keep the blade at right angles to the wire.

Root hook

Before root pruning, use the rounded end of this tool, in a radial movement from the trunk, to disentangle the roots of a larger bonsai without damage. You can buy a purpose-made, metal root hook like this one, or make one for yourself. For smaller bonsai, use a chopstick, a small-pronged rake, or a piece of wooden dowel with a rounded end.

Disentangling the rootball
A "raking" action helps to untangle the outer roots.

Basic bonsai methods

The two main methods of creating a bonsai could be described as the "subtraction" and the "addition" methods. Subtraction shapes the tree by pruning away unnecessary branches and twigs. In the addition method, you start the plant from seed or a cutting, and gradually encourage it to develop into the shape you want for your finished design.

These two methods are analogous to those used in sculpture: indeed, bonsai is often described as "living sculpture". In the subtraction method of real sculpture, the carver cuts away the wood or stone to reveal the basic design, and subsequently refines the surface detail. The addition type of sculpture involves the craftsman building up a pliable material like clay and shaping it until the final image is complete.

However, because a bonsai tree is formed from living material that grows and changes, the addition and subtraction methods are not mutually exclusive: most bonsai are made from a combination of the two methods. A tree may be grown from seed for some years, then severely pruned to reduce and shape the branches. The new growth that sprouts from the cut-back branches is pruned in its turn.

Another technique is to prune a young tree from a garden centre drastically, then allow it to grow freely for another year or two before you shape and refine it by less severe pruning. You can repeat these processes over a period of time, as often as is necessary.

Wiring is another process that enables the grower to refine an already pruned tree and alter its basic shape by training the branches and trunk into a different growth pattern from their natural one. Wiring will not damage the tree and, with practice, you can easily learn the skill (*see pp. 138–46*).

Pruning a bonsai to shape

You can create a bonsai within minutes by buying a vigorous, well-shaped young shrub, such as this pyracantha, from a garden centre or nursery and pruning its branches into a more refined shape. This is the basic "subtraction" method of creating a bonsai (*see also pp. 132–3*).

The first illustration shows the chosen pyracantha as it arrived from the garden centre, with a mass of narrow branches radiating out at all angles, and thickly covered with shiny green leaves.

The second illustration shows the effect of pruning and repotting. The pruning has revealed a slanting trunk line. Thinning and shortening the branches has produced a pleasing triangular-shaped bonsai. The apex is slightly domed, and the lower branches spread out in a balanced asymmetry. After the roots were pruned, the whole bonsai was planted into a speckled cream, oval pot.

Pyracantha 'Teton'
FIRETHORN

A six-year-old specimen, newly purchased from the garden centre

Pruning and repotting reveal an attractive, slanting trunk

Wiring a bonsai

If the branches and trunk of a tree are fairly flexible, you can wire them into a different direction, or give the tree a different shape. Wiring can also improve a bonsai created by pruning a ready-made shrub, or one grown from seed, or a design created by a combination of the two methods.

Detailed information on types of wire and wiring techniques is given on pp. 138–46, but the general principle is as follows. Wind the wire in a spiral, at a 45-degree angle, along a branch or up a trunk. Bind it tight enough to encourage the branch or trunk to maintain the new angle or curve into which you will twist or bend it when adjusting the tree's shape. Leave the wire in place for up to a year, but be sure to remove it before it bites into the surface of the bark, or it will create an ugly, long-lasting scar that may take years to fade away.

Juniperus
× *media*
'Blaauw'
CHINESE
JUNIPER

A six-year-old, garden-centre plant

Same plant after pruning and wiring

Propagating a bonsai

By propagating a plant, you can encourage bonsai characteristics which a garden-centre plant may lack. Grow a seedling, or a cutting, in a pot until it is big and strong enough to be planted out in the ground. This will thicken the stem and branches, producing growth in two years that could take twenty in a pot.

Trim the branches to encourage bushy growth. For a fibrous root system close to the trunk, prune the roots in winter by severing them with a sharp spade, or by digging up the plant, pruning, and then replacing it.

When the plant is ready, lift it and prune the roots and branches into the basic bonsai shape. Plant it in a pot to grow on, and continue to prune and train each year.

Larix kaempferi
JAPANESE LARCH

Two-year-old tree   **Three-year-old tree**   **Six-year-old tree**   **Ten-year-old tree**

Pruning for shape

For beginners, one method of creating a bonsai is especially recommended. This is to visit a nursery or garden centre, and buy a healthy small shrub or tree. Study it from all angles before pruning it to a more distinctive style and shape.

The advantages of this method are several. Firstly, you obtain an instant result instead of waiting for years to create a bonsai from seeds or cuttings: the example of a rockspray cotoneaster shown below was pruned in only 15 minutes. Secondly, you can obtain material much more easily than find a suitable tree in the wild. It is also a relatively cheap method. Finally, if you are not happy with your first attempt, your second may turn out to be a veritable masterpiece.

Of course, to have success with this method of pruning, it is vital to buy a suitable plant.

Pyracanthas and cotoneasters are ideal for this method, as well as the smaller shrubby varieties of *Lonicera, Jasminum nudiflorum*, and *Chaenomeles japonica*. The species should be one that is hardy and adaptable, with small leaves that will suit the scale of a bonsai. If you want seasonal features, the flowers and fruit of the original plant should be small and neat. A deciduous species is best for a first attempt, because its basic structure is clearly visible when the branches are bare, and you can prune it to shape in late winter, or in early spring just before the leaves unfold.

Select a shrub with a thick, sturdy trunk, that has a good line, to form a basis for your bonsai. The shrub should have many branches in sufficient numbers to complement the weight of the trunk, and the foliage or twigs should be compact, and growing up to the trunk.

Pruning a cotoneaster

A fine choice for a first bonsai is *Cotoneaster horizontalis*, the rockspray cotoneaster, which often makes an interesting trunk without any training. It grows vigorously, producing many branches which take readily to pruning. New buds form on old wood. The branches of a young plant grow in a herringbone pattern, but after pruning they will send out new shoots in all directions.

This example came from a garden centre and was then planted in a growing bed for several years to thicken the trunk. Now six to eight years old, it has just been lifted. It is late winter, so the mass of twiggy, intertwining, knobbly-looking branches and the strong, twisting trunk line

can easily be seen on the leafless shrub. The illustrations on the opposite page show the stages of pruning. The branches are trimmed to an interesting shape, and the mass of roots cut back to encourage new feeder roots, and to help the plant fit more comfortably into a bonsai dish. The aim is to produce a shallow root system while keeping as many fibrous roots as possible. More details about root pruning are given on p. 175.

A potential bonsai
Just lifted from the growing bed, the rootball of the shrub is still clogged with soil. Some of the long, slender branches show the typical herringbone pattern of fine twigs.

PRUNING A COTONEASTER

1 With a root hook, gently loosen the soil in the rootball and carefully disentangle the roots, working around the trunk base in a radial pattern.

2 Prune longer roots, cutting away any that grow downwards. Turn the shrub around, at eye level if possible, to find the best view for the front of the bonsai.

3 Expose the trunk by trimming off twiggy growth. Shorten the branches, leaving an interesting structure for new foliage to grow close to the trunk.

Cotoneaster horizontalis
ROCKSPRAY COTONEASTER

4 Repot the pruned tree in a container of appropriate size and shape (*see pp. 176-7*). Here, a shallow oval pot balances the design of the bonsai.

The tree in leaf
In a few months, the bonsai's tree-like shape has filled out with new foliage, and the well-balanced design is apparent.

Clothed with leaves
Fresh green, small leaves grow close to the trunk.

Balanced silhouette
The outer curves of the trunk support the major branches and foliage masses, giving balance to the design.

Sinuous shape
Selective pruning has revealed the natural curve of the trunk, creating a good informal upright bonsai specimen.

Clip and grow method

This method combines subtraction (pruning away unnecessary material) and addition (allowing new branches to grow and form the shape of the bonsai). You can use the clip and grow method to produce a more dramatic bonsai than you could achieve by pruning alone. This method emphasizes the acute angles between branches and trunk, and also encourages a rugged or aged effect.

The clip and grow method is done over two stages, and thus takes more time than simple pruning for shape. First, the original material is drastically pruned, and then allowed to regrow so that the shape of the bonsai forms during the following growing season. The autumn cherry shown opposite has been grown for a period of slightly over one year after the original pruning.

Styling a young autumn cherry tree

This grafted autumn cherry was bought at a garden centre. It has been grown on for two or three years after grafting to form a bushy, but narrow, plant. Instead of each branch being cut right back to the trunk at the initial clipping, small stumps or shoulders were left on the tree, because cherry trees produce new shoots which grow at a suitable downward angle from beneath such shoulders. The shoulders will be trimmed back more tidily as soon as the new shoots are strong and established. An advantage of this method is that the tree has a

sturdy trunk from the start, whereas it would take many years of growing on the tree in the ground to reach this stage if the tree had been propagated from seed or a cutting.

The autumn cherry, *Prunus subhirtella* 'Autumnalis' makes a splendid subject for bonsai. Most flowering cherries produce quite coarse leaves and twigs, and flower over only a short period, but the autumn cherry has fine leaves and neat twigs that grow in an elegant branching pattern. Flushes of small pink or white flowers appear in mild weather between late autumn and spring.

The tree also looks impressive in autumn when the leaves turn from their summer green to shades of yellow and orange.

STYLING A FLOWERING CHERRY

1 Select a strongly growing shrub with a well-developed trunk. Rotate it to find the view of the bonsai that looks best from the front (*see p. 24*).

2 Shorten any thick roots, and trim fibrous ones, to encourage the formation of a compact root system at the base of the trunk.

3 Holding the plant so that it is slightly tilted, prune off the heavy roots underneath the rootball, to make a flat root system that will fit comfortably into the pot.

Seasonal interest
Small, oval, green leaves follow the flowers and turn orange in autumn.

Prunus subhirtella **'Autumnalis'** AUTUMN CHERRY

Tree in bloom
The tree bears successive flushes of flowers in winter and spring. Future pruning will create twiggier growth and more flowers.

Tree-like shape
The branches form the beginnings of a balanced structure.

One year on (above)
After a year, in late winter, the cherry shows a quantity of new, straight stems, extending from points where previous branches were removed. Flower buds are forming on the new growth.

Sturdy trunk
With this method, a substantial trunk exists from the start.

Further training (right)
Two months on, the tree is in bloom. In future seasons, it will be potted into a bonsai pot, and the branches wired to refine the shape and encourage flowering.

Deep training pot
This retained moisture and gave frost protection while the severely pruned roots developed healthy growth.

4 Remove branches with concave branch cutters, leaving each wound with a small shoulder from which new shoots can grow.

5 Smear on a wound sealant such as cut paste over the cut surfaces. This helps to preserve moisture in the trunk and to prevent the bonsai from drying out.

6 After pruning the shrub, plant it in a ceramic training pot to grow on. The ceramic container will promote good drainage and thus healthy root development.

Pruning and wiring

Dwarf conifers, or shrubs such as pyracantha or cotoneaster, can easily be styled into bonsai by pruning alone, but taller-growing trees often need more attention to create a well-balanced design. Usually, you will need to wire the tree, so that you can more easily control its structure and the way in which the bonsai develops.

This example of pruning and wiring a Japanese white pine demonstrates how you can improve and refine a pruned design by wiring. More details on wiring techniques are described and illustrated on pp. 138–46.

You will seldom find a suitable plant of a conifer such as a pine in a garden centre, so you may need to grow the tree yourself. You can find full details of how to propagate a tree from seed on pp. 164–5. It will take you a very long time, but does mean that you will obtain suitable material for your bonsai, with a tapered trunk, closely spaced branches, and compact foliage. After several years, you can prune and wire your young tree into a balanced shape with attractively positioned branches. Pot it into a bonsai container, and gradually refine the design over several more years.

A Japanese white pine grown from seed

To make a pine into a good bonsai, you need a tree with a tapering trunk, many branches radiating from it at short intervals, and compact foliage close to the trunk. Usually, you have to grow such a tree yourself, as most garden centre pines are quite unsuitable for bonsai: they are fairly large, with straight trunks, branches radiating out at intervals of about 60–90cm (2–3ft), and foliage at about the same distance from the trunk.

The illustrated specimen of *Pinus parviflora*, the Japanese white pine, was developed from a one-year-old seedling into a nine-year-old tree ready to train as a bonsai.

The one-year-old seedling was moved from the seed tray to a 6.25cm (2½in) pot. It grew on without pruning for another three years, being potted on into successively larger pots as its roots developed.

The trunk of the four-year-old was still thin, but the internodal distances (spacing of branches and foliage) were suitably close. The tree was then planted in open ground for five years to thicken the trunk. It was fed and watered well; every spring, the new candles were trimmed back to encourage the production of densely massed foliage.

One-year-old seedling
The young plant, transferred from the seed tray to a small pot, was left untrimmed for three years.

Four-year-old tree
To develop its trunk and branches, the pine will be set in a growing bed, and fed and watered well.

Nine-year-old tree
New young shoots, or candle growth, have been trimmed each year for a dense clothing of foliage.

GROWING A JAPANESE WHITE PINE FROM SEED

1 Use a metal root hook to disentangle crossing roots. Shorten roots only as much as necessary to fit the bonsai container.

2 Rotate the tree to choose the front view. Refine it by cutting off branches, a little way from the trunk, with concave branch cutters.

3 By now, about half the foliage has been removed. The stub left near the base of the trunk can make a jin (*see p. 147*).

Wiring the bonsai
Once pruned, the basic form is refined by wiring to adjust trunk line or branches. Here, wiring was used also to correct an imbalance in the apex. There was no branch to the left of the apex, so the top part of the trunk was twisted slightly to utilize a branch formerly on the right of the tree.

Rectangular pot
Placing the tree off-centre helps to balance the design.

Pinus parviflora
JAPANESE WHITE PINE

The result
The tree now has a well-balanced, asymmetrical shape. Removing old needles and downward-hanging foliage has clarified the horizontal lines.

Triangular apex
The evenly weighted apex results from twisting the top with wiring.

Informal upright style
This specimen has a naturally strong trunk line. Styling has given it a graceful spread of branches.

Pleasing structure
Wiring has attractively accentuated the horizontal emphasis of the design.

Impression of age
Pruned lower branches have been treated as jins to give an aged look.

Wiring

Mastering the skill of wiring will give you much more scope when creating or refining your bonsai. You can change the direction of the branches or trunk, wire an upward branch into the horizontal, turn a branch on a young tree downwards to simulate age, or maintain and refine new growth. These pages and others throughout the book show the various ways in which wiring can enhance a bonsai style.

The best time to wire

Although in theory you can wire at any time, some seasons are better than others. It is easiest to wire deciduous trees just before the leaf buds unfold in spring, or before they become dormant in autumn. Leaf-cut trees like maples and elms are best wired just after you remove the leaves. Wire evergreens at any time, but conifers are best done when dormant from late autumn to early spring.

How long to leave the wire

Check regularly that wire is not biting into the growing bark as the tree continues to thicken, or long-term damage may be caused. When the limb is firmly set in its new position, remove the wire completely. How soon depends on the species of tree, the age and quality of the wood, and the thickness of the branches or trunk: a flexible young branch will hold its new position more quickly than resistant

older wood. As a rule, leave wiring three to six months on deciduous trees, about twice as long as on evergreens.

How to remove the wire

You can unwind the wire, but there is less risk of damaging the tree if you cut it away in little pieces. Wire left on too long will bite into the tree: this must be unwound very carefully, retracing its original direction. Paint any deeply cut bark with a wound sealant.

Some branches may slowly revert to their former position after the wire is removed, and will need rewiring in the original direction; if, however, the bark is badly scarred, wire in the opposite direction.

Cedrus atlantica glauca
BLUE CEDAR

Without wiring

Shaping the tree

This slanting-style bonsai was last wired five years ago. Branches that were trained in a downward direction have begun to lift towards the light once more. It will be rewired (*far right*) to refine the shape by adjusting the direction and growth pattern of the branches.

Removing wire
Cut the wire away carefully in little pieces, rather than unwinding it, to prevent any damage to the bark of the tree.

Wire too tight
The branch of this conifer is swelling because the wire has been left on too long. As a result, scarring has occurred.

Wire damage
Scarring to the branch caused by wire shows clearly when the wire is removed. The wound may not grow out for years.

Adjusting the apex
The branches have been opened out at the top to achieve a more balanced shape for the tree.

Horizontal spread
Detail wiring has spread the foliage horizontally, creating the flat planes typical of the mature cedar in nature.

Downward direction
Lower branches have been wired and brought downwards to create a more elegant and natural silhouette.

With wiring

Creating visual depth
A branch formerly growing on the left-hand side has been taken to the back of the tree to give depth to the silhouette.

New container
The rewired tree has been repotted into a wider pot that balances the growing branches.

Wire types

Copper and aluminium are the most common types of bonsai wire. Copper is less obtrusive, because it has an attractive colour, and is strong enough to be used in smaller gauges than aluminium. Copper wire is best for conifers, because it supports the flexible wood firmly. It does have the disadvantage of hardening over time, so it may scar the bark when removed. It also needs to be made more pliable by annealing. Sometimes you can buy it pre-annealed; if not, non-annealed wire is easy to find. Heat it over a low-temperature fire until it glows a bright cherry red; if overheated, it becomes brittle. Cool it slowly. It can be re-used after re-annealing.

The lighter, softer aluminium wire is better for deciduous trees, as it is less likely to damage the bark. It can also be re-used. It is, however, not so strong as copper wire, so you need to use it in a thicker gauge. Ordinary aluminium wire is a bright, silvery colour that does not blend with the tree; it is better to use aluminium wire treated with a dull coppery finish. This is readily available in specialist shops, and is the most commonly used type.

Wire gauges

Wire comes in many different thicknesses, so match the gauge carefully to the size and vigour of the trunk or branch. Generally, choose a gauge between one-sixth and one-third of the diameter of the wood, but you should also consider the age and resistance of the wood, and how much you need to bend it when shaping the bonsai.

Wiring techniques

Beginners find it takes much time and practice to master the technique of wiring. It is very important to learn first how to wire a bonsai specimen accurately and neatly; once you have mastered this, you will soon gain speed. Many people do not take the trouble to wire neatly, but it is not possible to shape the tree well with careless wiring.

Other methods of shaping (tying branches down with strings or wires, tying them to canes, or suspending weights from them) are used less, because they are less effective.

Before starting to wire, collect together enough wire in the gauges you think you will need. You should have wire cutters strong enough to cut the wire. Pliers will help you to hold the wire easily and to finish off the ends. Cut your wire a third as long again as the branch or trunk you intend to wire, so that you can wind it at a 45-degree angle, the best angle for effective wiring.

To protect the bark on heavy branches that you may have to bend drastically, you will find raffia useful. Wind it around the branches before wiring. If you are wiring delicate or soft twigs, it is often best to wrap the wire with strips of paper before using it.

WIRING THE TRUNK

1 Choose wire of the correct thickness. Cut it to length, and push one end into the soil behind the trunk of the tree.

2 To anchor the wire securely, bend it around the trunk almost parallel with the soil in the container.

3 Wind the first coil of wire around the trunk. Continue to wind up the trunk at an angle of 45 degrees.

4 If a second wire is necessary, wire it close to the first. Do not allow it to cross the first wire, or it will be ineffective.

It is important to anchor the wire securely, or it will not be effective. When wiring a low branch or trunk, anchor the wire in the soil of the container. For branches higher up the tree, the common practice is to use the same piece of wire to work on two branches at once, after taking a turn with the wire around the trunk for anchorage.

Do not cross wires: not only will they not look attractive, but they may bite into the wood and act as a tourniquet, cutting off the limb's sap and killing the upper part.

It is usual to start wiring at the heaviest part of the tree, and work up to the most delicate areas; if you have to wire the trunk, start with that and move on to the branches.

Wiring to reshape
Here you can see how a tree has been wired to bend the trunk into a curve and to direct the branches downwards into the required shape.

Apex
This has been wired together with one of the topmost branches. The wire is of a finer gauge than that used on the trunk.

Upper trunk
As the trunk tapers towards the apex, it is necessary to use just a single thickness of wire.

Tips of branches
In order to support the tip of the branch or shoot, the end of each wire is bent back on itself and wound again.

The branches
Once past the lowest level, two branches are wired with a single wire, taken around the trunk for a secure anchorage.

Shaping the lower trunk
A curve is maintained in the bottom part of the trunk by using two thicknesses of heavy wire.

The lowest branch
As this is isolated from the other branches, a thin wire is anchored in the soil, wound following the trunk wiring, and then bent out along the branch.

Wiring branches

Once the trunk of the bonsai tree has been fully wired, you can start on the branches. Always wire the branch at the lowest level on the trunk first and work upwards.

There are two schools of thought in the bonsai world about how to wire branches. One of the preferred techniques is to wire the length of each branch with its principal wire and continue until you have finished the whole tree. You follow by adding subsidiary wiring to shape the finer twigs – again beginning with twigs on the lowermost branches. The second method is to complete the wiring of one branch at a time, applying both its main and subsidiary wires before starting on the next branch. Whichever method you choose, make sure your wiring is precise and neat.

Beginning to wire
Take the first turn of wire over the branch as shown on the left. If you start by passing it underneath, as seen on the right, there is a tendency for the branch to snap when bent.

Wire secured around the trunk

Wiring two branches at the same time
The usual practice is to wire two branches with one wire. Take the wire around the trunk between one branch and the other to keep it firmly in place.

End of wire secured under turns

Anchoring wire to a lone branch
Where a limb is too isolated to be wired together with another branch, secure the end of the wire by trapping it under the first few turns.

Smaller gauge wire on end of tapering branch

Wire supports outer point of curve

Creating a bend in the trunk
When a trunk is to be bent into a curve, the maximum support is needed at the outer point of the curve. The support of the wiring is weaker between spirals.

Changing the gauge of the wire
As a trunk or branch tapers, you will need to change to a wire with a smaller gauge. Run the thinner wire alongside the thicker one for a number of turns, to secure it and to ensure that it adequately supports the taper. This technique also is used to bring a thin branch up to form the apex.

WIRING A TYPICAL BRANCH

Unwired branch

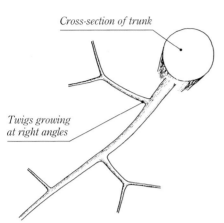

Cross-section of trunk

Twigs growing at right angles

Branch after wiring

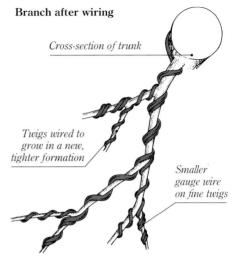

Cross-section of trunk

Twigs wired to grow in a new, tighter formation

Smaller gauge wire on fine twigs

Natural state
The branch, as it extends from the trunk, shows twigs growing at right angles to it. These should be wired to close up the whole arrangement.

Wiring the whole branch
Where it is necessary to wire the complete branch, as well as the twigs, the wire is anchored by a couple of turns at the trunk.

ANCHORING SUBSIDIARY WIRING

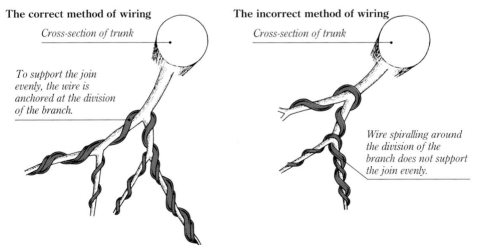

The correct method of wiring

Cross-section of trunk

To support the join evenly, the wire is anchored at the division of the branch.

The incorrect method of wiring

Cross-section of trunk

Wire spiralling around the division of the branch does not support the join evenly.

Even support
When it is necessary to wire just the twigs, not the full branch, the wire is anchored at the division of the branch, as shown here in cross-section, so that the join is evenly supported.

Uneven support
If a pair of twigs is wired so that the wire spirals around the division of the branch, as seen here, the join is not evenly supported and might very easily suffer damage.

Wiring a juniper

Junipers are ideal subjects for a first attempt at wiring, with flexible branches, and evergreen foliage that immediately shows an effect. Some junipers have prickly, needle-like foliage, and others neat, scale-like foliage, or a mixture of both. Begin with a scale-like specimen. This *Juniperus × media* 'Blaauw' was grown in a nursery for garden use. It has been growing for a year in its plastic pot, without any bonsai training. The first task is to thin out the foliage to reduce its density.

Unbalanced, dense structure

Before wiring
This tree, shown as it came from the nursery, has an upright trunk with a well-thickened base and good taper. It has scale-like leaves and a mass of upward-growing branches, which are strong but flexible.

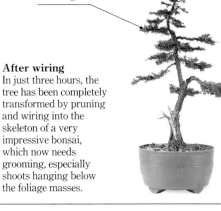

Elegant, tree-like design

After wiring
In just three hours, the tree has been completely transformed by pruning and wiring into the skeleton of a very impressive bonsai, which now needs grooming, especially shoots hanging below the foliage masses.

Wiring details

The branches must be wired downwards to simulate age, the foliage thinned out, and the subsidiary growth wired into neat, flat pads of foliage. During the growing season after such wiring, the tree must be groomed: the shoots growing downwards will be removed, upward ones finger pruned. After a year, the artificial look will be obscured by new foliage, producing the "cloud-shaped" foliage pads that grow on the tree in the wild. The grooming procedure will continue during subsequent growing seasons.

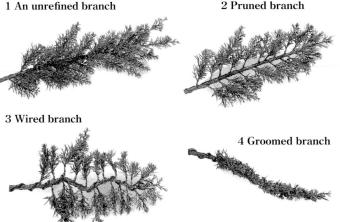

1 An unrefined branch

2 Pruned branch

3 Wired branch

4 Groomed branch

Grooming a branch
1 This is a typical branch structure, seen from above, before training.
2 The branch has a more balanced shape after trimming of longer shoots and of surplus foliage.
3 The stem has been gently curved by wiring with 2.5mm copper-coloured aluminium wire; 1.5mm wire was used on the shoots.
4 This profile view shows the shape of the wired branch. It leads downwards from the trunk, but has a slight upward movement at the tip.

WIRING THE JUNIPER

1 Place the tree at eye-level and choose the front view. Prune off heavy branches near the base. Thin out the upper branches. Treat any stubs left on the lower part of the trunk to create jins (*see p. 147*).

2 Cut a length of wire, a third longer than the combined lengths of the first two lower branches. Wind this wire around the trunk to anchor it and hold it firmly against the trunk.

3 Wind the first loop of wire over the top of the lowest branch. Take a turn around the trunk to anchor the wire and then take it over the top of the second branch. Wire the length of each branch.

4 Here are the first two levels of branches wired into their approximate positions. Later, when you have wired the whole tree, you can refine the shapes of both branches and foliage by secondary wiring and by pruning.

5 Carry on wiring. Carefully bend the upper branches into place and support them while you wind on the wires. If possible, work on pairs of branches rather than single ones, so that the wire can be anchored to the trunk.

6 The wiring is almost finished, the longer branches being shaped. Now wire the apex and adjust the branch positions. Groom foliage masses to clarify shapes and take out any dangling foliage (*see left*).

POTTING THE JUNIPER

1 Take the wired tree out of its original pot. Comb out the roots in a radial pattern with a metal root hook. Prune them into a shallow root system that suits the weight of the trunk and fits the bonsai pot (*see p. 175*).

2 Prepare the new pot with mesh and anchorage wires (*see p. 125*). Add a layer of potting mixture. Place the tree facing front in the pot. Secure it by twisting anchorage wires over the roots. Top up the pot with soil.

Maintaining the design
With this species, the wiring remains in place for about a year. It must be checked regularly and wires removed if they start biting into the bark. The bonsai will be rewired regularly every two or three years to accommodate new growth. As the tree grows, numerous refinements will be made to its shape. For instance, it might be necessary to prune out some branches in three to five years to open up the structure.

Well-balanced framework
The branch structure now makes an elegant outline which will soon be clothed in foliage.

Weathered look
Stubs left after pruning lower branches have been carved into jins to create a feeling of age.

Evergreen foliage
Well-formed foliage pads will gradually fill out over the seasons.

Improved trunk
The naturally graceful line of the trunk has been refined by careful wiring and is now easily seen.

Red-brown, unglazed pot
The colour and texture of this Tokoname oval echo reddish tones in the bark and complement the ruggedness of a forest tree.

Driftwood, jins, and shari

In nature, a tree often has areas of dead wood. You can achieve a similarly dramatic effect in a bonsai by using such dead wood, or live wood not wanted in the design. A design with extensive dead wood is called a "driftwood" design. The Japanese word *shari* is used for dead wood that is carved or torn down the trunk. Similarly damaged branches are given the Japanese word *jin*, which has no English equivalent; it is also a verb ("to jin"), and an adjective ("jinning pliers").

You can create driftwood, jins or shari by carving the dead wood on a bonsai, and then bleaching and preserving it with lime-sulphur solution. Alternatively, you can use any live branches surplus to your design. Cutting them off completely will scar the tree, but you can achieve an impressively aged effect by stripping them of bark, and then carving or tearing them to make the bonsai look as if it has been naturally damaged by thick snow or strong winds.

MAKING THE JINS ON THE JUNIPER

1 The lower branches were pruned to leave stubs (*see p. 145*). Score a ring in the bark around the base of the stub and close to the trunk with a concave branch cutter.

2 With jinning pliers, grip the bark and crush it, to loosen the bark from the white wood underneath. Grip the crushed bark with the pliers and pull it away from the stub.

3 To make the jin look more natural, grip the wood with the pliers. Tear it downwards to reveal the grain until you are satisfied with the shape of the jin.

4 With a wire brush (either a manual or, as here, an electrically driven, rotating one), clean up the surface of the exposed wood.

Planting on rock

If you want to increase the impact of your bonsai, introducing one or more rocks is a good idea. Solid, elemental-looking rocks can give the impression that a bonsai is part of a landscape. A single rock can resemble a rugged cliff, a towering mountain, or a rocky island. A group of smaller rocks, positioned as outcrops protruding from the soil of the bonsai container, can recall the rocky terrain in which the tree lives. Use a slab of rock or slate instead of a traditional container to make a design look especially natural.

The next few pages show how to achieve various effects with rock plantings. The clasped-to-rock style, where the trees appear to grow out of the rock, is shown opposite and on pp. 150–51. Root-over-rock plantings, where the rock enhances the sturdy roots of the bonsai, are depicted on pp. 152–5. Saikei, the tray landscape style, where a dramatic and rugged effect is created in a flat dish or tray, is shown on pp. 160–61.

Choosing the rock
The first element of a successful rock planting is to find a beautiful rock, and then set it off with one or more appropriate bonsai plants, so that all elements of the design seem as one.

Many types of rocks exist around the world, but some are better than others for rock plantings. The best kind for bonsai work is a hard rock that will not crumble away. It should also have attractive colour, shape, and texture. A popular choice is the Japanese Ibigawa rock shown opposite; it is a volcanic conglomerate, a mixture of different rock types welded together by the heat of a volcano.

Do not use marble or quartz because their shiny, glittering textures will detract from the natural effect of the trees. Frost may split the strata lines of sandstone and other types of sedimentary rocks.

Soft rocks are seldom useful for root-over-rock and clasped-to-rock styles, as they erode too quickly and easily. Soft, non-sedimentary rocks like lava rock and tufa, however, are easy to shape, so you can hollow out a section and plant the tree in it as if in a pot.

Rocks for clasped-to-rock plantings
The rock is the most important part of the design, because it dictates what type and size of tree or trees you will use. A round, smooth rock suggests a watery scene, so you will enhance it with waterside trees like willows. Choose a craggy rock, and you will need to plant it with trees of the mountainside, like birch, juniper, pine, and spruce.

Pay particular attention to the rock's shape and type. It should be intrinsically interesting: a bland rock is unlikely to result in a good planting. On the whole, pick a rock with a natural-looking shape, but you should not find this a limitation because nature produces a wide range of fantastically contorted mountains, boulders, and rocks. Pleasing texture and colour are also important: black and shades of grey are usually impressive.

Deciding on a clasped-to-rock planting
Look at the rock from all angles to choose the best view for the "front" of the design. Next, decide what scale the design will be, whether the rock is to represent a mountain, a cliff, or a boulder, as this will dictate the kind and size of plants you plant on. A forest of small trees would make the rock seem a distant mountain, whereas a single tree two-thirds the size of the rock would make it look like a boulder.

Watery setting
This type of planting is enhanced by setting it in a shallow water tray, such as this unglazed, embossed suiban.

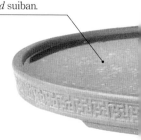

A complete rock planting

In this clasped-to-rock style of bonsai, the impression of a mature, dramatic landscape is created in a very short space of time. Although the plants are still relatively young, they already look as though they have been growing on this rock for many years. The passage of time can only enhance further an already striking and established-looking bonsai design.

Textural interest
Outcrops of quartz in the rock break up the surface.

White pine
The white stripes on the foliage pick up the colour of the quartz in the rock.

Complementary shapes
The rounded, irregular forms of the trees echo the contours of the Ibigawa rock.

Neat wiring
Each tree has been wired so that the curves of its trunk follow those of the rock.

Colour contrast
The blue-green foliage of the pines and the autumnal colours of the nearby small plants make a striking contrast to the bright leaves of the evergreen cotoneaster.

Natural effect
The shape of the rock enables water to collect under the overhang, giving the impression of a cascading stream.

Planting a clasped-to-rock design

The collected piece of Japanese Ibigawa rock chosen for this design already had a very attractive combination of texture and colour. It was subsequently cut and chiselled to refine its shape. Acid was used to eat away the softer parts and make the surface more irregular. Sawing the base flat gave added stability.

Preparing the materials

The rock was examined carefully to find the best view for the front, and to establish the design of the planting – a simulation of small trees clinging tenaciously to a rocky outcrop or island. Several young, partly trained white pines, and other small plants, were selected to establish the correct sense of scale.

After assembling all the necessary materials (*see below*), the trees were held up against the rock to check their proportions and shapes, and to choose the best places for planting them, places where they would complement the characteristics of the rock.

How to prepare anchorage wires

In a clasped-to-rock planting, you need anchorage wires to fix plants to the rock. Cut a length of wire and hold the centre against a fine chopstick or knitting needle, or any tool about 6mm (¼in) in diameter with a tapered end. Wind the centre of the wire once around the chopstick to form a circle or base, leaving two long ends. Slip the circle of wire off the chopstick, and hold it down flat with pliers while you pull each end of the wire up vertically. Glue the circle of wire to the rock, leaving the long ends free. Make sufficient of these anchorage wires (*see below*) to form a network that will hold down the roots of all the plants.

Hard-textured Ibigawa rock

Evergreen cotoneaster

White pines

White pine

Dwarf thyme

Yellow heather

Anchorage wires

Anchorage wire
Long ends either side of the circle secure the planting.

Finding the best angle
Before starting to design the planting, study the rock from all sides, choosing the most interesting aspect for the front view.

The choice of materials

The three white pines (*Pinus parviflora*) are all about 10cm (4in) tall. Other plants are included to enhance the idea of a lone island, and for textural and colour interest. Well-soaked mosses complete the planting. You will need anchorage wires and a strong adhesive. Planting is in peat muck (*see opposite*).

THE CLASPED-TO-ROCK PLANTING

1 Use a strong, waterproof adhesive, such as epoxy resin, or the quick-drying adhesive that is purpose-made in Japan (beware of sticking your fingers!) to stick the prepared anchorage wires to parts of the rock where you plan to plant the trees. There should be enough wires in position to provide a web-like framework that will secure all the roots.

2 Take some pre-soaked peat muck (one part peat to one part clay, presoaked and kneaded into a sticky mass) and press a layer on to the part of the rock where you intend to plant the first tree. Set the tree in position, carefully spread its roots over the peat muck, and cover them with some more peat muck.

3 Cross the anchorage wires over the roots. It is better to bring together two individual wires from different anchorages rather than fix the two ends of one anchorage wire to each other. To fasten the wires, grasp the ends of each wire with pliers. Twist them together, taking care not to allow the wires to bite into the roots, and fix the tree in place.

4 Add some more peat muck and press it in place over the roots of the tree, so that they are covered completely. Keep the peat muck continually moist, using a mist-sprayer of water if necessary, until you cover it up with moss (*see step 6*). The moss should have been soaked in water for several hours before being used on the planting.

5 Fix the other plants in position in the same way as the first one. You should secure the pines first, followed by the smaller plants. If necessary, keep spraying the peat muck with the mist-sprayer, so that it stays damp.

6 When all the plants have been positioned, cover the peat muck with soaked moss. This will make the planting look attractive and will also help to prevent erosion. Set the whole rock in a shallow tray. Scatter some fine gravel in the tray and top up with a little water. The water will set off the design and provide a humid atmosphere for the plants.

Root-over-rock style

Bonsai designed in root-over-rock style are recreating situations in mountainous or rocky terrain where trees grow up from seeds deposited in crevices. Desperately seeking food and moisture, the roots of such small trees fan out over the rock. When at last the tips locate some soil and sink into it, the exposed parts of the roots thicken up as they cling tightly to their rocky support.

In bonsai, trees that naturally form strong surface roots, like Chinese elms and trident maples, are popular for root-over-rock designs. You can use many other species, especially with smaller bonsai sizes which do not need such excessively heavy roots. It is essential to choose a suitable rock, as the tree's roots fuse with it to make it a permanent part of the planting. Choose a very hard, frost-resistant rock, with an interesting, craggy texture – not a soft rock that will crumble in frost, or one with a boringly flat surface.

The most popular choice is Japanese Ibigawa rock (*see p. 149*), available all over the world from bonsai suppliers. It fulfils all the bonsai criteria, being hard and rugged, with interesting colours and textures. In some areas, you may be able to find a local rock that will serve as a suitable substitute.

Planting a maple in root-over-rock style

This elegant young Japanese mountain maple (*Acer palmatum*) gained an appearance of maturity by being styled over one year in a root-over-rock design.

The two- or three-year-old tree was a bare-rooted seedling grown in a field. It was first attached to the Japanese Ibigawa rock by binding strips (*see p. 154*). Then both tree and rock were potted as a single unit in sand in a plastic container, to give the roots time to thicken up and grip the rock firmly. How long this thickening process will take varies according to the size of tree. Small to medium bonsai usually take a year, but a large bonsai subject may need two or three times as long.

Check the roots to ensure that they look substantial enough to be an interesting part of the bonsai design. Then examine them gently to ascertain that they have permanently attached themselves to the rock and will not come away when you remove the original binding material (*see p. 155*).

Plastic grafting tape

Japanese Ibigawa rock

Assembling the materials
Make sure that the shape of the rock fits inside the root structure of the tree. For the first stage, you need plastic grafting tape – or strips of plastic bag – to bind the roots to the rock, sharp sand, and an ordinary plant pot. For the final planting one year later, you will need a bonsai container and potting soil.

Two- to three-year-old, field-grown, bare-rooted seedling

The final planting

The young mountain maple is now 16.5cm (6½in) tall and has come into leaf, three months after it was planted in a bonsai pot. The basis of a good design is already apparent and, over the next few years, the tree will be left to develop more twiggy growth. The rock balances the design and gives the small bonsai greater authority. To enhance the naturalistic feel of the setting, the surface of the soil has been covered with sand and planted with mosses.

Elegant silhouette
Hard pruning at the potting stage has produced a good basic structure of branches on which the graceful, arching leaves are carried.

Balanced design
The rock adds textural interest and provides weight at the slender base of the young tree.

Speckled, oval container
The soft blue-green glaze, speckled with cream, enhances summer foliage and forms a striking contrast to the scarlet leaves of autumn.

Firm grip
One strong root is very prominent in this frontal view of the root system clasping the rock.

TRAINING THE ROOTS OVER THE ROCK

1 Use a root hook to comb out the roots. Shake off any remaining soil. Hold several pieces of the rock against the tree's roots to decide which has the best shape to fit snugly over it.

2 Wrap the roots over the rock. You will need a helper to secure the roots at the top, middle, and base of the rock by binding on plastic tape, while you hold them firmly in place.

3 The helper should bind all the roots tightly to the rock, covering them over to prevent any new horizontal roots from developing. Leave longer roots free at the base to grow downwards.

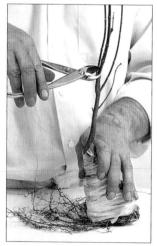

4 With a concave branch cutter, prune the tree back hard, trimming each branch to within no more than one or two buds from the trunk.

5 Moisture is essential for new buds to grow. To prevent trimmed branches from drying out, seal their cut ends with wound sealant or cut paste.

6 Bury all the roots and the entire rock in a pot of clean, sharp sand, making sure that they are covered up to the base of the trunk. You do not need to use any other growing medium.

POTTING THE TREE

7 Over the next year, water the tree in the pot daily during the growing season. Keep the sand just moist in winter. Feed fortnightly in summer. Prune vigorous new growth to within one or two buds of the trunk. After a year, follow steps 8 to 11.

8 In late winter or early spring, roughly trim the branches. Remove the tree from its pot, and use a hosepipe, watering can, or bowl of clean water to wash the roots and tape clean of sand.

9 Cut away the tapes with small, sharp scissors – take care not to cut any roots. Unwrap and remove the plastic to release the rock and roots.

11 When satisfied with the way the roots have developed, choose the best front view (*see p. 24*). Trim the branches to suit this view. Plant the tree in a bonsai pot (*see p. 125*), treating the rock as an extension of the trunk.

The tree's main roots now follow the contours of the rock.

10 The roots should have thickened and be clinging firmly to the rock. If not, rebind them, following steps 2 and 3. Replant the tree and rock in sand for a further year.

Group plantings

The natural beauty of a clump of trees, a woodland or a forest can be recreated with a group bonsai planting. Use this style also for trees that may not make good single specimens, such as young and slender trees or ones with few or one-sided growth of side branches.

Do not base your design on a photograph or another bonsai, but observe carefully the way trees grow in nature. In a group, a tree develops differently from a solitary specimen. Each tree has to compete for its share of light, water, and food, so it tends to grow upwards rather than outwards, developing a tall, slender trunk instead of a short, thick one. Only the branches of the outermost trees receive enough light to spread out well. Weaker and younger trees lean away from more dominant ones towards the sun.

Species for group plantings

Many species of evergreen and deciduous trees are suitable for group plantings, especially those that grow naturally upright. For a small to medium-sized group, choose trees with small leaves; use large-leaved and coarse-growing forms for bigger groups.

It is usually better to use trees of the same species; mixing, say, a wisteria, beech, cherry, and oak in one group never looks realistic. Scale is another problem when mixing species: a background tree with larger leaves than the foreground tree destroys the illusion of distance. Also, different species require different soil types, watering, and feeding.

Creating perspective and space

In a group planting, you must create an illusion of distance and space. Positioning tall trees at the front and smaller ones at the back gives a feeling of depth, even in a narrow container. Stagger the arrangement slightly, with two or three smaller groups, each diminishing in height. Keep the silhouette of the background trees simple, and the eye will register them as more distant than the elaborate trees placed in the foreground.

Arrange the trees asymmetrically, and keep the open spaces on either side of the container unequal in size. A large, shallow pot or a flat slab of slate or rock helps to recreate an effect of openness, so that you can feel that you could walk between the trees.

Planting a group

Ideal species for group planting are beech, birch, cedar, cryptomeria, elm, hornbeam, juniper, larch, maples, and spruce. It is often necessary to grow the maples, elms, and cryptomeria species from seedlings or cuttings, before you prune them into a more slender, upright shape than a single bonsai would require.

To make any group look natural, you should use an odd number of trees. Remember that you will need more trees to choose from than you will actually use. After root pruning each tree (see p. 175), work out a rough arrangement for the group. Select a large enough pot for your chosen group, and cover its drainage holes (see p. 125). Put a shallow layer of grit in the pot, and cover this with a layer of potting soil.

Pre-trained for group planting
Five Japanese dwarf cedars, *Cryptomeria japonica* 'Yatsubusa', were grown from cuttings and pre-trained over eight years. Varying in height and trunk thickness, they are now suitable for a small group.

PLANTING A GROUP

This will be the central tree of the group.

1 Take the first tree out of its training pot. Comb out the roots carefully with a root hook, and trim them to fit the pot with large-handled shears. Repeat this process on each of the other trees.

2 Decide on the front view of the tallest tree (*see p. 24*). When planting the tree in the prepared pot, position the tree nearest the viewer, towards the front of the container, and a third away from one side.

3 Choose a shorter and thinner tree. Place it close to the first tree, allowing it to lean slightly away from the taller one, as if it is seeking the light.

The composition has a realistic asymmetry.

Fill in between the trees with potting soil as you go.

4 Set the third tree on the opposite side of the central tree, and position it slightly back in the container. Vary the spacing between the central tree and the ones on either side of it, to make the grouping look natural.

5 To increase the illusion of perspective, position the fourth, thinner-trunked tree at the back of the pot. Set the fifth tree at the extreme right of the group, so that it is leaning away slightly from the other trees.

The intermediate stage
Already the well-balanced planting gives a realistic feeling of depth and perspective.

Pleasing silhouette
The grouping has a stable, triangular shape and attractive outline, but the dense foliage needs refining.

Interesting contrast
Upright and leaning trunks give variety and interest to the structure.

The setting
The asymmetrical group is well placed in the container.

GROOMING AND FINISHING THE DESIGN

1 Remove crossing branches and downward shoots with scissors or shears to open up the structure.

2 For a balanced silhouette and also to let in more light, groom the foliage as necessary.

3 Water the soil well. Add fresh moss, using a spatula to settle it firmly in place.

From the side
This viewpoint clearly shows the distribution of trees from front to back which creates perspective in the design.

Highest point
The tallest tree leans slightly forwards near its apex.

Staggered heights
The dominant tree is at the front, and the smallest at the back, of the group.

Distribution of space
There is more open "ground" in the foreground of the design.

The final arrangement
The five-tree group was finished in less than two hours. This included all stages from preparation for planting through to the final grooming. The strength of the design lies in careful planning and the application of natural logic to its every aspect.

Groomed foliage
Pruning has resulted in a sound basic shape. Further, repeated trimming will be necessary because the foliage grows quickly. Branches may be wired later on to refine the structure of the bonsai.

Triangular shape
The planting creates an attractive, asymmetrical silhouette.

Well-conceived design
The two inclined trunks lead the eye through the design towards the open space on the right.

Spacing
All trunks can be clearly seen from the front. Uneven spacing gives a natural look.

Unglazed, brown oval
The relatively large, Japanese Tokoname container helps to give a feeling of space within and around the trees.

The finishing touch
Velvety green moss adds to the naturalistic feel of this landscape style of planting.

Landscape styles

A saikei, or living landscape, planting combines living plants with materials such as rock, soil or sand to create the ambience of a natural landscape. The saikei can vary as much as natural landscape does. It does not even have to be totally realistic. Although you can reconstruct a favourite view using materials from a particular habitat, your inspiration could be an exotic location, or even the realms of your imagination. Whatever type of saikei you plan, make sure that all of the components blend in with each other, and that the plants can all flourish in their environment.

Components of a saikei design
The possibilities of saikei planting are endless, bounded only by your ideas and expertise. Often, rocks add an air of drama to a design, with their cragginess and height enhancing the

effect of distance and space. The frequently used Ibigawa rocks can suggest a landscape similar to that of their native Japan, or, as illustrated here, rocky islands off south-west England, or Brittany in France. Low, smoother stones with horizontal strata lines will achieve a softer effect, maybe of a moorland or heath.

If you mould low banks of soil into the design, and cover them with grasses, mosses and low-growing ground cover, a more open, rolling landscape is simulated. You can create a coastal, riverside or lakeside view by using a container with a water reservoir, but skilful deployment of sand or grit will often achieve the same effect.

The living material can be seedlings or cuttings that you have propagated, plants from a garden centre that you have shaped as you require, or trained bonsai.

Creating a saikei design

This design is based around two large, and several smaller, pieces of Ibigawa rock; the largest rock appears to have caves and inlets. The rocks should be positioned to look pleasing and make an interesting composition in themselves.

The trees are two dwarf Hinoki cypresses, *Chamaecyparis obtusa* 'Yatsubusa', thinned to reveal the trunk lines but retaining their natural shape. Fill-in plants are two heathers (simulating small trees on the more distant rock), and low-growing ground-cover plants (*Thymus, Acaena,* and *Cotula*). Their roots also prevent soil erosion.

A shallow oval pot in unglazed, red-brown Tokoname ware provides a broad base, its dark colour adding to the rugged effect of the scene. The illusion of an open landscape is increased by fine gravel filling the container almost to its low rim. The plants are set behind the rocks in a basic soil mix and, finally, the mosses are planted in peat muck (*see p. 151*).

The right size
Correct relative scale between the elements of the design is crucial to its success.

PLANTING THE SAIKEI

1 Place the large rock close to the front of the container, and the small rock nearer the back to

create a sense of perspective (*see overhead view, left*). Make sure the rock strata all run the same way, as in nature. Seen in elevation (*right*), the highest point is one third away from the side of the container. The composition is an asymmetrical triangle, with one side more than twice as long as the other.

2 Hold the plants in their pots against the rocks to choose the best positions for perspective. Position the trees first, then the low-growing plants and mosses.

3 Place a shallow layer of gravel around the rocks. Pour potting soil between and behind the rocks. Support soil behind the rocks with smaller retaining stones.

4 Plant trees in soil behind the large rock. Plant ground-cover plants in soil around the base of the trees, choosing those with the best height and texture.

Tree-like form
The heathers resemble the cypresses in colour and shape and so represent distant trees.

5 Trim heathers to resemble the trees, so that they will appear to be further away. Plant the heathers behind the secondary rock.

6 Cover the soil with peat muck and press soaked moss gently into it. To retain the surface in steeply raked areas, push U-shaped wires through the moss into the soil.

Unglazed, shallow, oval container
The rocks stand on gravel to emulate water. The planting is watered as usual because the container has drainage holes.

CHAPTER FOUR

PROPAGATING BONSAI

Propagating plants is a fascinating exercise, and an excellent method of acquiring and selecting the best specimens for bonsai training. It is also very satisfying to produce a mature bonsai that you have nurtured from its very beginnings. You could apply the techniques of propagation described in this chapter to produce new material from a plant that you have bought at a nursery or garden centre, or even to use clippings (that would otherwise be destined for the compost heap) from an existing bonsai. Step-by-step examples show you the basic techniques of propagating from seeds or cuttings, or by layering or grafting. The recommended method or methods of propagation are given for each of the trees or shrubs featured in the "A–Z of Bonsai Species" and the "Dictionary of Trees and Shrubs for Bonsai". You can then refer from these notes to the greater detail provided in this chapter.

New plants from old
A beautiful bonsai group such as this one of trident maples, Acer buergerianum, *may be grown from bonsai material obtained from seeds, softwood or hardwood cuttings, or by air layering.*

Propagating from seed

Growing trees or shrubs from seed will give you many seedlings, but needs much time and space. You are not "growing bonsai", only cultivating material that may, after several years, be suitable for training into bonsai.

First, ensure the required species is one that can be readily propagated from seed (*see* "A-Z Species Guide", *pp. 38–113*). Tree seeds must be fresh to germinate, even if stored at a suitable humidity and temperature. Collect the seeds yourself, or buy them from a good seed merchant. "Bonsai kits" are an unreliable and costly way of buying seeds.

Many hardy tree seeds need a period of cold to germinate. A refrigerator or freezer provides this for sowings out of season in, say, midsummer, but such seedlings may be too immature to survive a winter. Sow seed in early autumn or winter and expose it to cold weather, but protect it from birds and rodents.

Stratified seeds

Some seeds need stratification before sowing. Bury them in pots of wet sand, then either expose to frost or place in plastic bags in a refrigerator for some months. Soak seeds with hard husks or shells in water: viable seeds sink. Discard empty shells that float. A few drops of detergent in the water prevent viable smaller seeds from floating.

Pines grown from seed

The illustrations show *Pinus parviflora*, the Japanese white pine. If you have collected the pine cones, leave them in a warm room for a few days to open. Then remove the seeds and soak them (*see above*).

Pines are usually propagated from seed or by grafting, rather than from cuttings as their high resin content inhibits callousing. Grafting is often preferable, because seedlings do not always come true to the parent plant; however, the rootstocks for grafting still have to be propagated by seed.

The process of developing the seedling into material suitable for training as bonsai is shown on p. 136. If you require a small bonsai, grow the tree on in a pot, transplanting it into larger-sized pots as necessary. For a large bonsai with a heavy trunk, allow the young tree to develop in open ground.

SOWING THE SEEDS

1 Fill a seed tray with a suitable soil mixture for seeds. For pines, this consists of one part perlite to one part moss peat.

2 Make furrows in the surface so that the seeds can be sown evenly. Sprinkle a fine layer of sand over the soil first to make the seeds more visible.

3 Place the seeds in the furrows, spacing them evenly. The distance between seeds depends on their size: the larger the seed, the wider the spacing.

4 Cover the surface of the soil with coarse grit to a depth of just less than twice the size of the seed. Water well and place the tray in the open.

Transplanting seedlings

A seedling transplanted into open ground after its first year will grow more quickly into a tree suitable for bonsai. If this is not possible, pot the seedling up into a 7.5cm (3in) plastic pot filled with free-draining soil mix. Spread the roots carefully into a wheel-spoke pattern to prevent them from tangling as they thicken, and to encourage a radial root system. Pot on annually to allow space for growing roots.

2 In order to encourage the growth of more and finer roots at the base of the stem, trim back the tap root and other long roots, but avoid cutting the fine, fibrous roots close to the stem.

1 After leaving the seedlings undisturbed for a year, lift them carefully from the tray by gently working loose their long, straggly roots.

3 Leave each potted-up seedling to grow on unrestricted for a number of years. This will allow it to become established, as well as enable the trunk to thicken and the branch structure to develop.

Cuttings

Propagating bonsai material from cuttings has several advantages. It is very easy and reliable. The new plants always have the same characteristics as the parent. You can often use the prunings that you would otherwise throw away from routine pruning.

There are two kinds of cuttings: softwood and hardwood. Softwood cuttings come from the current season's soft new growth. Usually, therefore, you should take softwood cuttings from around late spring to the early summer when the parent plant is growing vigorously.

Hardwood cuttings
Hardwood cuttings come from wood that is fully ripened, and sometimes even several

years old. Take these during the fall and winter. Many bonsai enthusiasts, however, successfully take cuttings at what is supposed to be the "wrong" time of year, recycling prunings from their existing bonsai rather than throwing them on the compost heap.

Make sure the cuttings material is healthy and vigorous. To prevent the cutting from losing moisture, maintain humidity around it until it has calloused over and begun to root. Use a mist-spray, or cover the cutting with some glass or plastic protection, such as a propagator, a cold frame, or a greenhouse. However, hardwood cuttings from many species will "strike" from material pushed into the open ground without such protection.

Softwood cuttings

These softwood cuttings are taken from *Cryptomeria japonica* 'Yatsubusa', the dwarf Japanese cedar. Nip off the chosen shoot just below the junction of a side shoot (where most of the natural plant hormones congregate and promote root production in the cutting).

You can use a standard plastic seed tray, although an earthenware pot will allow the cuttings extra depth for root growth, and its clay walls will provide better drainage and insulation for the soil. Use an appropriate potting mixture for the species (*see pp. 177 and 186–209*); here, a mixture of one part perlite and one part moss peat forms the rooting medium.

PROPAGATING THE CUTTINGS

1 First, prepare the pot. Cover any large drainage holes with plastic mesh to prevent the soil from trickling out (*see p. 125*). Add a layer of coarse grit, and then fill up the container with the soil mixture.

2 Hold the chosen cutting material upright and trim it off the parent plant. Use very sharp scissors to make a really clean cut.

3 Trim away all needles and side shoots from the bottom third of the cutting. If you fail to do this, the cutting will rot at the base when it is inserted into soil and the cutting will fail.

4 Make a hole in the soil with a chopstick, dibber, or pencil. (It is important that the severed end of the cutting is not damaged when it is inserted into the container.)

5 Carefully place each cutting in its hole; lightly press down the surrounding soil to keep it in place. Do this for each cutting until you have filled the container.

6 Water with care to avoid disturbing the cuttings. It is important also to label the pot with the plant name and the date on which the cuttings were taken.

After care of cuttings

Place the container in an unheated greenhouse or a cold frame and leave the cuttings to root and grow on. Water regularly; otherwise the cuttings need no further attention for a year.

One year later
The cuttings should be showing considerable growth, roots should be growing through the drainage holes, and the container will be quite crowded. It is then time to transplant the cuttings into individual pots to give them the space they need to develop into bigger plants.

Potting up
Always use free-draining soil mix for repotting your cuttings. Lift each cutting from the container and trim back the long roots as described on p. 175. Replant it in a 7.5cm (3in) pot and leave to grow on for a year, before planting it out in open ground, or a larger pot, to thicken the trunk.

Layering and grafting

To increase a plant by layering, you peg down the shoot of a garden plant at ground level or bury it in the soil, to encourage it to root while still attached to the parent plant. You can sometimes use this method in bonsai, but the parent plant must be multi-trunked, and growing in open ground.

The technique more frequently used for bonsai is air layering, a very quick way of producing a bonsai, because you can first choose a well-shaped branch that can be pruned into a suitable bonsai shape.

Commercial growers usually propagate trees and shrubs by grafting, but this process is more difficult for beginners or amateur gardeners to master, and only the basic principles of grafting are explained here.

Propagation is a fascinating subject, and there are many specialist books to give you more information on all possible methods.

Air layering

The container-grown hawthorn shown here, *Crataegus laevigata* 'Paul's Scarlet', came from a garden centre, so it had not been trained as a potential bonsai. Although the plant is very spindly, the twiggy section at the apex should make a pleasing small tree that can be trained into a bonsai.

In the usual method of air layering, sphagnum moss is wrapped around the stem, and covered with clear plastic to make a "parcel". The roots will grow out from the stem into the moss. In this case, however, a pot of soil was used instead of the moss.

This method has the advantage that, after the roots have developed, you can sever them at the base of the pot and thus avoid disturbance of the tree by repotting it.

Maiden tree
This tree is in its first year after grafting, with one slender trunk. Such specimens are readily available in garden centres.

HOW TO AIR LAYER A SHRUB

1 Using a sharp knife, make two encircling cuts in the bark, spaced at a distance of one and a half times the stem diameter. Remove the bark between the cuts.

2 Cut a plastic pot down the side and halfway across the bottom towards the centre. Trim to fit around the trunk and position, preferably supported by branches.

3 Close the pot back together again and secure with wire. Fill the pot with some of the same free-draining soil mixture that is used for cuttings.

Air layering at low level

This specimen shows how you can use air layering to improve a tree's appearance. This flowering hawthorn is the same type as the hawthorn shown opposite. It was originally a grafted plant, but a clumsy graft located about 2.5cm (1in) above soil level had seriously disfigured the trunk.

Air layering can eliminate such a fault by stimulating new roots to grow above the graft, so that the tree can be repotted. This is done by enclosing the lower trunk in a pot of soil. After a suitable period of time, the pot can be temporarily removed to monitor how the roots are developing. It can then be fitted back around the rootball and the wires replaced.

Once a new root system has developed satisfactorily above the graft, the original rootstock can be removed, whenever the tree

An air layer in place
This specimen has been air layered with the base of the plastic pot at the original soil level. The pot has been in position for a year.

is not flowering. The air layered tree is grown on, with the new root system above the original soil level. The tree can be repotted in early spring before the new leaves open from the buds.

Grafting

The propagation technique of grafting is especially appropriate for certain species, such as pines (*see pp. 81–91*). Fruiting trees are frequently grafted, because a tree grown from seed will need many years' growth before it is sufficiently mature to produce flowers and fruit; it takes crab apples (*Malus*) 15–20 years to do so. Also, crab apples grown from seed seldom resemble their parent plant, and may have unattractive flowers and fruit. A grafted tree will always come true to type, and will produce plenty of flowers and fruits.

The part of the tree that is grafted on to the rootstock is called the scion. To make sure the graft will "take", you must align the cambium layers (the green layers just under the bark) of the scion and the rootstock. Here, a crab apple seedling that is two years old is used as a rootstock for a mature crab apple scion. Graft it in late winter or early spring, and the scion's flower buds will open three months later.

If you plan to do much grafting, it would be useful to read a specialist book that gives advice on practical details and on suitable rootstocks for species you plan to grow.

Preparing the scion
Using a very sharp grafting knife, scalpel or single-edged razor blade, cut the scion's base into a wedge shape.

HOW TO GRAFT A TREE

1 Make a clean cut across the stock, then split down the stem, using a sharp blade. Next, carefully fit the scion into the split stem.

2 Bind the graft firmly with clear plastic tape, from the uncut part of the stock to the scion's upper stem. Remove the tape after a year.

· CHAPTER FIVE ·

MAINTAINING BONSAI

Once you have trained, or started to train, a bonsai into a chosen style, it is vital to keep the plant growing well. To do this, you need a knowledge of the basic horticultural skills, such as placing the tree in a suitable position, and watering and feeding it correctly. You also need to know how to root prune and repot the bonsai from time to time. Routine pruning is also necessary to maintain the shape of the bonsai. Finally, you need to be vigilant in guarding the plant against pests and diseases. The "A–Z of Bonsai Species" and the "Dictionary of Trees and Shrubs for Bonsai" outline the routine care needed by each tree or shrub. Refer to this chapter, and you will find all such maintenance techniques explained in detail, with helpful step-by-step illustrations, so that you can give each bonsai the day-to-day care it needs to stay healthy, and so develop into a fine plant.

Routine tasks in bonsai care
*Judicious root pruning (*far left) *and finger pruning of the top growth (*top left) *play a part in the regular care and grooming of a bonsai to maintain its refined silhouette (*bottom left).*

Siting a bonsai

It is vital to position your bonsai trees in a location that gives them a suitable climate, light, and humidity levels. The position should also provide a good viewpoint, so that you can admire the trees, and sufficient room for you to work comfortably on the bonsai.

Listed below are some general points to help you site the bonsai, but the precise location must depend on the individual tree, and the local conditions. Check pp. 38–113 and 187–209 for the position that is best for each species. If you are a newcomer to bonsai, or have only recently moved to a new area, contact the local bonsai society for advice.

Climate
It is a popular misconception that bonsai should be grown indoors as houseplants. In fact, most are hardy trees that need to be grown outdoors in the open. If you bring them inside, it should be only for a day or so. Even outside, however, the bonsai will need more attention than full-sized specimens of the same species in the open garden. Roots growing in bonsai pots are less protected than roots in the ground, and easily become too cold, hot, wet or dry, according to weather conditions.

The best advice is to avoid extremes. In temperate countries like England, most bonsai can stay outdoors all year, but in areas such as California and parts of Australia, bonsai need shading against the hot sun. In cold places like Scandinavia, the north-eastern USA, and Canada, the trees must always be protected adequately against frost.

Viewing level
Bonsai look best on shelves or raised stands, so that they are at eye level. Eye level varies, of course: the height of the raised area will depend on whether the viewer will be sitting or standing. Viewed from a sitting position, bonsai should be 1m (3ft) above ground level; or at 1.2–1.5m (4–5ft) when seen from a standing position. However, this level is too high for easy day-to-day maintenance, so a compromise is often made, and the trees are set slightly lower, at table-top height.

Care in winter
How much winter protection is needed varies from species to species (see pp. 38–113 and 187–209), and depends on the conditions where you live. Protect hardy trees against wind and frost, but do not bring them indoors; a heated room will break their dormancy into new sappy growth. They do need maximum light, so a cold frame or a well-ventilated greenhouse will make good winter quarters. Alternatively, place the trees, especially those with delicate twigs, underneath their display bench, dropping a clear plastic "curtain" down in front of them to screen off the worst of the weather. Cold winds are particularly damaging to the foliage of evergreens.

Take particular care of the plant's roots, especially fleshy ones such as those on a trident maple. Even if you leave the main part of the tree unprotected, plunge the pot into the ground or, better still, into a prepared bed of pine needles or similar insulation material.

Bonsai indoors
Over recent years, bonsai enthusiasts in temperate climates have become increasingly interested in growing tropical and sub-tropical bonsai indoors. This is a difficult operation: most trees have been developed outdoors in their home country and exported to temperate countries where they are kept in heated, humid greenhouses before going on sale. An ordinary suburban living room can perhaps provide the level of warmth of the tree's native Taiwan or Philippines, but not the humidity and light it needs. To keep such "indoor" material happy, grow it in a conservatory or greenhouse, displaying it in the house for only a few days at a time. Certainly, it does seem to be difficult to keep an indoor subject happy in the average living room for more than a year. As indoor bonsai become more popular, growers will learn how to maintain them for longer periods.

Bonsai in an English garden
This formal display offers interest at various levels, as well as giving plenty of space to allow for routine maintenance of the trees and shrubs.

Watering and feeding bonsai

Various factors affect the amount of water and fertilizer you should give your bonsai. Some trees are "thirstier" than others. The time of year also affects the quantity of water and nutrients that a tree needs. The type and quality of the potting soil is a factor: the more water and fertilizer that are retained by the soil, the less water and food you need to give the plant, and vice versa.

Watering bonsai

More bonsai die from unsatisfactory watering than from any other problem. Their roots dry out much more quickly in their shallow pots than if they were planted in open ground. Most bonsai can survive, if not thrive, when grown in an inadequate soil without added nutrients, but if they do not have water they will soon dehydrate and die.

Usually, you need to water bonsai daily in spring, summer, and autumn. In winter, dormant trees kept outside in the rain and snow need little extra watering, but make sure that any specimens kept in a cold frame or unheated greenhouse do not dry out. Continue to water any tropical and sub-tropical bonsai indoors, because they will keep on growing throughout the winter, although at a slower rate than in summer, and need to be kept constantly moist.

How to water

Water your bonsai in the evening after sunset. The moisture will then be retained in the soil and available to the roots all night and into the next morning. If you water in the morning, the soil may dry out completely within a few hours; also, any water splattered on the leaves during daytime watering can act as a lens for the sun's rays and cause leaf scorch.

Water from above, using a watering can or a hosepipe that has a very fine rose. You can purchase sprinklers and cans especially designed for bonsai work. The watering can needs a long neck to create a sufficient "head" of water for the spray. The head of a sprinkler is removable, so that you can clean the tiny holes of the rose.

Feeding bonsai

It is essential to feed your bonsai for good growth; if you do not, they may not die, but they certainly will not flourish.

From spring to autumn, it is customary to apply a general, balanced fertilizer; many successful growers use nothing else. In the autumn, it is advisable to switch to a feed high in potassium and phosphorus, but low in nitrogen, because it is then that the trees' growth rate slows and they start to become dormant. When growing *Rhododendron* cultivars (azaleas), *Enkianthus*, stewartia, and other lime-hating plants, choose an ericaceous fertilizer specifically created for such plants.

The main elements in any fertilizer are printed on the packaging in the order NPK (N for nitrogen, P for phosphorus, and K for potassium). A typical autumn feed is in the ratio 0:10:10. Always follow the instructions on the packet; it is not worth buying such a specialized product if you deliberately interfere with its effectiveness.

Fertilizer types

There are many brands of fertilizers on sale, although their names may vary. You can choose between liquid or solid fertilizers. Solid fertilizers come as powder, granules, or small cakes or blocks. Buy granules if possible: they take several weeks to break down, and each time it rains or you water the bonsai, a little more fertilizer dissolves. The granules remain visible on the soil, thus reminding you when it is time to add some more.

Liquid fertilizer acts more quickly, but it is more difficult to see just how much has been absorbed. Heavy rain just after you have applied the product may wash the nutrients through the soil before the plant has absorbed them. The same problem applies to the powder form of solid fertilizer.

Japanese growers frequently add nutrients in the form of small blocks or cakes of rape seed or fish meal. These break down slowly in the same way as fertilizer granules, but do not look attractive on the soil. They can also act as a breeding ground for maggots.

Root pruning and repotting

After a few years, the roots of a bonsai completely fill the pot. When an ordinary pot plant is "pot-bound" like this, you simply pot it on into a bigger container with more soil. When repotting a bonsai, however, you will want to retain the original container that you chose so carefully to complement the tree. You therefore prune the bonsai's roots, so that you can add some fresh potting soil when you replace the tree in its original pot.

Such root pruning of bonsai is popularly, but erroneously, thought to result in stunting or dwarfing of the tree. In fact, a root-pruned bonsai grows more vigorously because the extra soil allows new, fibrous feeder roots to develop from each cut root. Inspect the rootball annually to see if root pruning (*see below*) is necessary. The approximate rate at which you reprune each tree or shrub is indicated on pp. 38–113 and 187–209.

Root pruning

The aim of root pruning is to trim the roots into a flat root system that will fit comfortably back into the pot. It is usually done in spring, but Japanese larches like this *Larix kaempferi* are hardy enough to be tackled in mid to late winter, if the soil is not frozen. Return the

repotted tree to an open position; frost protection is usually unnecessary. Larches grow fast and dislike being pot-bound, so they usually need annual root pruning. When making the wedge-shaped cuts in Step 3, do not damage any surface roots that show above the soil: the shape and spread of the exposed roots on a mature bonsai are an important part of the design and should not be destroyed.

Checking the rootball
Inspect the tree each year to see if root pruning and repotting are necessary. Cut the anchorage wires and ease the plant from the pot, tilting it to check the underside of the soil. If there is a dense mass of long roots coiled around the rootball, they need to be pruned, and the tree must be repotted.

Circling roots indicate the necessity of root pruning and repotting.

ROOT PRUNING TECHNIQUE

1 Use a metal root hook to comb out roots gently. Do not damage the surface radial roots.

2 The long, circling roots need to be cut away with shears. Trim roots on the underside.

3 Cut out wedge-shaped sections from the rootball. This stimulates fibrous roots by the trunk.

Repotting a bonsai

When you repot a bonsai, you will usually replace it in its original container. After removing the tree, you should clean the pot thoroughly. Use a stiff brush to remove any potting soil clinging to the inside of the container. Frequently, this is all that is necessary, but if the pot is still dirty, scrub it out thoroughly with a little washing-up liquid dissolved in clean water.

It is not horticulturally necessary to change the bonsai's container when you repot, although you would do if it were an ordinary plant whose roots needed to expand into a larger area. Sometimes, however, you may feel the container does not suit the design of the bonsai as well as you originally thought, so take this opportunity to use a different pot. In this example, it was decided that a plainer pot would suit the larch better than its original, more rounded one.

Whether you use a new container or the old one, insert or refurbish the plastic mesh over the drainage holes (*see p. 125*). Do the same with the anchorage wires, before covering the bottom of the container with an even layer of a potting soil suitable for the species (*see opposite*). After any necessary root pruning (*see p. 175*), replant the tree as shown below.

Before repotting
It is essential to inspect the rootball annually, to check the root mass and see if the tree needs to be repotted.

REPOTTING THE SPECIMEN

1 Position the bonsai in the prepared pot to give the required front view. Fix it in place with the anchorage wires, bringing them up and over the rootball and twisting them together.

2 With a chopstick, thoroughly work more soil mixture into the root mass. Push it well down into the cut sections. Keep adding soil until it reaches just below the rim of the container.

3 Give the tree a thorough watering. Place pads of damp moss on top of the soil and press them down with a small trowel.

Soil mixtures for bonsai

Different bonsai require different types of soil. A good potting soil should be able to retain enough moisture for the roots to absorb what they need. However, the soil should also be sufficiently well-draining to prevent the soil from becoming waterlogged and causing root-rot. The soil texture should be loose and open enough to help retain the moisture, and to provide good ventilation, so that oxygen circulates and enables the roots to "breathe".

Three kinds of soil mixtures are given for the plants covered in the "A–Z of Bonsai Species" on pp. 38–113, and there are suggestions for other plants in the "Dictionary" on pp. 187–209. With experience, you will learn to mix your own potting soil. The ingredients of the three mixes are as follows.

- *Basic soil mix*
  One part loam, two parts sphagnum moss peat, two parts granite grit.
- *Free-draining soil mix*
  One part loam, one part sphagnum moss peat, three parts granite grit.
- *Lime-free (ericaceous) soil mix*
  One part loam, three parts sphagnum moss peat, one part granite grit.

Fertilizers will scorch new roots, so you should not feed a repotted or newly planted bonsai until two or three weeks after the initial new growth of spring. Once the plant is established, you can add any necessary nutrients (*see p. 174*).

Larix kaempferi
JAPANESE LARCH

The repotted tree
The only visible difference after the tree has been repotted is the change to a different pot, which was felt to be a better complement to the bonsai. Larches like this one usually need repotting each year to maintain healthy growth; other species may not need this treatment so often.

Routine pruning

With correct positioning, watering, feeding, and repotting, your bonsai should grow vigorously. Then the skills of shaping and grooming the tree come into play, partly to maintain the design you have created, and also to improve and refine it.

One technique of maintenance pruning is called pinching back or finger pruning. This encourages secondary growth further back on the branch or twig, producing bushy foliage that makes the tree look more mature.

Without pinching back, the most vigorous shoots, usually on the topmost branches, grow strong and thick, resulting in a top-heavy look as the lower branches wither and die. Trim top shoots early on to prevent this, but allow the lower branches to spread out and thicken before trimming. This method produces delicate twigs at the apex and strong lower branches. It will also thicken trunks on developing bonsai. You must, of course, accompany pruning with correct watering and feeding.

Finger pruning a conifer

Conifers such as cedars, cryptomerias, larches, spruces, and this juniper, are usually finger pruned; trimming with scissors turns the cut shoots brown and temporarily spoils the bonsai. You will not cause any damage if you use the soft pads of your fingertips. The two types of conifer foliage – scale-like and needle-like – require different methods of finger pruning (*see below and opposite*). The trees mentioned above and some junipers have needles, cypresses and other junipers have scale-like foliage. Some junipers have one type of foliage; others have needles when young, and scale-like leaves when mature. Such foliage is known respectively as "juvenile" and "adult".

FINGER PRUNING SPECIES WITH SCALE-LIKE LEAVES

1 Leading shoots are removed with a twisting movement. Hold the branch with one hand. Using the thumb and forefinger of the other hand, grasp the leading shoot so that you twist the shoot as you pull it.

2 The objective is to break the shoot cleanly and neatly from the branch without causing damage to the remaining foliage. Do this by using a twisting motion at the same time as you firmly pull the shoot away from the tree.

3 Continue finger pruning over the whole tree to refine the lines of the design and create a balanced shape. Pay particular attention to the apex of the bonsai to prevent it becoming ragged and untidy.

The apex has been heavily finger pruned.

The growing foliage is obscuring the branches.

The sinuous line of the trunk is revealed.

Juniperus squamata 'Meyeri'
before finger pruning
After initial shaping, this bonsai specimen grew on for two months without further training. The line of the trunk and the overall structure started to be lost among a mass of foliage.

The same tree after finger pruning
The bonsai has been quite heavily pinched back to reveal its elegant lines and to bring order to the overall design. Now that balance and harmony have been restored, the process of finger pruning will be repeated regularly to flesh out the shape.

FINGER PRUNING SPECIES WITH NEEDLES

1 Grasp the branch with the finger and thumb of one hand and gently but firmly take hold of the leading shoot between the pads of the thumb and forefinger of the other hand.

2 In a single, sharp movement, pull the branch straight towards you. If you do this correctly, the shoot will break away neatly from the shoot leaving the rest of the foliage intact.

3 Pinch out the shoots over the entire apex of the bonsai and do as much work as necessary to tidy up the branches. Finger pruning in this way creates a more compact refined shape which emphasizes the trunk line.

Scissor trimming

The Chinese elm, *Ulmus parvifolia*, shown here demonstrates how careful scissor trimming throughout the growing season can refine a bonsai's shape and encourage bushier growth.

You can use scissors to cut stems, but never foliage, which will look untidy and turn brown at the edges. Fingernails are best for pinching out very soft, young stems, and also for pine "candles" (the extending buds of pine trees), if they have not hardened. You will, however, have to use scissors to cut off tougher stems and candles, or you will tear the tissues of the stem.

This bonsai is being grown in root-over-rock style.

Before trimming
Straggly growth has "blurred" the silhouette.

TRIMMING A DECIDUOUS TREE WITH SCISSORS

The trimmed bonsai has regained balance.

1 Hold the shoot at the top and cut the stem directly above a leaf. Never cut through foliage as this will turn brown.

2 Remove all long shoots that mar the outline of the bonsai. These cut shoots can often be used as propagating material.

After trimming
The tree now has an attractive conical shape.

TRIMMING PINE CANDLES WITH SCISSORS

1 Position scissors with fine, sharp points carefully at the base of a candle so that you do not cut the surrounding needles.

2 Make a single, neat cut through the base of the candle, ensuring that you leave no ragged ends.

3 Cutting away the candles refines the shape of the tree and encourages new buds to develop.

Leaf cutting

Some species such as birches, elms, and this Japanese maple produce leaves in continuous or successive flushes. If you remove all the leaves in summer, a second crop will sprout: this gives you two years' growth in one, because the new leaves emerge from next year's buds. They are usually smaller, and their autumn colour brighter, than those of the first flush of leaves. The leaf-cut Japanese maple (*below*) produces a second crop of its bright red spring foliage. Timing of leaf cutting is vital. If you do it too soon, the new buds will not have formed; too late, and the new leaves may not harden off before autumn, leaving insufficient time for replacement buds to form.

LEAF CUTTING TECHNIQUE

1 Using scissors, remove leaves carefully and systematically, starting at the top of the tree and working your way downwards to the lowest branches.

2 Cut off each leaf directly behind its base, leaving the petiole (leaf stalk) sticking out from the trimmed branch.

3 Allowing petioles to stay in place conserves moisture for the dormant buds at their bases. The petioles will drop off before the new buds open.

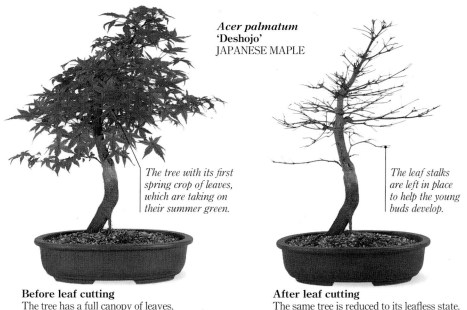

Acer palmatum
'Deshojo'
JAPANESE MAPLE

The tree with its first spring crop of leaves, which are taking on their summer green.

The leaf stalks are left in place to help the young buds develop.

Before leaf cutting
The tree has a full canopy of leaves.

After leaf cutting
The same tree is reduced to its leafless state.

Pests and diseases

These pages show the more common pests and diseases that might attack your bonsai. Fortunately, most bonsai trees and shrubs are hardy species that are not notably susceptible to pests and diseases, but, if a problem should arise, you should recognize it quickly and "nip it in the bud". A useful preventative measure is to spray the bonsai monthly, from early spring and through the summer, with a systemic insecticide and fungicide. This should be ninety per cent effective, penetrating the sap and helping the plant to counter-attack any enemy over the following two or three weeks. Check that the brands of fungicide and insecticide are compatible, and follow the manufacturer's instructions. Only spray leaves that are in bud or fully open; unfolding ones may be damaged.

PESTS

Blackfly
Aphids such as blackfly are common in many climates and suck sap from stems, leaves, and fruit of garden plants, and also carry viruses. Once spotted, they must be eradicated. They are easy to see; you may notice leaves and new shoots curling up.

Greenfly
Like most of the aphids, greenfly were named after their colour. Aphids attack thin-leaved, deciduous trees in particular. They lurk on undersides of leaves and on young shoots, and secrete a sticky "honeydew". Prune out damaged shoots.

Cuckoo spit
Larvae of this insect, found in many climates, inhabit the spit-like masses on leaves and shoots. They thrive on plant sap. The damage is similar to that done by aphids. Remove the "spit" by wiping with a damp cloth or spraying with clean water.

Scale insects
These are a group of tiny, sap-sucking insects which look like hard white, yellow, red or brown blisters on leaves and stems. Signs of damage are a sooty mould and sticky "honeydew" coating the leaves. A systemic insecticide is effective.

Orbital mites
These red or black "pinhead" mites, found in most climates, can be seen under branches or in bark crevices. They feed on algae on the bark, but do no damage to the tree's growth. They are unsightly, but can be brushed away with a toothbrush.

Caterpillars
As soon as they hatch out in the spring, caterpillars begin feeding voraciously on young foliage and stems. It is best to pick them off by hand or use a contact spray. Remove any damaged leaves to improve the appearance of the tree.

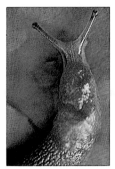

Damage (above) caused by the adult vine weevil (right)

Slugs and snails
These attack roots, shoots, and leaves, making large holes in the latter. Liquid slug-killers, which must be watered in, are not very suitable for bonsai, because there is not much soil in the pot. Instead, leave a cream or pellet type of slug bait near the pot.

Vine weevils
The adult beetle nibbles foliage, leaving notched edges; the larvae feed off roots. Getting rid of larvae in regions where they occur can be a problem as they can live in the soil for up to six months and may not be noticed until repotting. Soak pots in a solution of gamma-HCH.

Leaf miners
If you notice brown or white markings on leaves, this is probably caused by leaf miners which feed on the soft, interior tissues. These pests are the larvae which hatch from eggs laid on the undersides of the leaves by moths and flies. They have a blister-like appearance. On bonsai, remove spoilt leaves and spray regularly with a systemic insecticide.

A leaf damaged by leaf miners

DISEASES

Peach leaf curl
This problem, which causes leaf damage and so weakens the tree, occurs in many climates but is limited to a few *Prunus* species. Reddish blisters form on leaves, grow bigger, and turn white. Leaves distort, discolour, and drop. The fungus can survive over winter. Destroy affected leaves and spray with a copper fungicide.

Powdery mildew
These fungal spores, which thrive in damp conditions, appear as white, powdery patches on leaves and stems, of oak, hawthorn, and crab apple in particular. They leach sap, causing the tree to lose vigour. Remove the affected shoots on which the disease overwinters. Routine preventive treatment is important.

CHAPTER SIX

DICTIONARY OF TREES AND SHRUBS FOR BONSAI

To give you the widest choice when you select material for a bonsai, this dictionary extends the range of the "A-Z of Bonsai Species" on pp. 36–113, thus providing a total list of over 300 trees and shrubs which are suitable for bonsai cultivation. This dictionary has been devised to follow the same principles as the "A-Z of Bonsai Species". It lists the plants in alphabetical order of their botanical names, followed by their common names. Sub-species, forms, and cultivars are listed alphabetically immediately after the entry on the main species. Every entry briefly describes the characteristics of the tree or shrub, and suggests, or gives a cross-reference to, bonsai styles and sizes that specially suit it. Advice on cultivation is also included, classified under the same symbol headings as in the "A-Z of Bonsai Species".

Selection of bonsai
A bench display at a bonsai nursery shows off some of the immensely varied range of species and styles which make up the amazing and exciting world of bonsai.

How to use the dictionary

Over 300 trees and shrubs that are suitable for bonsai are listed on pp. 187–209 in this dictionary. Most of them are species, but many excellent subspecies, hybrids, varieties, and cultivars are included with their parent species, and both the similarities or differences to the species are pointed out. The dictionary also recapitulates all the plant entries in the "A-Z of Bonsai Species", with a brief description of each plant, and a cross-reference to the relevant page for styles, sizes, and cultivation details.

The plants are listed under their botanical names in alphabetical order. If a plant has two names, its main entry is under the name most commonly used, with the synonym given in brackets. The synonym is also included in the correct alphabetical order, with a cross-reference to the main entry. The common name of every plant is also given.

Descriptions

Every tree and shrub featured, including those in the "A-Z of Bonsai Species", is described briefly, indicating characteristics such as growth rate, size, and hardiness, leaf shape and size, as well as any autumn tints or unusual colouring. Flowers or fruit are also detailed, together with bark texture.

Styles and sizes

Styles given are those likely to succeed, rather than absolute definitions: the individual tree's species and character will affect your choice. See pp. 116–21 for more details. Good accent or accessory plants are also noted. Sizes given are based on a plant's natural size or the fineness of its leaves or twigs. These are: extra-large, over 90cm (36in); large, 45–90cm (18–36in); medium, 20–45cm (8–18in); small, 10–20cm (4–8in) and extra-small, up to 10cm (4in).

Cultivation details

The plant's needs and propagation are given under the same symbols as in the "A-Z of Bonsai Species" (see box below). Further care details are on pp. 170–83. If two forms suit the same style or size, or have similar cultivation needs, these details are not repeated. Instead, there is a cross-reference to the earliest entry, in the dictionary or "A-Z of Bonsai Species". If an aspect of care, styling, or size differs from the earliest entry, it is noted in the dictionary entry.

Cultivation symbols
◉ Position ◌ Watering ⦂ Feeding
▣ Repotting ◈ Pruning ⚇ Propagation

General description
This includes the plant's natural habit, hardiness, leaf type, and flowers or fruit, if any. Suitable bonsai styles and sizes are also listed.

Identification
This dictionary is an alphabetical order of botanical names (in bold italics). Common names, in italic type, follow each botanical name.

Ulmus × elegantissima **'Jacqueline Hillier'**,
'Jacqueline Hillier' elm
A deciduous tree with a neat, dense habit and small, toothed leaves. Suitable for all styles and sizes.
◉ Full sun. Protect from frost.
◌ Daily during growing season, more frequently if necessary in very hot weather. Keep moist in winter.
⦂ Weekly for first month after leaf buds open; then fortnightly until late summer.
▣ Annually in early spring. Free-draining soil mix.
◈ Trim new shoots during growing season.
⚇ Cuttings; grafting.

Ulmus glabra, *Wych* or *Scotch elm*
In autumn, the dull green leaves of this deciduous tree turn yellow. The bark is grey-brown. Styles, sizes, and most cultivation as for *U. × elegantissima* 'Jacqueline Hillier'.
⚇ Seeds; cuttings; root cuttings.

Cultivation
Plant care required is listed under relevant symbols (see above). Propagation is also detailed, in ascending order of difficulty.

Cross-references
Species or forms with similar styles, sizes, and cultivation needs have a cross-reference to the earliest entry. Any entry for a plant illustrated in the "A-Z of Bonsai Species" has a cross-reference to the relevant page.

Abies alba, *Silver fir*
An evergreen conifer with cylindrical cones and dark green, needle-like leaves. Suitable for formal upright, informal upright, slanting, semicascade, literati, twin-trunk, clump, straight line, sinuous, multiple-trunk, group, and saikei styles. Medium to extra-large sizes.
- ◉ Slight shade.
- ◹ Daily during summer.
- ⚘ Fortnightly from early spring to mid autumn.
- ▦ Every other year, in spring or autumn, using basic soil mix.
- ⊗ Finger pinch new shoots during growing season.
- ✄ Seeds; layering; cuttings.

Abies koreana, *Korean fir*
A slow-growing, small, evergreen conifer with dark green leaves. The cones are purple even on a young tree. Styles, sizes, and cultivation as for *A. alba*.

Abies koreana 'Compact dwarf',
Dwarf Korean fir
A dwarf form of *A. koreana* that does not produce cones. Suggested sizes: extra-small and small. Styles and most cultivation as for *A. alba*.
- ✄ Grafting.

Abies lasiocarpa, *Alpine fir*
An evergreen conifer with grey-green, needle-like leaves. Styles, sizes, and cultivation as for *A. alba*.

Abies lasiocarpa arizonica, *Cork fir*
A variety with silver-grey, needle-like leaves and thick, corky bark. Styles, sizes, and cultivation as for *A. alba*.

Abies lasiocarpa arizonica 'Compacta',
Dwarf cork fir
A dwarf form, with notable silvery blue-grey foliage. Styles, sizes, and most cultivation as for *A. alba*.
- ✄ Grafting.

Acer buergerianum (A. trifidium),
Trident maple
A deciduous tree, with wonderful orange and red colours in autumn. (*See pp. 40–41.*)

Acer buergerianum formosanum,
Formosan trident maple
A more compact subspecies, with thick, leathery leaves. For styles, sizes, and cultivation, see pp. 40–41.

Acer buergerianum 'Mino Yatsubusa',
Dwarf trident maple
This dwarf variety has a pointed apex. In autumn, its long, narrow, shiny leaves look as if they are lacquered red and orange. For styles, sizes, and cultivation, see pp. 40–41.

Acer campestre, *Field maple*
A small deciduous tree with a fairly coarse structure. In autumn, the leaves turn bright yellow. (*See p. 42.*)

Acer davidii, *Snake bark* or *Père David's maple*
A deciduous tree with striking, snake-like bark striped in white and green. The leaves are heart-shaped and grow on red stalks; in autumn, they turn rich yellow. Suitable for all styles, except broom. Good in medium to large sizes, but also extra-small. For cultivation, see p. 42.

Acer ginnala, *Amur maple*
This is a deciduous tree that greatly resembles *A. buergerianum*, but very frost-tolerant, so planted frequently as a replacement in colder climates. For styles, sizes, and most cultivation, see pp. 40–41.
- ◉ Full sun.
- ▦ Annually in early spring. Free-draining soil mix.

Acer japonicum, *Full moon maple*
A deciduous tree with fan-shaped leaves that turn red, orange, and bright yellow in autumn. All styles except broom. Good in medium to large sizes, but also extra-small. For most cultivation, see p. 42.
- ✄ Seeds; cuttings; grafting; layering; air layering.

Acer japonicum 'Aureum',
Golden full moon maple
A variety with yellow leaves that turn orange in autumn. For styles, sizes, and most cultivation, see p. 42.
- ✄ Grafting; layering; air layering; cuttings.

Acer palmatum, *Japanese maple*
This classic bonsai subject is a deciduous tree, with five-lobed leaves that turn red in autumn, and bark that turns silver with age. There are over 250 cultivars. (*See pp. 43–5.*)

Acer palmatum 'Chishio', *Japanese red maple*
Similar to the species above, but with crimson spring foliage. Once the most frequently grown red maple in bonsai, but now mainly superseded by 'Deshojo'. For styles, sizes, and most cultivation, see pp. 44–5.
- ✄ Grafting; cuttings; layering; air layering.

Acer palmatum 'Deshojo', *Japanese red maple*
The hardiest of the *palmatum* cultivars, with red spring foliage that is particularly brilliant. For styles, sizes, and most cultivation, see pp. 44–5.
- ✄ Grafting; cuttings; layering; air layering.

Acer palmatum 'Dissectum',
Cut-leaf Japanese maple
This acer has finely cut, green leaves with seven to eleven lobes. In autumn, they turn red. The best styles are informal upright, slanting, semicascade, cascade,

twin-trunk, and clump. All sizes are suitable. For most cultivation, see pp. 44–5.

☒ Grafting; cuttings; layering; air layering.

Acer palmatum 'Dissectum atropurpureum',
Cut-leaf purple maple
A variety with purple leaves that turn bright orange in autumn. Suitable for informal upright, slanting, semicascade, cascade, twin-trunk, and clump styles, and all sizes. For most cultivation, see pp. 44–5.

☒ Grafting; cuttings; layering; air layering.

Acer palmatum 'Dissectum atropurpureum' 'Inaba shidare',
Cut-leaf purple maple
The leaves of this outstanding cultivar are a deep purple-red throughout spring and summer, before they turn crimson in autumn. Styles are informal upright, slanting, semicascade, cascade, twin-trunk, clump. Grow this shrub in all sizes. For most cultivation, see pp. 44–5.

☒ Grafting; cuttings; layering; air layering.

Acer palmatum 'Kagiri Nishiki',
Japanese maple 'Kagiri Nishiki'
The leaves are a deep bluish-green with creamy white margins suffused with pink. In autumn, they turn rose-red. For styles, sizes, and cultivation, see p. 43.

Acer palmatum 'Kashima',
Japanese maple 'Kashima'
A very dwarf form, with leaves that appear early in spring as a light yellow-green with a reddish margin. They deepen to rich green, before turning bright yellow in autumn. Best styles are informal upright, slanting, semicascade, cascade, twin-trunk, and clump. All sizes are suitable. For cultivation, see pp. 44–5.

☒ Grafting; cuttings; layering; air layering.

Acer palmatum 'Katsura',
Japanese maple 'Katsura'
The foliage of this dwarf 'Yatsubusa' form is apricot in spring and, in autumn, changes to orange and yellow. Grow this shrub in informal upright, slanting, semicascade, cascade, twin-trunk, and clump styles, and in all sizes. For most cultivation, see pp. 44–5.

☒ Grafting; cuttings; layering; air layering.

Acer palmatum 'Kiyohime',
Japanese maple 'Kiyohime'
This very early 'Yatsubusa' form is very small and grows horizontally without a central leader shoot. Suitable in all styles and sizes except literati, but especially good in broom style and smaller sizes. For most cultivation, see pp. 43–5.

☒ Cuttings; grafting; layering; air layering.

Acer palmatum 'Kotohime',
Japanese maple 'Kotohime'
A very small 'Yatsubusa' form, strongly vertical, with some of the smallest leaves. All styles except semicascade, cascade, and literati; small and extra-small sizes. For most cultivation, see pp. 44–5.

☒ Grafting; cuttings; layering; air layering.

Acer palmatum 'Nishiki gawa',
Pine bark maple
The corky bark of this variety becomes very thick while the tree is fairly young. The leaves turn red in autumn. Informal upright, slanting, semicascade, cascade, twin-trunk, and clump styles are best, and all sizes are suitable. For most cultivation, see pp. 44–5.

☒ Cuttings; grafting; layering; air layering.

Acer palmatum 'Sango Kaku',
'Sango Kaku' maple
A variety with vivid coral-pink bark. The pink twigs are best appreciated in winter; in spring, the green leaves have red margins. For styles, sizes, and most cultivation, see pp. 44–5.

☒ Grafting; cuttings; layering; air layering.

Acer palmatum 'Seigen', *Japanese red maple*
In spring, the foliage is a translucent pink and red, although very sensitive to wind at this time. In autumn, it turns red and orange. For styles, sizes, and most cultivation, see pp. 44–5.

☒ Grafting; cuttings; layering; air layering.

Acer palmatum 'Shigitatsu Sawa',
Japanese maple 'Shigitatsu Sawa'
A maple with yellow-green leaves prominently veined in bright green; the autumn colour is red. For styles, sizes, and most cultivation, see pp. 44–5.

☒ Grafting; cuttings; layering; air layering.

Acer palmatum 'Ukigomo',
Japanese maple 'Ukigomo'
The light green leaves are subtly variegated in white and pink, some being completely white or pink. For styles, sizes, and most cultivation, see pp. 44–5.

☒ Grafting; cuttings; layering; air layering.

Acer palmatum 'Ukon', *Ukon maple*
In autumn, the lime-green leaves turn yellow and gold. The branches and twigs are also lime-green. For styles, sizes, and most cultivation, see pp. 44–5.

☒ Grafting; cuttings; layering; air layering.

Acer trifidium, see Acer buergerianum.

Amelanchier lamarckii, *Snowy mespilus*
This deciduous shrub has scented, white flowers in spring and purple fruit in autumn. Suitable for

informal upright, slanting, semicascade, cascade, root-over-rock, twin-trunk, straight line, sinuous, or saikei styles, and extra-small to large sizes.

- ◉ Full sun.
- ◔ Daily during growing season.
- ⠶ Fortnightly from spring to autumn.
- ▦ Every other year in early spring. Basic soil mix.
- ▨ Trim new growth after flowers fade.
- ▧ Seeds; cuttings; layering; air layering.

Andromeda japonica, see *Pieris japonica*.

Andromeda polifolia, *Bog rosemary*
A shrub with narrow, evergreen leaves; in early summer, it produces heather-like, pink flowers. Hates lime. Good styles are clump and saikei; also grown as an accent plant. Extra-small and small sizes.

- ◉ Slight shade.
- ◔ Keep soil moist during growing season.
- ⠶ Monthly during summer. Use ericaceous feed.
- ▦ Annually in spring. Use lime-free soil mix.
- ▨ Trim new growth after flowering.
- ▧ Cuttings; division.

Arundinaria nitida, *Bamboo*
Grass-like, evergreen leaves are borne on strong, arching canes. (*See pp. 46–7.*)

Arundinaria pygmaea, *Dwarf bamboo*
This dwarf species grows up to 25cm (10in) in nature, but much less in a shallow pot. Suitable for multiple-trunk styles in extra-small and small sizes. For cultivation, see pp. 46–7.

Azalea indica, see *Rhododendron indicum*.

Berberis buxifolia, *Barberry*
The box-like leaves on this semi-evergreen shrub are deep green on top and grey underneath. In spring, yellow flowers are produced, followed in autumn by purple fruits. Styles are informal upright, slanting, root-over-rock, clasped-to-rock, twin-trunk, clump, straight line, sinuous, group, and saikei. The best sizes are extra-small to medium.

- ◉ Full sun or shade.
- ◔ Daily during growing season.
- ⠶ Fortnightly during summer.
- ▦ Every other year, in early spring before bud break. Use basic soil mix.
- ▨ Trim new growth during summer.
- ▧ Seeds; cuttings; division; layering.

Berberis darwinii, *Barberry*
This evergreen shrub has dark green, holly-like leaves. In very early spring, it is covered with clusters of small, golden-orange flowers, followed in autumn by blue fruits. Styles, sizes, and cultivation as for *B. buxifolia*.

Berberis thunbergii, *Barberry*
In autumn, the leaves of this thorny shrub turn red before they fall. Other features are the small, yellow flowers it produces in spring, and the bright red fruits that follow in autumn. Styles, sizes, and cultivation as for *B. buxifolia*.

Berberis thunbergii 'Bagatelle',
Dwarf purple barberry
The compact foliage of this very hardy dwarf variety is red-purple in spring, and turns dark red in summer. It is best in extra-small and small sizes. Styles and most cultivation as for *B. buxifolia*.

- ▧ Cuttings; division; layering.

Betula nana, *Dwarf birch*
The tiny, serrated leaves on this shrub turn rich gold in autumn before they fall. The trunk is copper-coloured. (*See p. 48.*)

Betula pendula, *European white* or *Silver birch*
This tree has a distinctive silver-white bark, and heart-shaped, deciduous leaves that turn gold in autumn. (*See p. 49.*)

Bougainvillea buttiana, *Bougainvillea*
This tender climber has deep-red, flower-like bracts and semi-evergreen, oval leaves. It is suitable for all styles except formal upright, broom, and literati, and for medium to extra-large sizes.

- ◉ Full sun. Minimum temperature 7°C (45°F).
- ◔ Daily during summer, sparingly in winter.
- ⠶ Fortnightly during summer.
- ▦ Every three to four years in spring. Use free-draining soil mix.
- ▨ Continually trim back straggling shoots for a more compact plant.
- ▧ Cuttings.

Bougainvillea buttiana 'Orange King',
'Orange King' bougainvillea
The flower-like bracts on this variety are orange. Styles, sizes, and cultivation as for *B. buttiana*.

Bougainvillea glabra, *Bougainvillea*
This tender climber has semi-evergreen, oval leaves and cerise, flower-like bracts. Styles, sizes, and cultivation as for *B. buttiana*.

Bougainvillea glabra 'Magnifica', *Bougainvillea*
The flower-like bracts of this variety are rosy purple. Styles, sizes, and cultivation as for *B. buttiana*.

Bougainvillea glabra 'Snow White',
White bougainvillea
A form with white, flower-like bracts. Styles, sizes, and cultivation as for *B. buttiana*.

Buxus microphylla, *Japanese box*
This compact shrub produces small, oblong, dark green leaves which are evergreen. It is suitable for informal upright, slanting, semicascade, root-over-rock, clasped-to-rock, twin-trunk, clump, group, and saikei styles, and all sizes.
[●] Full sun or shade. Protect from frost and cold winds.
[◌] Daily during growing season. In winter, keep always moist.
[⋯] Fortnightly during growing season.
[▦] Every second year in spring. Use basic soil mix.
[◱] Continually trim new growth.
[▨] Cuttings; division; layering.

Buxus sempervirens, *Common box*
This small, evergreen tree or shrub with tiny, dark green leaves is almost indistinguishable from *B. microphylla*, but is more generally available. Styles, sizes, and cultivation as for *B. microphylla*.

Calluna vulgaris, *Heather*
The many cultivated varieties of this small, lime-hating, evergreen shrub have fine-textured foliage in different colours. The flowers are often purple, but can be in shades of pink, white, or red. Stems are woody. Suitable styles are informal upright, slanting, semicascade, literati, clasped-to-rock, twin-trunk, clump, multiple-trunk, saikei; also used as an accent plant. Grow it in extra-small and small sizes only.
[●] Full sun.
[◌] Daily during summer.
[⋯] None: feeding will discourage flowering.
[▦] Every three to four years. Use lime-free soil mix.
[◱] Scissor trim foliage to keep compact.
[▨] Cuttings; layering; seeds.

Calluna vulgaris 'County Wicklow',
'County Wicklow' heather
In summer, this dwarf compact heather bears double, shell-pink flowers. Styles, sizes, and most cultivation as for *C. vulgaris*.
[▨] Cuttings.

Calluna vulgaris 'Foxii Nana', *Dwarf heather*
This heather is grown more for its fine, moss-like foliage than for its light purple flowers, which appear only rarely. The best styles are clasped-to-rock and saikei. Sizes and most cultivation as for *C. vulgaris*.
[▨] Cuttings.

Camellia japonica, *Common camellia*
An impressive, lime-hating shrub with shiny, evergreen leaves. In spring, it produces pink, red, or white flowers. Grow it in informal upright, slanting, semicascade, cascade, twin-trunk, and clump styles, and in large or extra-large sizes.

[●] Partial shade. Protect from frost.
[◌] Daily during growing season. Use lime-free water. In winter, keep soil always moist.
[⋯] Fortnightly during growing season. Use ericaceous fertilizer.
[▦] Every two to three years in late spring. Use lime-free soil mix.
[◱] Trim new growth after flowers fade.
[▨] Cuttings; layering; seeds.

Camellia reticulata, *Camellia*
A lime-hating, evergreen shrub with large, single or double flowers in red or pink. Styles, sizes, and most cultivation as for *C. japonica*.
[▦] Annually in late spring. Use lime-free soil mix.

Camellia sasanqua, *Camellia*
This is the smallest of the camellias, and thus often used for bonsai. It is a lime-hating, evergreen shrub, with small, fragrant, white flowers in winter and early spring. It needs more winter protection than other camellias. Styles, sizes, and most cultivation as for *C. japonica*.
[●] Partial shade. Protect from frost and cold winds.

Caragana arborescens, *Chinese pea tree*
The compound leaves of this shrubby tree are deciduous, and the pea-type flowers yellow. This native of Siberia is very tough, and can withstand temperatures below freezing. As an indoor bonsai, it also tolerates high temperatures. (*See p. 50.*)

Caragana chamlagu, see *C. sinica.*

Caragana sinica (*C. chamlagu*),
Mongolian redshrub
This shrub bears glossy, oval, serrated, dark green leaves on spiny branches. It is semi-evergreen. For styles, sizes, and most cultivation, see p. 50.
[●] Full sun indoors or out. Protect from frost and freezing winds.

Carmona microphylla (*Ehretia buxifolia*),
Fukien tea
This tender, evergreen shrub has small, shiny, dark green leaves, white flowers, and red fruits. (*See p. 51.*)

Carpinus betulus, *European hornbeam*
This tree has striped and ridged grey bark. Its grooved, oval leaves turn yellow in autumn before they fall. For styles, sizes, and cultivation, see p. 52.

Carpinus japonica, *Japanese hornbeam*
This tree has prominently grooved, deciduous leaves and produces long catkins in spring. For styles, sizes, and cultivation, see p. 52.

Carpinus laxiflora, *Loose-flowered hornbeam*
This hornbeam with smooth trunk and smallish, glossy leaves bears loose clusters of flowers, that, in autumn, form green fruiting "keys". For styles, sizes, and cultivation, see p. 52.

Carpinus turczaninowii, *Korean hornbeam*
Delicate, branching twigs bear very small leaves that turn orange-red in autumn. For styles, sizes, and cultivation, see p. 52.

Castanea, *Chestnut*
A tree with large, toothed, deciduous leaves and, in spring, white or red flower spikes. Informal upright, slanting, semicascade, twin-trunk, clump, and group styles look good, as do large and extra-large sizes.
☀ Full sun.
◌ Daily during growing season.
⚘ Every two or three weeks during growing season.
▦ Every other year in spring. Use basic soil mix.
◔ Trim new growth continually.
✂ Seeds.

Cedrus atlantica, *Atlas cedar*
This evergreen conifer has grey bark, needle-like leaves, and cylindrical cones. (*See p. 53.*)

Cedrus atlantica glauca, *Blue cedar*
A variety with blue-grey bark and foliage. For styles, sizes, and most cultivation, see p. 53.
✂ Grafting.

Cedrus brevifolia, *Cyprian cedar*
This slow-growing evergreen conifer has very short, dark green needles. Suitable for extra-small to large sizes. For styles and most cultivation, see p. 53.
✂ Grafting.

Cedrus deodara, *Deodar* or *Indian cedar*
An evergreen conifer with drooping branches and leader stem covered by large needles. For styles, sizes, and cultivation, see p. 53.

Cedrus libani, *Cedar of Lebanon*
This long-lived, slow-growing conifer carries its dark green, evergreen leaves on horizontal, spreading branches. For styles, sizes, and cultivation, see p. 53.

Celastrus orbiculatus, *Oriental bittersweet*
In autumn, the leaves of this deciduous climber turn yellow, and its green fruits split open to reveal golden linings and brilliant red seeds. (*See p. 54.*)

Celtis sinensis, *Chinese hackberry*
A small, deciduous tree that resembles *Zelkova serrata*, with delicate twigs and glossy leaves. It is suitable for formal upright, informal upright,

slanting, semicascade, cascade, broom, root-over-rock, clasped-to-rock, twin-trunk, clump, multiple-trunk, group, and saikei styles. Grow it in all sizes.
☀ Full sun.
◌ Daily during summer. Keep moist at other times.
⚘ Weekly for first month after buds open, then fortnightly during summer.
▦ Annually in early spring. Use basic soil mix.
◔ Trim new shoots as they grow during summer.
✂ Seeds; cuttings; layering.

Cercidiphyllum japonicum, *Katsura tree*
This deciduous tree is often confused with *Cercis siliquastrum*. Its small leaves are heart-shaped with a rounded point, and turn brilliant yellow and pink in autumn. Grow it in informal upright, slanting, semicascade, cascade, broom, twin-trunk, clump, multiple-trunk, and saikei styles. The sizes may be small to extra-large.
☀ Sun or half shade.
◌ Daily during growing season, sparingly in winter.
⚘ Fortnightly during summer.
▦ Every two to three years in early spring. Use basic soil mix.
◔ Trim back new growth continually.
✂ Seeds; cuttings; layering; air layering.

Cercis canadensis, *American redbud*
Pale pink flowers in early summer and bright green, heart-shaped leaves adorn this deciduous tree. Informal upright, slanting, semicascade, cascade, broom, root-over-rock, twin-trunk, clump, multiple-trunk, and group styles are best, as are medium and large sizes.
☀ Full sun.
◌ Daily during summer, sparingly in winter.
⚘ Fortnightly during summer.
▦ Every other year in early spring. Use basic soil mix.
◔ Trim back new growth continually.
✂ Seeds; cuttings; layering; air layering.

Cercis siliquastrum, *Judas tree*
This tree has small, heart-shaped, deciduous leaves. In spring, rose-lilac flowers are borne on the bare branches. Styles, sizes, and cultivation as for *C. canadensis*.

Chaenomeles japonica, *Maul's flowering quince*
A shrub with deciduous, oval leaves, brilliant red flowers on bare branches in early spring, and yellow fruits. For styles, sizes, and cultivation, see p. 55.

Chaenomeles japonica 'Chojubai',
Dwarf Japanese flowering quince
This dwarf variety produces flushes of red or white flowers throughout the year. For styles, sizes, and most cultivation, see p. 55.
✂ Cuttings; division.

Chaenomeles sinensis (*Pseudocydonia sinensis*), *Chinese quince*
This small tree has attractive, flaky-textured bark, and glossy, semi-evergreen leaves that in autumn turn from gold through to purple. Small, pink flowers in spring are followed by fragrant, yellow fruits. (*See p. 56.*)

Chaenomeles speciosa, *Flowering quince*
This deciduous flowering shrub with oval leaves is very similar to *C. japonica*. In early spring, red flowers are produced on the bare branches. Yellow fruits are borne in autumn. For styles, sizes, and most cultivation, see p. 55.
- ⚬ Fortnightly from spring to autumn.
- ⚬ Grafting; cuttings.

Chaenomeles speciosa 'Nivalis',
White flowering quince
This variety is unusual in producing white flowers in early spring, instead of the pink or red flowers of other forms. For styles, sizes, and most cultivation, see p. 55.
- ⚬ Fortnightly from spring to autumn.
- ⚬ Grafting; cuttings.

Chaenomeles × superba
(*japonica × speciosa*), *Flowering quince hybrids*
All these small to medium-sized flowering shrubs have oval leaves, but flowers in different colours. For styles, sizes, and most cultivation, see p. 55.
- ⚬ Grafting; cuttings.

Chaenomeles × superba 'Crimson and Gold',
Flowering quince
A variety producing dark red flowers with very conspicuous yellow anthers in spring. For styles, sizes, and most cultivation, see p. 55.
- ⚬ Grafting; cuttings.

Chaenomeles × superba 'Etna',
Flowering quince
This variety has vermilion flowers. For styles, sizes, and most cultivation, see p. 55.
- ⚬ Grafting; cuttings.

Chaenomeles × superba 'Incendie',
Flowering quince
Semi-double flowers in orange-red adorn this form. For styles, sizes, and most cultivation, see p. 55.
- ⚬ Grafting; cuttings.

Chaenomeles × superba 'Pink Lady',
Flowering quince
A variety with rose-pink flowers. For styles, sizes, and most cultivation, see p. 55.
- ⚬ Grafting; cuttings.

Chamaecyparis obtusa, *Hinoki cypress*
This evergreen conifer has flat, fan-shaped branches. The cones are the size of a pea, and the undersides of the scale-like leaves are edged with blue. For styles, sizes, and cultivation, see p. 57.

Chamaecyparis obtusa 'Nana Gracilis',
Dwarf Hinoki cypress
This slow-growing, dwarf variety is cone-shaped with glossy, dark green foliage. Especially suitable for extra-small to medium sizes. For styles and most cultivation, see p. 57.
- ⚬ Grafting; cuttings.

Chamaecyparis obtusa 'Yatsubusa',
Dwarf Hinoki cypress
A compact, dwarf form that is slow-growing and naturally cone-shaped. Especially suitable for extra-small to medium sizes. For styles and most cultivation, see p. 57.
- ⚬ Cuttings.

Chamaecyparis pisifera, *Sawara cypress*
This evergreen conifer has scale-like leaves that are dark green with white markings. The bark is ridged, peeling, and red-brown, and the cones are very small. For styles, sizes, and most cultivation, see p. 57.
- ⚬ Cuttings.

Chamaecyparis pisifera 'Boulevard',
Boulevard or *Blue moss cypress*
Soft steel-blue foliage, tinged in winter with purple. For styles, sizes, and most cultivation, see p. 57.
- ⚬ Cuttings.

Chamaecyparis pisifera 'Plumosa',
Cypress 'Plumosa'
When young, the frond-like foliage is bright green. Another form, *C. p.* 'Plumosa Aurea', has golden foliage. Formal upright, informal upright, slanting, twin-trunk, clump, straight line, sinuous, multiple-trunk, and saikei styles; and all sizes. For most cultivation, see p. 57.
- ⚬ Cuttings.

Cornus kousa, *Kousa dogwood*
This deciduous shrub produces numerous white flowers in early summer. In autumn, the foliage turns rich bronze and red. The best styles are informal upright, slanting, semicascade, cascade, root-over-rock, twin-trunk, group, clump, and multiple-trunk. Suitable sizes are medium to extra-large.
- ● Full sun, slight shade in summer.
- ⚬ Daily during summer. Do not allow to dry out.
- ⚬ Fortnightly during summer.
- ⚬ Every other year in spring. Use basic soil mix.
- ⚬ Trim new shoots after flowers fade.
- ⚬ Cuttings; layering.

Cornus officinalis, *Japanese cornelian cherry*
In early spring, clusters of yellow flowers appear on the bare wood of this deciduous shrub or small tree. Red fruits follow, and the foliage turns red in autumn. Suitable styles are informal upright, slanting, semicascade, cascade, root-over-rock, twin-trunk, clump, multiple-trunk, straight line, and sinuous. Grow the plant in medium to extra-large sizes.

- ● Full sun, partial shade in summer.
- ◔ Daily during summer. Keep moist in winter.
- ⁛ Fortnightly during summer.
- ▦ Every other year in early spring or early autumn. Use basic soil mix.
- ✎ Trim new shoots after flowers fade.
- ✂ Layering; seeds.

Corylopsis pauciflora, *Buttercup winter hazel*
When young, the small, oval leaves on this lime-hating, deciduous shrub are pink. In early spring, fragrant, yellow flowers are produced. Informal upright, slanting, root-over-rock, twin-trunk, clump, straight line, sinuous, multiple-trunk, and group styles; medium to extra-large sizes.

- ● Full sun.
- ◔ Daily during growing season. Use lime-free water.
- ⁛ Fortnightly during growing season. Use ericaceous fertilizer.
- ▦ Every other year in early spring. Lime-free soil mix.
- ✎ Trim new shoots after flowers fade.
- ✂ Cuttings; layering; air layering.

Corylopsis spicata, *Spiked winter hazel*
A deciduous shrub with oval leaves and, in spring, fragrant, bright yellow flowers. Grow it in informal upright, slanting, semicascade, cascade, root-over-rock, twin-trunk, clump, straight line, sinuous, multiple-trunk, and group styles. Best sizes are medium to extra-large.

- ● Full sun, slight shade in summer.
- ◔ Daily during summer.
- ⁛ Fortnightly during summer.
- ▦ Every other year after flowering. Basic soil mix.
- ✎ Trim new shoots after flowers fade.
- ✂ Cuttings; layering; air layering.

Corylus avellana, *Hazel*
Large, coarse leaves make this deciduous shrub unattractive as a bonsai in summer, but in winter its structure and twigs can be appreciated. It produces yellow "lambs' tails" catkins in late winter, and nuts the following autumn. It is suitable for all styles, except broom and literati, and for medium to extra-large sizes.

- ● Full sun, slight shade in summer.
- ◔ Daily during summer. Keep soil moist, especially when nuts are swelling.
- ⁛ Fortnightly during growing season.

- ▦ Annually in early spring. Use basic soil mix.
- ✎ Continually trim back new shoots as they grow.
- ✂ Seeds; cuttings; layering.

Corylus heterophylla, *Japanese hazel*
This is like *C. avellana*, but the leaves are smaller. Styles, sizes, and cultivation as for *C. avellana*.

Cotinus coggygria, *Smoke tree*
A deciduous shrub with smooth, rounded leaves that turn orange-red in autumn. In summer, the pale, plume-like flowers look like smoke. Informal upright, slanting, semicascade, cascade, twin-trunk, clump, and multiple-trunk styles; medium to extra-large sizes.

- ● Sun or shade.
- ◔ Daily during summer.
- ⁛ Fortnightly from spring until flowering, then monthly until late summer.
- ▦ Every other year in early spring. Basic soil mix.
- ✎ Trim new growth during growing season.
- ✂ Cuttings; seeds.

Cotoneaster adpressus, *Cotoneaster*
In early spring, pink flowers speckle this small, deciduous shrub. In autumn, the small leaves turn scarlet, and there are bright red fruits. For styles, sizes, and cultivation, see pp. 58–9.

Cotoneaster adpressus praecox, *Cotoneaster*
The autumn tints in this small, deciduous flowering shrub are more brilliant than those on *C. adpressus*, and the fruits are brighter. For styles, sizes, and cultivation, see pp. 58–9.

Cotoneaster congestus, *Dwarf cotoneaster*
This tiny, evergreen shrub has oval leaves and produces white flowers and red fruit. For styles, sizes, and cultivation, see pp. 58–9.

Cotoneaster conspicuus decorus, *Cotoneaster*
A small-leaved, evergreen shrub with fragrant, white flowers, which open fully like those of a wild rose. The fruits are red. For styles, sizes, and most cultivation, see pp. 58–9.

- ▦ Each year in late spring for the first ten years, then as necessary.

Cotoneaster horizontalis, *Rockspray cotoneaster*
This evergreen shrub has small, round, dark green leaves that turn red in autumn. In spring, it bears pink flowers, which become red fruits. (*See pp. 58–9.*)

Cotoneaster horizontalis 'Variegatus',
Variegated rockspray cotoneaster
A variety with pink and red fruit, and leaves marked in green and cream; not as vigorous as *C. horizontalis*. For styles, sizes, and cultivation, see pp. 58–9.

Cotoneaster microphyllus, *Cotoneaster*
This evergreen shrub bears slender, pointed, glossy, dark green leaves. The flowers are white, the fruits red. For styles, sizes, and cultivation, see pp. 58–9.

Cotoneaster simmonsii, *Cotoneaster*
A semi-evergreen shrub with small, leathery leaves that turn scarlet in autumn, pink flowers, and red fruits. For styles, sizes, and cultivation, see pp. 58–9.

Cotoneaster 'Skogholm', *Cotoneaster*
Large, coral-red, oval fruits are the main feature of this dwarf, evergreen flowering shrub. (*See pp. 58–9.*)

Crassula arborescens, *Jade tree*
An evergreen succulent with smooth, rounded leaves, and pale pink flowers. (*See p. 60.*)

Crassula sarcocaulis, *Crassula*
This dwarf evergreen succulent has grey-green leaves and pink flowers that are beautiful but evil-smelling. Informal upright, twin-trunk, and clump styles are best, as are extra-small to medium sizes.
- ◉ Full sun. If kept dry, will tolerate cold; otherwise, protect in winter.
- ◔ Moderately, every three to four weeks if conditions are cool.
- ⚡ Monthly from late spring to early autumn.
- ▦ Every other year in spring.
- ◎ In spring, pinch back new shoots; during growing season, prune branches. Remove leaves from trunk.
- ✂ Cuttings.

Crataegus cuneata, *Japanese hawthorn*
This deciduous tree has small, lobed leaves. In spring, it produces white flowers and large, rosehip-type fruit. For styles, sizes, and cultivation, see p. 61.

Crataegus laevigata (**C. oxyacantha**),
English hawthorn
A deciduous tree with white flowers and, in autumn, orange-red fruit. For styles, sizes, and most cultivation, see p. 61.
- ✂ Cuttings; seeds; grafting (for hybrids).

Crataegus laevigata 'Paul's Scarlet',
Double red-flowering hawthorn
A hybrid that produces scarlet double flowers, but rarely fruits. (*See p. 61.*)

Crataegus monogyna, *Common hawthorn*
This deciduous tree bears extremely fragrant, white flowers that give way in autumn to red fruits called haws. For styles, sizes, and cultivation, see p. 61.

Crataegus oxyacantha, see **Crataegus laevigata.**

Cryptomeria japonica, *Japanese cedar*
The needle-like foliage of this evergreen conifer is a bright blue-green. The red-brown bark peels away in strips. The best sizes are medium to large. For styles and most cultivation, see pp. 62–3.
- ✂ Seeds; cuttings.

Cryptomeria japonica 'Yatsubusa',
Dwarf Japanese cedar
This dwarf variety is narrowly conical, with compact foliage. (*See pp. 62–3.*)

Cycas revoluta, *Cycad*
This tender evergreen has fronded leaves like those of a palm tree. Clump and multiple-trunk styles are best, and small to large sizes.
- ◉ Full sun. Keep warm in winter.
- ◔ Twice weekly in summer, very sparingly in winter.
- ⚡ Once a month during spring and summer.
- ▦ Every other year in late spring. Use basic soil mix.
- ◎ No pruning necessary.
- ✂ Division.

Cydonia oblonga, *Common quince*
A deciduous tree similar to *Chaenomeles sinensis*, the Chinese quince. This bears pink and white single flowers, followed in autumn by golden fruits. Informal upright, slanting, semicascade, cascade, twin-trunk, clump, multiple-trunk, straight line, sinuous, and group styles are all suitable. Grow it in medium to extra-large sizes.
- ◉ Full sun.
- ◔ Daily during growing season.
- ⚡ Every two to three weeks during growing season.
- ▦ Every other year in spring. Use basic soil mix.
- ◎ Allow new shoots to develop and lengthen before shortening and wiring.
- ✂ Seeds; cuttings; layering; air layering.

Daphne burkwoodii, *Daphne*
This semi-evergreen shrub has oval leaves and, in early summer, scented, pink flowers. Informal upright, slanting, semicascade, cascade, twin-trunk, clump, multiple-trunk, and saikei styles; small and medium sizes.
- ◉ Full sun.
- ◔ Daily during summer.
- ⚡ Fortnightly during summer.
- ▦ Every other year in early spring. Use free-draining soil mix.
- ◎ Trim new growth after flowers fade.
- ✂ Cuttings; layering.

Daphne odora, *Daphne*
An evergreen shrub with fragrant, pink flowers in winter and early spring. Styles, sizes, and most cultivation as for *D. burkwoodii*.
- ▦ Every other year in early spring. Basic soil mix.

Deutzia gracilis, *Deutzia*
In early summer, pure white flowers cluster on this deciduous shrub. Informal upright, slanting, semicascade, cascade, twin-trunk, clump, and multiple-trunk styles; medium and large sizes.
- ◉ Full sun, slight shade in summer. Protect from spring frosts.
- ◍ Daily during growing season.
- ⚘ Fortnightly during growing season.
- ▣ Annually in early spring. Use basic soil mix.
- ◲ Cut back hard after flowering. Shorten the ensuing new shoots.
- ✂ Cuttings; layering.

Deutzia scabra, *Deutzia*
Several cultivars of this deciduous shrub exist, with single or double flowers in white and shades of pink. Styles, sizes, and cultivation as for *D. gracilis*.

Deutzia scabra 'Azaleiflora', *Deutzia*
A variety that produces small, white flowers with petals that curve backwards. Styles, sizes, and cultivation details as for *D. gracilis*.

Deutzia scabra 'Nikko', *Deutzia*
This very dwarf variety has white flowers. Styles, sizes, and cultivation as for *D. gracilis*.

Deutzia scabra 'Plena', *Deutzia*
A form with double white flowers flushed with pink. Styles, sizes, and cultivation as for *D. gracilis*.

Diospyros kaki, *Chinese persimmon*
The autumn colour of this deciduous tree is purple and orange; the tomato-like, edible fruits are orange. Informal upright, slanting, semicascade, cascade, literati, twin-trunk, clump, straight line, sinuous, and group styles; medium to extra-large sizes.
- ◉ Full sun.
- ◍ Daily during growing season.
- ⚘ Fortnightly during growing season.
- ▣ Annually in early spring. Use basic soil mix.
- ◲ Trim new growth during summer.
- ✂ Grafting; layering; air layering.

Ehretia buxifolia, see **Carmona microphylla**.

Elaeagnus multiflora, *Elaeagnus*
This deciduous shrub has green leaves with silvery undersides, small, fragrant cream flowers in spring, and in midsummer, blood-red fruits. (*See p. 64*.)

Elaeagnus pungens, *Thorny elaeagnus*
The shiny leaves on this evergreen shrub have white undersides speckled with brown. In autumn, it bears fragrant, cream flowers. For styles, sizes, and cultivation, see p. 64.

Enkianthus campanulatus, *Enkianthus*
In autumn, the smallish, dark green leaves on this lime-hating, deciduous shrub turn brilliant yellow, orange-red, and purple. In spring, creamy-white, bell-like flowers are produced. Informal upright, slanting, semicascade, root-over-rock, twin-trunk, clump, multiple-trunk, and group styles; small to large sizes.
- ◉ Full sun, slight shade in summer.
- ◍ Daily during growing season.
- ⚘ Fortnightly in summer. Use ericaceous fertilizer.
- ▣ Annually in early spring. Use lime-free soil mix.
- ◲ Trim back new shoots to shape.
- ✂ Cuttings; layering.

Enkianthus cernuus rubens, *Red enkianthus*
This lime-hating, deciduous shrub has red flowers in late spring, and excellent foliage colour in autumn. Styles, sizes, and cultivation as for *E. campanulatus*.

Enkianthus perulatus, *White enkianthus*
This compact, deciduous variety is more suitable than others for smaller bonsai sizes. White flowers appear at the same time as the leaves. Hates lime. Styles, sizes, and cultivation as for *E. campanulatus*.

Escallonia 'Apple blossom', *Escallonia*
A shrub with small, glossy, evergreen leaves, and apple blossom-like flowers in pink and white. There are many cultivars and hybrids, with red, pink, or white flowers. Informal upright, slanting, semicascade, cascade, twin-trunk, clump, and multiple-trunk styles; all sizes.
- ◉ Full sun. Protect from frost and freezing winds.
- ◍ Daily during summer. Keep moist in winter.
- ⚘ Fortnightly in growing season.
- ▣ Every second year in early spring. Use basic soil mix.
- ◲ Prune hard after flowering, then trim new shoots as they grow.
- ✂ Cuttings; layering.

Euonymus alatus, *Winged spindle*
Fascinating purple-pink autumn colour, and ridged, corky "winged" bark adorn this deciduous shrub. For styles, sizes, and most cultivation, see p. 65.
- ✂ Cuttings; layering; air layering.

Euonymus europaeus, *European spindle*
A deciduous tree with scarlet seed capsules. For styles, sizes, and most cultivation, see p. 65.
- ✂ Seeds; cuttings; layering; air layering.

Euonymus sieboldianus, *Japanese spindle*
Pale green flowers, pinkish-white fruits, and red seeds are features of this deciduous tree. For styles, sizes, and most cultivation, see p. 65.
- ✂ Seeds; cuttings; layering; air layering.

Fagus crenata, *Japanese white beech*
In autumn, the foliage of this deciduous tree turns bronze. The bark is pale grey. (*See p. 66.*)

Fagus japonica, *Japanese black beech*
The leaves on this small tree are deciduous, oval, and bright green. For styles, sizes, and cultivation, see p. 66.

Fagus sylvatica, *European beech*
This large tree has vivid green, deciduous leaves, whose bronze autumn colour lasts a long time. The bark is smooth and grey. (*See p. 67.*)

Fagus sylvatica heterophylla,
Fern-leaved beech
This variety has deeply cut, lobed leaves. For styles, sizes, and most cultivation, see p. 67.
☒ Cuttings; grafting.

Fagus sylvatica 'Riversii', *Purple beech*
A form with purple-black leaves. For styles, sizes, and most cultivation, see p. 67.
☒ Cuttings; grafting.

Fagus sylvatica 'Rohanii',
Purple fern-leaved beech
Deeply cut purple leaves distinguish this graceful variety. For styles, sizes, and cultivation, see p. 67.
☒ Cuttings; grafting.

Ficus benjamina, *Weeping fig*
In temperate countries, this tender evergreen is grown as a houseplant. The weeping stems have pointed, oval leaves, variegated in some forms. For styles, sizes, and cultivation, see p. 68.

Ficus macrophylla,
Australian banyan or *Moreton Bay fig*
The mature trunk of this tender evergreen tree forms buttresses. The dark green leaves are glossy and leathery. For styles, sizes, and cultivation, see p. 68.

Ficus platypoda, *Australian fig*
In nature, this tender tree often has more than one trunk. It has smooth, elliptic, evergreen leaves and small, orange-red flowers. For styles, sizes, and cultivation, see p. 68.

Ficus pumila, *Creeping fig*
The evergreen leaves on this tender climbing shrub are oval to heart-shaped; they are smaller on younger plants. For styles, sizes, and cultivation, see p. 68.

Ficus retusa, *Banyan fig*
The leaves of this tender, banyan-like tree are small, glossy, and leathery. (*See p. 68.*)

Ficus rubiginosa, *Port Jackson* or *Rusty-leaved fig*
The undersides of this tender tree's glossy, dark green, oval leaves are normally covered with rust-coloured down. For styles, sizes, and cultivation, see p. 68.

Forsythia intermedia, *Forsythia*
This deciduous shrub is grown mostly for the bright golden yellow, bell-shaped flowers in spring, because most varieties except dwarf ones are coarse-growing. Informal upright, slanting, semicascade, cascade, twin-trunk, clump, and multiple-trunk styles; all sizes.
◉ Full sun.
◌ Daily during growing season, sparingly in winter.
⚬ Fortnightly during growing season.
▣ Every other year in autumn or late winter. Use basic soil mix.
▧ Prune branches back hard after flowering. Trim shoots to shape.
☒ Cuttings.

Forsythia intermedia 'Minigold',
Dwarf forsythia
A compact dwarf form. Styles, sizes, and cultivation as for *F. intermedia*.

Forsythia ovata 'Tetragold', *Dwarf forsythia*
The golden yellow flowers on this deciduous shrub appear earlier than those of other forsythias. Styles, sizes, and cultivation as for *F. intermedia*.

Fortunella hindsii, *Dwarf orange*
Fruits like miniature oranges, as well as small, fragrant, white flowers, and glossy, oval leaves are features of this tender, evergreen shrub. All styles except broom and literati; extra-small to large sizes.
◉ Full sun. Warm location, minimum temperature 4°C (40°F).
◌ Daily during summer, weekly in winter.
⚬ Fortnightly during summer.
▣ Every two to three years in spring. Basic soil mix.
▧ Trim back new shoots as they grow.
☒ Seeds; cuttings; grafting.

Fraxinus excelsior, *Common* or *European ash*
A deciduous tree that is very hardy, but has a coarse structure with large, compound leaves. It has white flowers in mid spring, and good autumn colour. Informal upright, slanting, twin-trunk, clump, and multiple-trunk styles; large or extra-large sizes.
◉ Full sun.
◌ Daily during summer, sparingly in winter.
⚬ Fortnightly during summer.
▣ Every other year in spring. Use basic soil mix.
▧ Trim shoots back hard continually to keep their shape neat and compact.
☒ Seeds; layering; air layering.

Fuchsia × bacillaris (microphylla × thymifolia), *Fuchsia*

The flowers on this shrub open bright crimson, and darken as they age. The outer petals tend to curve backwards. It does not flower as profusely as other fuchsias. The deciduous leaves are smallish, leathery, and oval. For styles, sizes, and cultivation, see p. 69.

Fuchsia 'Lady Thumb', *'Lady Thumb' fuchsia*

This deciduous, dwarf form produces a profusion of white and pink flowers. For styles, sizes, and cultivation, see p. 69.

Fuchsia microphylla, *Dwarf fuchsia*

A dwarf fuchsia with small, drooping, red flowers and dark green, deciduous leaves. *(See p. 69.)*

Fuchsia pumila, *Dwarf fuchsia*

A deciduous, dwarf form with dark purple and dark red flowers. For styles, sizes, and cultivation, see p. 69.

Fuchsia 'Tom Thumb', *'Tom Thumb' fuchsia*

A profusion of scarlet and violet flowers is the characteristic of this deciduous, dwarf variety. For styles, sizes, and cultivation, see p. 69.

Gardenia jasminoides radicans, *Gardenia*

This lime-hating, tender shrub bears shiny, dark green, evergreen leaves, and fragrant, white flowers. Informal upright, slanting, semicascade, cascade, root-over-rock, twin-trunk, clump, and multiple-trunk styles; all sizes.

- ● Avoid full sun, but give maximum light, with slight shade in summer. Minimum temperature of 13°C (55°F).
- ◔ Daily during summer, more sparingly in winter. Use lime-free water.
- ⚘ Fortnightly during summer, monthly otherwise. Use ericaceous fertilizer.
- ▦ Every other year in late spring. Lime-free soil mix.
- ✎ Trim new growth after flowering, and continue to maintain shape.
- ✄ Cuttings; layering; air layering.

Gingko biloba, *Maidenhair tree*

In autumn, the deciduous, broad leaves of this conifer turn gold, and yellowish fruits appear. *(See p. 70.)*

Gleditsia triacanthos, *Honey locust*

A deciduous tree with frond-like leaves that turn pale yellow in autumn. It has three-pointed thorns, and long, brown seed pods. *(See p. 71.)*

Hamamelis japonica, *Japanese witch hazel*

This deciduous shrub is grown for the effect of its small, yellow flowers, borne on bare branches from midwinter to early spring. In autumn, the leaves turn

a good orange colour. Grow it in informal upright, slanting, semicascade, cascade, root-over-rock, twin-trunk, clump, multiple-trunk, and group styles, and in medium to extra-large sizes.

- ● Full sun.
- ◔ Daily during summer.
- ⚘ Fortnightly during summer.
- ▦ Every other year, in late autumn, or in early spring after flowering. Use basic soil mix.
- ✎ Trim new growth to shape throughout summer.
- ✄ Cuttings; layering; air layering; grafting.

Hamamelis mollis, *Chinese witch hazel*

This deciduous shrub is similar to *H. japonica*, but its flowers are larger, earlier, and more fragrant. The oval leaves turn yellow in autumn. Styles, sizes, and cultivation as for *H. japonica*.

Hedera helix, *Common ivy*

An evergreen climber bearing yellowish flowers, berry-like black fruits, and glossy, dark green leaves with three to five lobes. Suitable for informal upright, slanting, semicascade, cascade, root-over-rock, twin-trunk, and clump styles, and all sizes.

- ● Partial shade.
- ◔ Daily during growing season.
- ⚘ Fortnightly during growing season.
- ▦ Every other year in spring or early autumn. Use basic soil mix.
- ✎ Trim shoots back hard to form a trunk.
- ✄ Cuttings; layering; air layering.

Ilex crenata, *Japanese evergreen holly*

This slow-growing, evergreen shrub has small, smooth leaves, neat twigs, and insignificant, white flowers. In autumn, the female plants produce shiny black fruits. *(See p. 72.)*

Ilex crenata 'Convexa', *Japanese evergreen holly*

This variety is more compact than *I. crenata*, and has glossy, convex leaves. *(See p. 72.)*

Ilex crenata 'Stokes', *Japanese evergreen holly*

A dwarf form with tiny leaves. For styles, sizes, and cultivation, see p. 72.

Ilex serrata (*I. sieboldii*), *Japanese deciduous holly*

In autumn, the thin, serrated leaves on this deciduous tree turn a variety of shades from yellow to purple. If grown near a male plant, female plants bear red fruits. *(See p. 73.)*

Ilex serrata 'Leucocarpa', *White-berried Japanese deciduous holly*

A form of *I. serrata* that produces white berries. For styles, sizes, and cultivation, see p. 73.

Ilex serrata 'Subtilis' ('Koshobai'),
Dwarf Japanese deciduous holly
This miniature has unusually small leaves and fruits.
It is a hermaphrodite, so it produces berries freely,
and acts as a pollinator for female trees of the main
species. It is suitable only for extra-small and small
sizes. For styles, sizes, and cultivation, see p. 73.

Ilex sieboldii, see **Ilex serrata**.

Jacaranda mimosifolia, see **Jacaranda
ovalifolia**.

Jacaranda ovalifolia (J. mimosifolia),
Jacaranda
A tender, lime-hating tree with deciduous, fern-like
leaves and, in spring, violet flowers. Informal upright,
slanting, semicascade, cascade, twin-trunk, clump,
multiple-trunk, and saikei styles; small to large sizes.
⬤ Maximum light, but protect from direct sunlight.
Warm location, minimum temperature 16°C (60°F).
◊ Daily with lime-free water.
⁙ Fortnightly in summer. Use ericaceous fertilizer.
▣ Every other year in spring. Use lime-free soil mix.
▨ Pinch soft terminal shoots to shape.
▨ Seeds.

Jasminum nudiflorum, *Winter jasmine*
This deciduous shrub has narrow, dark green leaves.
In winter, starry, yellow flowers stud the bare
branches. (*See p. 74*.)

Jasminum officinale, *Common white jasmine*
This shrub has evergreen, pinnate leaves and, in
summer, fragrant, white flowers. The best styles are
informal upright, slanting, semicascade, root-over-
rock, twin-trunk, and clump. It is suitable for all sizes.
⬤ Full sun. Protect from frost.
◊ Daily during growing season.
⁙ Fortnightly during growing season.
▣ Every other year in late spring. Use basic soil mix.
▨ Trim shoots after flowers fade, and new shoots in
late spring or early autumn.
▨ Cuttings; air layering.

Juniperus communis, *Common juniper*
An evergreen conifer with many cultivars. The
foliage is needle-like, the pale undersides banded on
top with white. The fruit is black. For styles, sizes,
and most cultivation, see p. 75.
◊ Daily throughout growing season, mist spray in
summer.
▨ Seeds; cuttings.

Juniperus × media 'Blaauw', *Chinese juniper*
This evergreen shrub conifer has shaggy bark and
grey-blue, scale-like foliage. (*See p. 75*.)

Juniperus procumbens, *Creeping juniper*
A prostrate dwarf conifer with tight, needle-like
foliage. For styles, sizes, and cultivation, see p. 75.

Juniperus rigida, *Needle juniper*
Over two years, the green berries on this juniper ripen
to purple-black. The foliage is needle-like and
evergreen. (*See p. 76*.)

Juniperus sabina, *Savin juniper*
This evergreen conifer has a variable habit, with
grey-green, predominantly scale-like foliage. For
styles, sizes, and most cultivation, see p. 75.
◊ Daily during growing season; mist spray in
summer.

Juniperus sargentii,
Chinese or *Sargent's juniper*
The grey-green foliage on this evergreen conifer is
needle-like when juvenile, smoothly scale-like when
mature. The berries are blue-black. (*See p. 77*.)

Juniperus squamata 'Meyeri', *Blue juniper*
An evergreen conifer notable for its rough, shaggy
bark, and greyish-blue needles with a fine "bloom".
For styles, sizes, and most cultivation, see p. 75.
◊ Daily in growing season, mist spray in summer.

Kadsura japonica, *Scarlet kadsura*
An evergreen climber that is deciduous in temperate
zones. In late summer, it produces white flowers,
followed by red fruits. The shiny oval leaves turn red
in autumn. Informal upright, slanting, semicascade,
cascade, root-over-rock, twin-trunk, and clump styles;
medium to extra-large sizes.
⬤ Full sun. Protect from frost.
◊ Daily during summer.
⁙ Fortnightly during growing season.
▣ Every two to three years, at any time during
growing season. Use basic soil mix.
▨ Trim shoots throughout summer.
▨ Cuttings; layering.

Laburnum alpinum,
Scotch laburnum or *Golden rain tree*
A very hardy tree with deciduous, compound leaves
and, in late spring and early summer, drooping
racemes of yellow flowers. It looks best in informal
upright, slanting, semicascade, cascade, twin-trunk,
clump, and multiple-trunk styles; and small to
extra-large sizes.
⬤ Full sun.
◊ Daily during growing season.
⁙ Fortnightly during growing season.
▣ Annually in early spring. Use basic soil mix.
▨ Trim shoots to two or three buds.
▨ Seeds.

Laburnum anagyroides,
Common laburnum or *Golden rain tree*
This deciduous tree is similar to *L. alpinum*, but the racemes are shorter, and flower earlier. Styles, sizes, and cultivation as for *L. alpinum*.

Lagerstroemia indica, *Crape myrtle*
A trunk mottled in grey, pink, and cinnamon is a feature of this deciduous tree. In summer, the flowers are white or shades of pink or mauve. (*See p. 78.*)

Lagerstroemia indica 'Alba', *White crape myrtle*
This form bears white flowers that fade to cream. For styles, sizes, and cultivation, see p. 78.

Lagerstroemia indica 'Amabilis',
Purple crape myrtle
Purple flowers are the feature of this form. For styles, sizes, and cultivation, see p. 78.

Larix decidua, *European larch*
The needle-like foliage on this deciduous conifer is bright green in spring, turning to gold in autumn. The stems of new shoots are a light straw colour. (*See p. 79.*)

Larix × eurolepsis (decidua × kaempferi),
Dunkeld larch
The new shoots of this tough hybrid are pale yellow-orange. For styles, sizes, and cultivation, see p. 79.

Larix kaempferi (Larix leptolepis),
Japanese larch
This deciduous conifer has broader leaves than *L. decidua*. The red-orange new twigs darken by winter to almost purple. (*See p. 80.*)

Larix laricina, *Tamarack* or *American larch*
A deciduous conifer with longer and looser needles, as well as smaller flowers and cones, than other larches. For styles, sizes, and cultivation, see p. 80.

Larix leptolepis, see *Larix kaempferi*.

Lespedeza bicolor, *Japanese bush clover*
Purple-pink flowers in late summer and clover-like leaves distinguish this deciduous shrub. Good styles are informal upright, slanting, semicascade, cascade, root-over-rock, clasped-to-rock, twin-trunk, and clump. It is suitable for extra-small to medium sizes.
- ⦿ Full sun. Protect from frost.
- ◔ Daily during growing season.
- ⬥ Fortnightly in growing season.
- ▣ Every other year in spring. Use basic soil mix.
- ◩ Trim shoots after flowers fade. In late autumn, cut branches back hard to the trunk.
- ◪ Cuttings; seeds.

Ligustrum ovalifolium, *Oval-leaf privet*
White summer flowers and small, oval, semi-evergreen leaves are the features of this shrub. Grow it in informal upright, slanting, root-over-rock, clasped-to-rock, twin-trunk, clump, and group styles, and in all sizes.
- ⦿ Full sun or shade.
- ◔ Daily during summer.
- ⬥ Fortnightly during summer.
- ▣ Annually in early spring. Use basic soil mix.
- ◩ Trim shoots after flowering, new growth throughout growing season.
- ◪ Cuttings; layering; seeds.

Ligustrum vulgare, *Common privet*
A semi-evergreen shrub with dark, glossy leaves. Styles, sizes, and cultivation as for *L. ovalifolium*.

Liquidambar styraciflua, *Sweet gum*
In autumn, superb orange, red, and deep purple foliage clothes this deciduous tree. All styles, except literati and broom, and all sizes.
- ⦿ Full sun.
- ◔ Daily during growing season, sparingly in winter.
- ⬥ Fortnightly during summer.
- ▣ Every other year in spring. Use basic soil mix.
- ◩ Trim back new shoots as they grow.
- ◪ Seeds; cuttings.

Lonicera japonica, *Japanese honeysuckle*
This vigorous climber has semi-evergreen, oval leaves and, in early summer, scented, white flowers, that fade to yellow. Grow it in informal upright, slanting, semicascade, cascade, root-over-rock, clasped-to-rock, twin-trunk, clump, and multiple-trunk, and all sizes. For cultivation, see p. 81.

Lonicera morowii, *Honeysuckle*
This deciduous shrub has creamy-white flowers that change to yellow before being followed by red fruits. Grow in informal upright, slanting, semicascade, cascade, root-over-rock, clasped-to-rock, twin-trunk, clump, and multiple-trunk styles, and all sizes. For cultivation, see p. 81.

Lonicera nitida, *Dwarf honeysuckle*
This dwarf shrubby honeysuckle has small, evergreen leaves and responds well to constant clipping. For styles, sizes, and most cultivation, see p. 81.
- ◪ Cuttings.

Magnolia stellata, *Star magnolia*
Fragrant, white, starry flowers on this slow-growing, deciduous shrub appear before the leaves in late spring. Informal upright, slanting, semicascade, cascade, twin-trunk, clump, and multiple-trunk styles are suitable, as are medium and large sizes.

⦿ Full sun or shade. Protect flowers from spring frosts.
◔ Daily during growing season. Do not allow soil to dry out at any time.
⦙ Fortnightly during summer.
▣ Every three to four years in early spring. Use basic soil mix.
◩ Shape by shortening new shoots.
◪ Division; layering.

Malus cerasifera, *Nagasaki crab apple*
The many pink flower buds on this deciduous tree open to white, and turn into cherry-like, red fruits. For styles, sizes, and most cultivation, see pp. 82–3.
◪ Grafting; layering; air layering.

Malus 'Golden hornet', *Golden hornet crab apple*
The white flowers on this tree are followed by bright yellow fruits, which remain after the leaves fall. For styles, sizes, and most cultivation, see pp. 82–3.
◪ Grafting; layering; air layering.

Malus halliana, *Hall's crab apple*
This tree has narrow, dark green, deciduous leaves. Small, purple fruits follow the pink blossom. For styles, sizes, and most cultivation, see pp. 82–3.
◪ Grafting; layering; air layering.

Malus 'Profusion', *Purple crab apple*
A tree with purple deciduous leaves, wine-red flowers, and deep red fruits. For styles, sizes, and most cultivation, see pp. 82–3.
◪ Grafting; layering; air layering.

Malus 'Red jade', *Weeping crab apple*
The young leaves on this weeping tree are bright green. The pink and white flowers are followed by small, red fruits, which hang on the tree all winter. For styles, sizes, and most cultivation, see pp. 82–3.
◪ Grafting; layering; air layering.

Malus sieboldii (*M. toringo*), *Crab apple*
The pink buds on this small-leaved tree open as small, white flowers. The tiny crab apples are yellow or red. For styles, sizes, and most cultivation, see pp. 82–3.
◪ Grafting; layering; air layering.

Malus sylvestris, *Common crab apple*
A small deciduous tree, often with spurs. It has toothed, oval leaves. The flowers are white or suffused with pink, and turn into red-flushed or yellow-green fruits. For styles, sizes, and cultivation, see pp. 82–3.

Malus toringo, see *Malus sieboldii*.

Metasequoia glyptostroboides, *Dawn redwood*
A cone-shaped, deciduous conifer, with shaggy, cinnamon-coloured bark. The flattened, needle-like leaves are light green, and turn red-brown in autumn. Suitable styles are formal upright, informal upright, slanting, twin-trunk, clump, multiple-trunk, and group. Grow it in small to extra-large sizes.
⦿ Full sun.
◔ Daily during growing season.
⦙ Fortnightly during growing season.
▣ Every other year in early spring. Basic soil mix.
◩ Trim back new shoots continually as they grow.
◪ Seeds; cuttings.

Millettia japonica, *Japanese millettia*
An evergreen climber with mauve flowers in early summer, and small, dark green, pinnate leaves. Informal upright, slanting, semicascade, cascade, root-over-rock, twin-trunk, and clump styles are suitable, as are small to large sizes.
⦿ Full sun.
◔ Generously during year.
⦙ Fortnightly during growing season.
▣ Annually in early spring. Use basic soil mix.
◩ Trim new growth after flowers fade, and throughout summer.
◪ Cuttings; layering; grafting; seeds.

Millettia japonica 'Microphylla', *Dwarf wisteria*
The common name of this compact, evergreen climber derives from its minute compound leaves, which look very like those of a wisteria. It seldom flowers. It is suitable for extra-small and small sizes. Styles and most cultivation as for *M. japonica*.
◪ Division; cuttings; layering.

Morus alba, *White mulberry*
This deciduous tree has heart-shaped leaves and, in autumn, reddish, edible fruits. (*See p. 84.*)

Murraya paniculata, *Jasmine orange*
This shrub has small, pinnate, evergreen leaves. The white, bell-shaped flowers are scented. They are followed by orange-like fruits. (*See p. 85.*)

Myrtus apiculata, *Myrtle*
The cinnamon-coloured bark on this small, tender tree peels to show cream underneath. The oval, evergreen leaves are dull green. The small, white flowers of summer are followed by red and black fruits. Suitable for informal upright, slanting, semicascade, cascade, twin-trunk, clump, and multiple-trunk styles, and all sizes.
⦿ Full sun. Protect from cold and frost.
◔ Daily during summer. Keep soil always moist.
⦙ Fortnightly during summer.
▣ Every other year in early spring. Basic soil mix.
◩ Trim shoots to shape as they grow.
◪ Cuttings; layering.

Myrtus communis, *Common myrtle*
This shrub has aromatic, evergreen foliage. The
white flowers of summer are followed by black fruits.
Styles, sizes, and most cultivation as for *M. apiculata*.
- 🦗 Every other year in spring. Use basic soil mix.

Nandina domestica, *Sacred* or *heavenly bamboo*
An evergreen shrub with long, narrow leaves flushed
with red in spring and autumn. Suitable for twin-
trunk, clump, multiple-trunk, and saikei styles, and
all sizes. (*See also pp. 46–7.*)
- ◉ Full sun, partial shade in summer. Protect from
frost in winter.
- ◌ Daily during summer.
- ⋮ Fortnightly during growing season.
- 🦗 Every second year in spring. Use free-draining
soil mix.
- � Trim new shoots to shape.
- ✂ Cuttings; division; grafting; seeds.

Nothofagus antarctica, *Antarctic beech*
This deciduous tree has small, glossy, heart-shaped
leaves. The foliage is dark green, but turns bright
yellow in autumn. Suitable for all styles except
literati, and for all sizes.
- ◉ Full sun.
- ◌ Daily during summer.
- ⋮ Fortnightly during summer.
- 🦗 Every other year in early spring. Basic soil mix.
- � Trim new shoots during summer. Prune
branches in winter.
- ✂ Seeds; cuttings; layering; air layering.

Nothofagus obliqua, *Roblé beech*
The oblong leaves on this very fast-growing,
deciduous tree have good autumn colour. Styles,
sizes, and cultivation as for *N. antarctica*.

Nothofagus procera, *Southern beech*
A fast-growing, deciduous tree with prominently
veined leaves that colour well in autumn. Styles, sizes,
and cultivation as for *N. antarctica*.

Olea europaea, *Olive*
The light-grey bark on this tender, evergreen tree
becomes gnarled with age. The shiny, narrow, dark
green leaves have light grey undersides. Its
insignificant, cream flowers develop into green fruits,
which ripen to black. Suitable for all styles except
broom, and for small to extra-large sizes.
- ◉ Full sun. Warm location, minimum temperature
7°C (45°F).
- ◌ Every other day during summer, weekly in winter.
- ⋮ Fortnightly during summer.
- 🦗 Every other year in spring. Free-draining soil mix.
- � Pinch back new shoots during growing season.
- ✂ Cuttings; seeds.

Osmanthus delavayi, *Osmanthus*
This evergreen shrub bears small, holly-like leaves
and, in spring, fragrant, white flowers. Informal
upright, slanting, semicascade, cascade, twin-trunk,
clump, multiple-trunk, and group styles; all sizes.
- ◉ Full sun, slight shade in summer.
- ◌ Daily during growing season.
- ⋮ Fortnightly during growing season.
- 🦗 Every other year in early spring. Basic soil mix.
- � Trim shoots after flowers fade, then subsequent
shoots as they occur.
- ✂ Cuttings; grafting; layering.

Parthenocissus tricuspidata, *Boston ivy*
In autumn, the three-lobed, deciduous leaves on this
climber turn brilliant red. The fruits are dark blue.
Suitable styles are informal upright, slanting,
semicascade, cascade, root-over-rock, twin-trunk,
and clump. Sizes range from small to large.
- ◉ Full sun, slight shade in summer.
- ◌ Daily during summer.
- ⋮ Fortnightly during summer.
- 🦗 Every other year in early spring. Basic soil mix.
- � Trim new growth back during growing season.
- ✂ Cuttings; grafting; layering; seeds.

Phyllostachys aurea,
Golden or *Buddha's belly bamboo*
The bright green canes on this evergreen turn yellow
as they mature. Clump and multiple-trunk styles;
medium to extra-large sizes. (*See also pp. 46–7.*)
- ◉ Partial shade. Keep warm during winter months.
- ◌ Daily during summer. Less often at other times,
but keep moist.
- ⋮ Fortnightly during summer.
- 🦗 Every other year in late spring. Use free-draining
soil mix.
- � Remove central bud when desired height reached.
- ✂ Division.

Phyllostachys nigra, *Black bamboo*
A clump-forming bamboo with striking stems that
are green in their first year, and deep black the next.
Styles, sizes, and cultivation as for *P. aurea*; see also
pp. 46–7.

Picea abies, *Norway spruce*
This evergreen conifer has dark green, needle-like
leaves, reddish shoots, and cylindrical cones. It is
suitable for medium to large sizes. For styles and
cultivation, see p. 86.

Picea abies 'Echiniformis', *Dwarf spruce*
This compact dwarf variety is slow-growing and has
tightly congested foliage. Suitable for extra-small and
small sizes. For styles and most cultivation, see p. 86.
- ✂ Cuttings.

Picea abies 'Little Gem', *Dwarf spruce*
A very compact dwarf form with tiny leaves. Suitable for extra-small to medium sizes. For styles and most cultivation, see p. 86.
▣ Cuttings.

Picea abies 'Maxwellii', *Dwarf spruce*
Coarse, spiny needles are a characteristic of this dwarf variety. Suitable for extra-small to medium sizes. For styles and most cultivation, see p. 86.
▣ Cuttings.

Picea abies 'Nidiformis', *Bird's nest spruce*
A dwarf variety with fresh green buds. Suitable for extra-small to medium sizes. For styles and most cultivation, see p. 86.
▣ Cuttings.

Picea glauca albertiana 'Conica',
Dwarf Alberta white spruce
This slow-growing dwarf conifer has a compact, conical habit and bright green, evergreen foliage. Suitable for small to large sizes. For styles and most cultivation, see p. 86.
▣ Cuttings.

Picea glehnii, *Sakhalin spruce*
This evergreen conifer is the preferred spruce species in Japan. It is a slender, conical tree, with blue-green leaves, and red-brown, flaking bark. Export from Japan is now banned, but there are still some stocks, and seed is freely available. Suitable for medium to large sizes. For styles, sizes, and cultivation, see p. 86.

Picea glehnii 'Yatsubusa', *Dwarf Sakhalin spruce*
This dwarf form of *P. glehnii* is almost identical in appearance to *P. abies* 'Little Gem'. Suitable for extra-small to medium sizes. For styles and most cultivation, see p. 86.
▣ Cuttings.

Picea jezoensis, *Yezo* or *Edo spruce*
The dark green leaves on this evergreen conifer are white underneath. The young shoots are light brown. Suitable for medium to large sizes. For styles and cultivation, see p. 86.

Picea jezoensis hondoensis, *Hondo spruce*
A variety of *P. jezoensis* with shorter leaves. Suitable for medium to large sizes. For styles and cultivation, see p. 86.

Picea mariana 'Nana', *Dwarf black spruce*
This dwarf, evergreen tree has grey-green, needle-like leaves. Suitable for extra-small to medium sizes. For styles and most cultivation, see p. 86.
▣ Cuttings.

Pieris japonica (Andromeda japonica),
Pieris
A lime-hating shrub with shiny, evergreen leaves that are copper-coloured when young. In spring, it bears panicles of white flowers. Suitable for informal upright, slanting, semicascade, cascade, root-over-rock, twin-trunk, and clump styles, and for small to large sizes.
◉ Slight shade.
◌ Daily during summer. Use lime-free water.
⬩ Fortnightly. Use ericaceous fertilizer.
▣ Every three or four years in early spring. Use lime-free soil mix.
▧ Trim back new shoots during growing season.
▣ Cuttings; layering.

Pinus densiflora, *Japanese red pine*
The blue-green needles on this evergreen conifer grow in pairs. The bark is reddish. All styles except broom are suitable, and all sizes.
◉ Full sun. Protect from frost and cold, drying winds.
◌ Daily during summer, unless soil is already moist, and mist-spray. Sparingly in winter. Keep fairly dry.
⬩ Monthly from midwinter to mid autumn.
▣ Every two to five years in early to mid spring. Use free-draining soil mix.
▧ Annually in spring, finger prune candles; every other year in early autumn, prune branch tips.
▣ Grafting; seeds.

Pinus mugo, *Mountain pine*
A small evergreen conifer with dark green needles and light green shoots. (*See p. 87.*)

Pinus parviflora (P. pentaphylla),
Japanese white or *five-needled pine*
This evergreen conifer carries its twisted bluish needles in bundles of five. It has smooth grey bark, and small flowers, that, if fertilized, turn into dark brown cones. (*See pp. 88–9.*)

Pinus parviflora 'Kokonoe',
Dwarf Japanese white pine
The dark green needles of this dwarf 'Yatsubusa' form are thick and slightly twisted. Very popular for small and extra-small sizes. For styles, and most cultivation, see pp. 88–9.
▣ Grafting.

Pinus parviflora 'Miyajima',
Dwarf Japanese white pine
This cultivar is among the most popular for bonsai, because of its compact growth and small, stiff, straight needles. Suitable for small and extra-small sizes. For styles, and most cultivation, see pp. 88–9.
▣ Grafting.

Pinus parviflora 'Nasumusume',
Dwarf Japanese white pine
Tiny needles are a feature of this dwarf 'Yatsubusa' form. Suitable for small and extra-small sizes. For styles, and most cultivation, see pp. 88–9.
▣ Grafting.

Pinus pentaphylla, see *Pinus parviflora*.

Pinus pumila, *Dwarf Siberian pine*
This conifer is a dwarf, with blue-green leaves in bundles of five, and red-brown young shoots. For styles, sizes, and most cultivation, see pp. 88–9.
▣ Monthly from midwinter through to mid autumn.

Pinus sylvestris, *Scots pine*
A distinctive, evergreen conifer with spreading outline and flattened top. The flaking bark is orange; the short, blue-green needles grow in pairs. (*See p. 90*.)

Pinus sylvestris 'Beuvronensis', *Dwarf Scots pine*
This dwarf form is very compact with short needles. For styles, sizes, and most cultivation, see p. 90.
▣ Grafting on to *P. sylvestris*.

Pinus sylvestris 'Watereri', *Dwarf Scots pine*
This variety is very slow-growing. For styles, sizes, and most cultivation, see p. 90.
▣ Grafting on to *P. sylvestris*.

Pinus thunbergii, *Japanese black pine*
This conifer has craggy bark and brown young shoots. The long, thick, stiff needles are dark green and carried in pairs. (*See p. 91*.)

Pinus thunbergii corticosa,
Cork-barked Japanese black pine
Corky bark which makes broad, vertical cracks with wing-like protrusions is a feature of this conifer. Formal upright, informal upright, slanting, semi-cascade, cascade, twin-trunk, clump, and multiple-trunk styles. For sizes and most cultivation, see p. 91.
▣ Grafting on to *P. thunbergii*.

Podocarpus chinensis, see *Podocarpus macrophyllus.*

Podocarpus macrophyllus (P. chinensis),
Chinese podocarpus
This slow-growing evergreen has yew-like foliage. Suitable for formal upright, informal upright, slanting, twin-trunk, clump, multiple-trunk, and group styles, as well as all sizes.
◉ Full sun.
◔ Daily during growing season.
▣ Fortnightly from spring to autumn, every four to six weeks in winter.

▣ Every other year in spring. Use basic soil mix.
▧ Finger pinch new shoots during growing season.
▣ Cuttings; layering.

Potentilla fruticosa, *Potentilla*
The bark of this deciduous shrub is shaggy and old-looking even when young. The grey-green leaves are small and divided. In summer, yellow, buttercup-like flowers are produced. There are many cultivars with a variety of habits and flower colours. All styles except literati are suitable. Sizes range from extra-small to large.
◉ Full sun.
◔ Daily during growing season. Do not allow soil to dry out at any time.
▣ Fortnightly during growing season.
▣ Every other year in early spring. Use basic soil mix.
▧ Continually trim back new shoots to maintain neat and compact growth.
▣ Seeds; cuttings.

Potentilla fruticosa 'Kobold', *Potentilla*
This small, compact variety bears yellow flowers. It is suitable for extra-small to medium sizes. Styles and most cultivation as for *P. fruticosa*.
▣ Cuttings; grafting.

Potentilla fruticosa 'Manchu', *Potentilla*
Pure white flowers characterize this compact, small form. It is suitable for extra-small to medium sizes. Styles and most cultivation as for *P. fruticosa*.
▣ Cuttings; grafting.

Potentilla fruticosa 'Tangerine', *Potentilla*
The flowers on this cultivar are an unusual yellow-orange colour. Suitable for extra-small to medium sizes. Styles and most cultivation as for *P. fruticosa*.
▣ Cuttings; grafting.

Prunus avium, *Gean* or *Wild cherry*
With age, the smooth, grey bark of this tree turns red, cracks, and peels. Attractive features are the white spring blossom, small, reddish-purple fruits in autumn, and deciduous foliage that turns crimson in autumn. Informal upright, slanting, semicascade, cascade, twin-trunk, clump, straight line, sinuous, multiple-trunk, group, and saikei styles are suitable. The wild cherry looks good in all sizes.
◉ Full sun.
◔ Daily during growing season.
▣ Fortnightly during growing season.
▣ Every other year in early spring. Use basic soil mix.
▧ Trim back new growth to create and maintain a good shape.
▣ Seeds.

Prunus avium 'Plena', *Double gean*
A form with double flowers. Styles, sizes, and most cultivation as for *P. avium*.
☒ Grafting.

Prunus cerasifera, *Myrobalan plum*
Masses of small, white flowers appear on this deciduous tree from late winter to early spring. Styles, sizes, and cultivation as for *P. avium*.

Prunus cerasifera 'Pissardii', *Purple-leaved plum*
In autumn, the dark red foliage of this tree turns deep purple. In early spring, there are masses of pink buds, that open to white. The fruits are purple. Styles, sizes, and most cultivation as for *P. avium*.
☒ Grafting; cuttings.

Prunus dulcis, *Almond*
In late winter and early spring, delicate pink flowers appear on this tree's bare branches. Styles, sizes, and most cultivation as for *P. avium*.
☒ Grafting.

Prunus 'Hally Jolivette', *'Hally Jolivette' cherry*
This elegant tree has delicate twigs upon which, in spring, cluster small, semi-double flowers that are white flushed with pink. Styles, sizes, and most cultivation as for *P. avium*.
☒ Grafting.

Prunus incisa, *Fuji cherry*
In autumn, the foliage of this tree turns orange. It bears a profusion of pinkish-white blossom. Styles, sizes, and most cultivation as for *P. avium*.
☒ Grafting.

Prunus mahaleb, *St Lucie cherry*
A tree with small, heart-shaped, bright green leaves that turn yellow in autumn. In early spring, it produces masses of fragrant, white blossoms. The fruits are black. Styles, sizes, and most cultivation as for *P. avium*.
☒ Seeds; grafting to hasten flowering.

Prunus mume, *Japanese flowering apricot*
There are many cultivars available from Japan of this classic bonsai subject, always called there the wild or flowering plum. In late winter, the distinctive, angular branches are enhanced by single or double flowers in whites, pinks, and reds (sometimes on the same tree). Literati is the most popular style. (*See pp. 92–3*.)

Prunus padus, *Bird cherry*
Small, bitter, purple-black fruits follow the spikes of small, white, scented flowers. Styles, sizes, and cultivation as for *P. avium*.

Prunus persica, *Peach*
The pale pink flowers on this tree in early spring are followed by the familiar edible, golden-red fruits. There are many ornamental varieties, which are more often used in bonsai. Styles, sizes, and most cultivation as for *P. avium*.
☒ Grafting.

Prunus persica 'Alboplena',
Double-flowered peach
A cultivar with double, white flowers. Styles, sizes, and most cultivation as for *P. avium*.
☒ Grafting.

Prunus persica 'Klara Meyer',
Double-flowered peach
Peach-pink, double flowers in mid-spring distinguish this ornamental tree. The leaves are slender, lance-shaped, and bright green. Styles, sizes, and most cultivation as for *P. avium*.
☒ Grafting.

Prunus persica 'Russell's Red',
Double-flowered peach
This tree has double, crimson flowers. Styles, sizes, and most cultivation as for *P. avium*.
☒ Grafting.

Prunus salicina, *Japanese plum*
In spring, small, white flowers are carried on the bare wood. In autumn, the leaves turn bright red. Styles, sizes, and most cultivation as for *P. avium*.
☒ Grafting.

Prunus serrulata, *Flowering cherry*
This tree is the parent of many cultivars that are bred for the garden, but are also good as bonsai. Single, semi-double, or double flowers appear from late winter to late spring, in shades of white, pink, or red. (*See p. 94*.)

Prunus serrulata 'Hisakura', *Flowering cherry*
A tree with deep pink, single flowers. For styles, sizes, and cultivation, see p. 94.

Prunus serrulata 'Kanzan', *Flowering cherry*
Double, purple-pink flowers are the feature of this tree. For styles, sizes, and cultivation, see p. 94.

Prunus serrulata 'Kiku-shidare Sakura',
Flowering cherry
In early spring, double pink flowers appear before the leaves on this cultivar. (*See p. 94*.)

Prunus serrulata 'Shirotae', *Flowering cherry*
This tree has fragrant, white, semi-double flowers. For styles, sizes, and cultivation, see p. 94.

Prunus spinosa, *Sloe* or *Blackthorn*
In early spring, small, white flowers stud the bare
spiny branches of this tree, and are followed by black
fruits. Styles, sizes, and cultivation as for *P. avium*;
see also pp. 92–3.

Prunus subhirtella 'Autumnalis', *Autumn cherry*
A deciduous tree with slender, graceful branches and
twigs. In autumn, the small, delicate leaves develop
bright colours. Semi-double flowers in white appear
on the bare branches at intervals from late autumn to
early spring. Styles, sizes, and most cultivation as for
P. avium.
[✂] Grafting.

Prunus subhirtella 'Autumnalis rosea',
Pink autumn cherry
This tree has pale pink, semi-double flowers, mostly
in spring, but sometimes in flushes throughout
autumn and winter. Styles, sizes, and most cultivation
as for *P. avium*.
[✂] Grafting.

Prunus subhirtella 'Fukubana',
Pink spring cherry
Deep pink, semi-double flowers in early spring are the
feature of this tree. Styles, sizes, and most cultivation
as for *P. avium*.
[✂] Grafting.

Prunus tenella, *Dwarf Russian almond*
In early spring, bright pink flowers cover the
branches of this tree. Suitable for all sizes, especially
extra-small and small. Styles and most cultivation as
for *P. avium*.
[✂] Grafting; cuttings.

Prunus tomentosa, *Downy cherry*
A tree with white or pale pink flowers in early spring,
followed by red fruits. The young growth and the
undersides of the leaves are downy. Styles, sizes, and
most cultivation as for *P. avium*.
[✂] Grafting; seeds.

Pseudocydonia sinensis, see **Chaenomeles
sinensis**.

Punica granatum, *Pomegranate*
This tender tree has shiny, oblong, deciduous leaves.
Scarlet flowers in late summer or early autumn
precede yellow-red fruits. (*See p. 95.*)

Punica granatum 'Nana', *Dwarf pomegranate*
Every aspect of this form is dwarf, from its overall
size, to its finer leaves, and smaller flowers and fruits.
Especially good for extra-small and small sizes. For
styles and cultivation, see p. 95.

Pyracantha angustifolia,
Pyracantha or *Firethorn*
An evergreen shrub with glossy, dark green, oval
leaves. The small, white flowers of summer precede
yellow, orange, or scarlet fruits. (*See p. 96.*)

Pyracantha coccinea, *Scarlet firethorn*
This shrub with smallish, evergreen leaves has small,
white flowers in early summer, followed by bright red
fruits. For styles, sizes, and cultivation, see p. 96.

Pyracantha coccinea 'Teton', *Dwarf firethorn*
A compact dwarf form which bears yellow-orange
fruits. Recommended for smallest sizes. For styles
and cultivation, see p. 96.

Quercus cerris, *Turkey oak*
This deciduous tree is tough and fast-growing. Its
lobed, downy leaves are grey-green in spring, bronze
in autumn. For styles, sizes, and cultivation, see p. 97.

Quercus palustris, *Pin oak*
Elegant, slender branches are a feature of this
deciduous tree. The sharp-pointed, lobed leaves are
bright green, but turn rich scarlet in autumn. For
styles, sizes, and cultivation, see p. 97.

Quercus petraea, *Sessile* or *Durmast oak*
This tree is very like *Q. robur*, but has longer leaves
and stalks, and likes slightly more moist conditions.
For styles, sizes, and cultivation, see p. 97.

Quercus robur, *English oak*
A long-lived, slow-growing tree. The lobed, deciduous
leaves are bright yellow-green, and turn to bronze in
autumn. (*See p. 97.*)

Rhododendron indicum (Azalea indica),
Satsuki azalea
There are many hundreds of Satsuki evergreen
azaleas, with smallish, narrow, dark green leaves.
They flower in early summer, in white, pink, red, and
purple. Often, different colours are found on the same
plant, as are striped, speckled or blotched forms. For
styles, sizes, and cultivation, see pp. 98–9.

Rhododendron indicum 'Chinzan',
Satsuki 'Chinsan'
This shrub has small, deep-pink flowers with red
throats. The leaves are small, narrow, and glossy.
For styles, sizes, and cultivation, see pp. 98–9.

Rhododendron indicum 'Hakurei',
Satsuki 'Hakurei'
Creamy-white flowers and small, glossy, dark green
leaves with a pointed shape characterize this form.
(*See pp. 98–9.*)

Rhododendron indicum 'Kaho', *Satsuki 'Kaho'*
A shrub with large trumpet-type flowers in soft, pale shades of pink. (*See pp. 98–9.*)

Rhododendron indicum 'Kazan',
Satsuki 'Kazan'
This compact, small-leaved form has small, red flowers. For styles, sizes, and cultivation, see pp. 98–9.

Rhododendron indicum 'Kinsai',
Satsuki 'Kinsai'
This form has deeply cut, red flowers and small, narrow leaves. For styles, sizes, and cultivation, see pp. 98–9.

Rhododendron indicum 'Korin', *Satsuki 'Korin'*
Small, pink flowers distinguish this compact form. For styles, sizes, and cultivation, see p. 98–9.

Rhododendron kiusianum,
Kurume or Kirishima azalea
This dwarf evergreen or semi-evergreen azalea has flowers in shades of purple, red, and pink. For styles, sizes, and cultivation, see pp. 98–9.

Rhododendron obtusum,
Japanese Kurume azalea
An evergreen or semi-evergreen with red flowers and small, shiny leaves. (*See pp. 98–9.*)

Ribes sanguineum, *Flowering currant*
In early spring, this deciduous shrub produces racemes of pink flowers. The small, lobed leaves have a characteristic pungent smell. Informal upright, slanting, semicascade, and cascade styles are good, as are extra-small to medium sizes.
- ● Full sun or shade.
- ◌ Daily during growing season.
- ⁛ Fortnightly during summer.
- ▣ Every other year in early spring. Use basic soil mix.
- ◪ Cut back hard after flowering, then shorten subsequent shoots as they grow.
- ⛏ Cuttings; layering.

Robinia pseudoacacia, *False acacia*
This tree has rough bark and pinnate, deciduous leaves. In early summer, it produces white, pea-type flowers. Suitable for informal upright, slanting, semicascade, cascade, twin-trunk, clump, multiple-trunk, and group styles, and all sizes.
- ● Full sun.
- ◌ Daily during growing season.
- ⁛ Fortnightly during growing season.
- ▣ Every other year in spring. Use basic soil mix.
- ◪ Trim back new growth continually during growing season to create and maintain shape.
- ⛏ Seeds; cuttings; layering.

Sageretia theezans, *Sageretia*
The rough bark of this tender shrub peels off in patches. The small, oval, evergreen leaves are borne on slender branches. White flowers are produced in summer and followed by blue fruits. (*See p. 100.*)

Salix babylonica, *Weeping willow*
A deciduous tree with long, narrow leaves on slender, flexible, pendent branches. (*See p. 101.*)

Salix helvetica, *Swiss willow*
This bushy shrub has small, downy, grey-green leaves and, in early spring, yellow catkins. The best sizes are extra-small to medium. For styles and cultivation details, see p. 101.

Salix repens, *Creeping willow*
This compact willow has small, greyish-green leaves that are silvery-white underneath. In spring, it produces yellow catkins. Styles, sizes, and cultivation as for *S. helvetica*. (*See also pp. 26–7.*)

Sasa veitchii, *Dwarf variegated bamboo*
An evergreen grass with purple-green canes, and narrow leaves that become variegated in autumn and winter. Good as an accent plant, although not suitable for bonsai. (*See also pp. 46–7.*)
- ● Slight shade.
- ◌ Water plentifully.
- ⁛ Weekly during summer.
- ▣ Annually in late spring. Use free-draining soil mix.
- ◪ Remove central shoot to control height, cut down stems to ground level in early summer.
- ⛏ Division.

Schefflera actinophylla, *Umbrella tree*
This tender, evergreen tree is grown as a houseplant in temperate climates. It produces shiny, bright green leaves on long stalks. The light-grey trunk tends to produce aerial roots. Informal upright, clasped-to-rock, twin-trunk, clump, multiple-trunk, group, and saikei styles; small and medium sizes.
- ● Bright light. Warm location, minimum temperature 16°C (60°F).
- ◌ Twice weekly in summer. Fortnightly in winter.
- ⁛ Monthly during summer.
- ▣ Every other year in spring. Free-draining soil mix.
- ◪ Prune top shoots hard to encourage branching.
- ⛏ Cuttings.

Sequoia sempervirens, *California redwood*
The world's tallest tree, 115m (377ft) high, is a Californian redwood. This conifer is conical and evergreen, with flattened, needle-like leaves and spongy, red-brown bark. Formal upright, informal upright, slanting, twin-trunk, clump, multiple-trunk, and group styles; small to extra-large sizes.

- ⬤ Full sun.
- ◔ Daily during growing season.
- ⬙ Fortnightly during growing season.
- ▣ Every three to four years in early spring. Use basic soil mix.
- ✄ Shorten new shoots as they grow to create and maintain shape.
- ✂ Seeds; cuttings.

Sequoiadendron giganteum, *Wellingtonia*
A conical, evergreen conifer with drooping branches covered in bright green, scale-like foliage. The bark is thick and spongy. (*See p. 102.*)

Serissa foetida, *Tree of a thousand stars*
Masses of small, white flowers appear in summer on this shrub. The evergreen leaves are small and oval; the bark and roots have an unpleasant smell. (*See p. 103.*)

Sophora japonica, *Japanese pagoda tree*
A deciduous tree with pinnate leaves. In late summer, older trees produce white, pea-type flowers. Informal upright, slanting, semicascade, cascade, twin-trunk, clump, multiple-trunk, and group styles; all sizes.
- ⬤ Full sun.
- ◔ Daily during growing season.
- ⬙ Fortnightly during growing season.
- ▣ Every other year in early spring. Use basic soil mix.
- ✄ Trim new growth constantly to create and maintain shape.
- ✂ Seeds; cuttings; grafting.

Sorbus aucuparia, *Rowan* or *Mountain ash*
In autumn, the pinnate leaves on this deciduous tree turn gold and orange. There are white flowers in spring and bright red fruits in autumn. (*See p. 104.*)

Sorbus cashmiriana, *Cashmiriana mountain ash*
A deciduous tree with white flowers and fruits, and dark green, pinnate leaves. For styles, sizes, and cultivation, see p. 104.

Sorbus commixta, *Korean mountain ash*
The young foliage of this deciduous tree is copper-coloured, turning into brilliant shades in autumn. Small, red fruits are produced. For styles, sizes, and cultivation, see p. 104.

Sorbus 'Joseph Rock', *'Joseph Rock' mountain ash*
Orange, copper, and purple autumn foliage are a feature of this deciduous tree, as are white flowers and yellow fruits. For styles, sizes, and most cultivation, see p. 104.
- ✂ Grafting.

Spiraea japonica, *Japanese spiraea*
From midsummer onwards, flat heads of pink flowers are produced on this deciduous shrub. The leaves are small, toothed, and oval. Informal upright, slanting, semicascade, cascade, clump, and saikei styles are suitable, as are extra-small to medium sizes.
- ⬤ Full sun.
- ◔ Daily during growing season.
- ⬙ Fortnightly during growing season.
- ▣ Every other year in spring. Use basic soil mix.
- ✄ Trim back new growth hard after flowering and again during summer.
- ✂ Cuttings.

Spiraea thunbergii, *Spiraea*
This deciduous shrub produces small, white flowers early in spring. The leaves are narrow and toothed. Styles, sizes, and cultivation as for *S. japonica*.

Stewartia grandiflora, see ***Stewartia pseudocamellia***

Stewartia monodelpha (**S. monodelpha**), *Stewartia*
In autumn, the oval, deciduous leaves of this lime-hating, dwarf shrub or small tree turn brilliant scarlet and purple. White flowers are produced in summer. The bark is shiny and copper-coloured. (*See p. 105.*)

Stewartia pseudocamellia (**S. grandiflora**), *Stewartia*
A lime-hating shrub or small tree with deciduous foliage that turns a good red-yellow in autumn. It has white summer flowers, and flaking bark. For styles, sizes, and cultivation, see p. 105.

Stuartia monodelpha, see ***Stewartia monodelpha***.

Styrax japonica, *Snowbell*
The fan-shaped branches of this lime-hating shrub or small tree bear oval, decidous leaves and, in early summer, white, bell-like flowers. Informal upright, slanting, root-over-rock, twin-trunk, and clump styles are suitable, as are all sizes.
- ⬤ Full sun.
- ◔ Daily during growing season.
- ⬙ Fortnightly in growing season. Use ericaceous fertilizer.
- ▣ Every other year in early spring. Lime-free soil mix.
- ✄ Trim continually during summer to create and maintain shape.
- ✂ Cuttings; layering; seeds.

Syringa velutina, *Korean lilac*
This shrub has oval, deciduous leaves and, in mid spring, lilac-pink flowers with a strong fragrance.

Suitable styles are informal upright, slanting, semicascade, cascade, root-over-rock, clasped-to-rock, twin-trunk, multiple-trunk, group, and saikei. Grow it in extra-small to medium sizes.
- ◉ Full sun.
- ◌ Daily during growing season.
- ⋮ Fortnightly during growing season.
- ▣ Every other year in spring. Use basic soil mix.
- ◿ Trim new growth after flowers fade, and again as necessary during summer.
- ◿ Cuttings; division; layering.

Tamarix juniperina, *Tamarisk*
Purplish or brownish-pink flowers in spring and summer, and scale-like foliage, are the features of this deciduous shrub or small tree. Its fragile, feathery appearance belies its toughness. (*See p. 106.*)

Taxodium distichum, *Swamp cypress*
A deciduous conifer with red-brown bark and light green, needle-like leaves that turn orange in autumn. Suitable styles are formal upright, informal upright, slanting, root-over-rock, clasped-to-rock, twin-trunk, clump, multiple-trunk, and group. Grow it in all sizes.
- ◉ Full sun, slight shade in summer.
- ◌ Daily during growing season. Stand in shallow water in summer; keep moist in winter.
- ⋮ Fortnightly during growing season.
- ▣ Every other year in late spring. Use free-draining soil mix.
- ◿ Finger pinch new shoots during growing season.
- ◿ Seeds; cuttings; layering.

Taxus baccata, *Common yew*
This evergreen has dark green, needle-like leaves. Female trees produce bright, pinkish-red fruits. (*See p. 107.*)

Taxus cuspidata, *Japanese yew*
This tree is very similar to *T. baccata*, but the leaves are a brighter green, with paler undersides. Deep pink fruit with distinctive protruding seeds are borne in female trees. (*See p. 108.*)

Taxus cuspidata 'Nana', *Dwarf Japanese yew*
Dense foliage is a feature of this dwarf form. Suitable for extra-small and small sizes. For styles and cultivation, see p. 108.

Thymus serpyllum, *Thyme*
A dwarf evergreen shrub with mauve, pink, or white flowers and small, aromatic leaves. If grown extra-small, it is suitable for all styles. Otherwise, use as an accent or accessory plant, particularly on rocks, for saikei, and as ground cover for groups.
- ◉ Full sun.
- ◌ Daily during growing season.

- ⋮ Fortnightly during growing season.
- ▣ Every other year at any time. Use basic soil mix.
- ◿ Clip to shape.
- ◿ Cuttings.

Tilia cordata, *Small-leaved lime*
This deciduous tree has lime-green, heart-shaped leaves, a smooth, grey trunk and, in summer, fragrant cream flowers. It is suitable for all styles except literati, and for all sizes.
- ◉ Full sun or shade.
- ◌ Daily during growing season.
- ⋮ Fortnightly during growing season.
- ▣ Every other year in early spring. Basic soil mix.
- ◿ Constantly trim back new shoots to create and maintain shape.
- ◿ Seeds; cuttings.

Tsuga canadensis, *Eastern hemlock*
This graceful conifer is similar to *T. heterophylla*, but in nature it usually grows with two or more trunks. It has evergreen, needle-like leaves. For styles, sizes, and some cultivation, see p. 109.
- ▣ Every second year in spring. Free-draining soil mix.
- ◿ Finger pinch new shoots during growing season.
- ◿ Seeds; cuttings; grafting for named cultivars.

Tsuga canadensis 'Nana', *Dwarf hemlock*
A delicate, compact dwarf form. Suitable for small and medium sizes. For styles and some cultivation, see p. 109.
- ▣ Every second year in spring. Free-draining soil mix.
- ◿ Finger pinch new shoots during growing season.
- ◿ Grafting.

Tsuga canadensis 'Pendula', *Dwarf hemlock*
Slender, arching growth distinguishes this weeping dwarf form. The bright green, new growth contrasts against deeper green, older foliage. Suitable for small and medium sizes. For styles and some cultivation, see p. 109.
- ▣ Every second year in spring. Free-draining soil mix.
- ◿ Finger pinch new shoots during growing season.
- ◿ Cuttings; grafting.

Tsuga heterophylla, *Western hemlock*
A graceful, delicate conifer. The short, glossy, evergreen, needle-like leaves are light green when young, darkening with age. (*See p. 109.*)

Ulmus × elegantissima 'Jacqueline Hillier', *Jacqueline Hillier elm*
A deciduous tree with a neat, dense habit and small, toothed leaves. Suitable for all styles and sizes.
- ◉ Full sun. Protect from frost.
- ◌ Daily during growing season, more frequently if necessary in very hot weather. Keep moist in winter.

⚬ Weekly for first month after leaf buds open; then fortnightly until late summer.
◼ Annually in early spring. Free-draining soil mix.
▧ Trim new shoots during growing season.
▨ Cuttings; grafting.

Ulmus glabra, *Wych* or *Scotch elm*
In autumn, the dull green leaves of this deciduous tree turn yellow. The bark is grey-brown. Styles, sizes, and most cultivation as for *U. × elegantissima* 'Jacqueline Hillier'.
▨ Seeds; cuttings; root cuttings.

Ulmus parvifolia, *Chinese elm*
This deciduous tree is the best elm for bonsai work. Its small, serrated, bright green leaves last into winter. The roots are long and flexible. (*See p. 110.*)

Ulmus parvifolia '**Hokkaido**', *'Hokkaido' elm*
This variety has tiny, bright green leaves on delicate twigs. Suitable for extra-small to medium sizes. For styles and most cultivation, see p. 110.
▨ Cuttings.

Ulmus parvifolia variegata,
Variegated Chinese elm
A tree with leaves variegated in green and white. For styles, sizes, and cultivation, see p. 110.

Ulmus procera, *English elm*
This deciduous tree has cracked, greyish bark, and dark green leaves that turn gold in autumn. (*See p. 111.*)

Vitis vinifera, *Grape vine*
This deciduous climber has dark green, lobed leaves and, in autumn, green or purple edible fruits. Suitable for informal upright, slanting, semicascade, cascade, and root-over-rock styles, and all sizes.
◉ Full sun.
◔ Daily during growing season.
⚬ Fortnightly during summer.
◼ Every other year in early spring. Basic soil mix.
▧ Trim new shoots during growing season.
▨ Cuttings; grafting; layering.

Weigela florida, *Weigela*
A shrub with trumpet-shaped, rose-pink flowers in early summer, and oval, deciduous leaves. Informal upright, slanting, semicascade, cascade, twin-trunk, clump, and group styles; medium and large sizes.
◉ Slight shade.
◔ Daily during growing season.
⚬ Fortnightly in growing season.
◼ Every other year in early spring. Basic soil mix.
▧ Trim shoots after flowers fade; shorten new shoots as they appear during summer.
▨ Cuttings; layering.

Wisteria floribunda, *Japanese wisteria*
Long racemes of fragrant, bluish-purple flowers in late spring, and bright green, pinnate leaves are the features of this deciduous climber. (*See p. 112.*)

Wisteria sinensis, *Chinese wisteria*
This very vigorous, deciduous climber is like *W. floribunda*, but its racemes are shorter and its flowers more fragrant. For styles, sizes, and cultivation, see p. 112.

Zelkova serrata, *Japanese elm*
In autumn, the serrated, oval leaves of this deciduous tree turn red and bronze. The bark is smooth and grey. (*See p. 113.*)

Zelkova serrata variegata,
Variegated Japanese grey-barked elm
This form is variegated in creamy-white and green. For styles, sizes, and cultivation, see p. 113.

Zelkova serrata '**Yatsubusa**',
Dwarf Japanese elm
This compact form has leaves roughly a quarter of the size of those on the species. For styles, sizes, and most cultivation, see p. 113.
▨ Cuttings.

Zelkova serrata '**Yatsubusa variegata**',
Variegated dwarf Japanese elm
The foliage of this dwarf form is variegated in green and creamy-white. For styles, sizes, and most cultivation, see p. 113.
▨ Cuttings.

Glossary

Accent plant A separate, often seasonal, planting of grasses, bulbs, or small herbaceous plants displayed with a formal bonsai.

Accessory plant Another term for an accent plant; also, an additional plant used in the same pot as underplanting for a bonsai group planting.

Adult foliage The mature leaves of a tree with a distinctly different type of young foliage.

Air layering Propagation method that encourages roots to form on a tree trunk or branch.

Apex In bonsai, this usually means the top part of the tree.

Aspect A position facing a certain direction, especially in relation to the direction of the prevailing winds and sunlight.

Broad-leaved Describing a plant that has broad, flat leaves, as opposed to needles.

Bud break Moment when a leaf bud opens sufficiently to show a green tip.

Bud burst Moment when newly opened leaves begin to unfurl.

Callus Corky-textured tissue that forms over a wound on a branch.

Cambium Narrow layer of cell tissue between the bark and wood of woody plants. The cambium of live wood is green and moist.

Collected tree A naturally dwarfed tree taken from the wild.

Compound leaf A leaf comprising two or more separate but similar parts, called leaflets.

Conifer A tree that bears cones containing the seeds. Most conifers are evergreen.

Cross A hybrid plant produced by deliberately cross-fertilizing species or varieties.

Crown The upper part of the tree where the branches spread out from the trunk.

Cultivar Variant plant produced in cultivation; indicated by single quotation marks in its botanical name (e.g. *Picea abies* 'Little Gem').

Cut-leaved Describing a tree or a shrub that has its leaves shaped in segments.

Cut paste Similar to wound sealant.

Deciduous Describing a tree or shrub that loses its leaves annually and often remains bare of leaves all winter.

Die-back The death of young shoots, due to bad weather or fungal disease.

Divided leaf A leaf that is composed of separate sections on a common base.

Division Propagation of shrubby plants by dividing the rootball and replanting the sections.

Dwarf A variety, form, or cultivar smaller than the species plant, but otherwise similar.

Ericaceous Describing plants in the family *Ericaceae*; generally, indicating lime-hating plants.

Evergreen Describing a tree or shrub that retains its leaves all year round.

Fruit The seed-bearing part of a plant; which may be a fleshy berry, nut or pod-like seed case.

Genus The unit of classification for a group of closely related plants; shown by the first word in the botanical name (e.g. *Picea*).

Germination The moment when a seed starts into growth.

Habit The characteristic growth pattern of a plant (such as an 'upright' or 'prostrate' habit).

Hardy Describing plants that are able to withstand winter frost.

Hermaphrodite A self-fertilizing plant with both male and female reproductive organs.

Humidity The amount of moisture in the atmosphere.

Internodal distance The length of stem between two nodes (leaf joints).

Juvenile foliage Young leaves of a tree that has distinctly different adult foliage.

Larva A wingless grub, or second stage in an insect's lifecycle.

Leader Generally, the main shoot, at the tip of a branch, that extends the branch growth; in bonsai, usually the uppermost continuation of the trunk.

Lifting Removing a plant from the ground with its rootball (roots and surrounding soil) intact.

Loam A loose soil composed of a balanced mixture of clay, sand, and decomposed organic matter.

Mist-spraying Using a sprayer to provide humidity, in a spray of very fine water particles.

Needle A leaf that is narrow and relatively hard in texture.

New wood Twig, branch, or stem of current season's growth.

Nitrogen (N) Essential element of plant nutrition; for growth above the ground, especially green tissue in leaves and stems.

Node The points on a twig or branch where leaf buds and twigs appear; also, may be the source of a new shoot.

NPK Abbreviation used to denote the relative proportions of the minerals nitrogen (N), phosphorus (P), and potassium (K) contained in a fertilizer.

Nursery bed The ground used for growing either seedlings or young plants.

Old wood A twig, branch, or stem of the previous growing season or earlier.

Ornamental Describing a tree grown for beauty of foliage and flowers, rather than for functional reasons such as fruit cropping.

Peat Partly decomposed organic matter, found in bogs, marshes or heaths. It helps to retain moisture in potting soil.

Perlite Lightweight, coarse granules heat-pressed from a type of volcanic rock, used to increase the moisture retention and ventilation in growing mediums such as potting soil.

Phosphorus (P) Essential element of plant nutrition: for root development and ripening of fruits and seeds.

Pinching out or **back** Training or shaping a tree by gently pulling off soft new shoots with finger and thumb.

Potassium (K) Essential element of plant nutrition: for strong new growth, flower buds, and fruit. In horticulture, it is commonly known as potash.

Pot-bound Describing a plant when its roots fill its pot and eliminate all air spaces.

Prostrate Describing a plant that grows along the ground.

Pruning Cutting or pinching back shoots, leaves, and stems in order to control growth and to shape the plant.

Raceme Elongated flowerhead made up of many individual flowers growing on their stalks from a central stem.

Repotting Regularly removing a plant from its pot, usually every year or so, and replanting in fresh soil to encourage root growth.

Rootball The mass of roots and soil seen when plant is lifted from container or ground.

Root pruning Cutting back roots of a pot-bound plant to add fresh soil and encourage growth of new roots.

Rootstock Root system and main stem used as basis of new plant in propagation by grafting. The rootstock enables the new plant to grow strongly.

Scion A woody stem or a small section of plant, used in the propagation of a plant by grafting it on to a rootstock from another plant; the characteristics of the new plant are held in the scion.

Scorch Foliage damage from strong sun or wind, or root damage from fertilizer overdose.

Species Unit of classification for a plant that has particular characteristics; identified by the second word of its botanical name (e.g. *Picea abies*).

Sphagnum moss Highly water-absorbent moss native to damp locations; used in air layering or to keep large wounds moist.

Standard Tree or shrub with a single stem up to 1.8m (6ft) below the branching head.

Stock, see **Rootstock**.

Stratification Encouraging tree seeds to germinate by dispersing them in sand and subjecting them to cold conditions before sowing.

Succulent Plant with fleshy stem or leaves capable of retaining large amounts of moisture for some time.

Subspecies A unit of plant classification, for a naturally occurring variant of a species that has some similarity to the species.

Suckering The growth habit of a plant with new shoots that travel out from its base, above or below the ground.

Synonym An alternative botanical name for a plant, usually an old or invalid classification.

Systemic Describing an insecticide or fungicide that enters a plant's sap and, over time, counterattacks from within the pest or disease afflicting the plant.

Tap root A long, anchoring root that grows vertically downwards in the soil; often, the first undivided root of a seedling.

Tender Describing a plant that cannot withstand frost and may die if kept outdoors in the cold.

Tokoname A region in Japan that is a major centre for the manufacture and export of containers for bonsai.

Topiary Pruning full-sized trees and shrubs regularly so that they form ornamental shapes.

Tufa rock A very porous, moisture-retentive type of limestone, that is easily worked and so used for some types of bonsai planting.

Variety The naturally occurring variant of a species.

Viability A seed's ability to germinate.

Winter kill Death of plant due to frost or freezing winds.

Woody Describing a hardened plant stem that will not die off in winter or during dormancy.

Wound sealant A compound that seals a cut in a branch or a trunk: it prevents sap bleeding and loss of moisture, and thus promotes healing.

'Yatsubusa' A particular type of dwarf form, with shorter internodal distances and more buds than usual, and thus denser top-growth.

Index

Figures in italic refer to illustrations

· Q & R ·

· S ·

Acknowledgments

Editor: Margaret Crush
Designer: Kelly Flynn

Dorling Kindersley
Managing editor: Jemima Dunne
Deputy art director: Tina Vaughan
Project editor: Annelise Evans
Art editor: Karen Ward
Designer: Glenda Tyrrell
Production: Maryann Rogers, Catherine Toqué

Photographic credits
All photography by Paul Goff except pp. 7 *top*, 184–5 author; p. 10 *inset* author; p. 16 author; pp. 34–5 author;
p. 41 Reiner Goebel (Canada); p. 102 Dan Barton (England); pp. 182–3 Bill Jordan (England).

Illustration
David Ashby

Thanks are due to the following people who helped in many ways, including allowing trees or containers they
owned or had created to be photographed: Mark Abbott; Bryan Albright; Dan Barton; Martin Bradder; Gordon
Duffet; Petra Engelke; Reiner Goebel; Paul Goff; Hoka-en (Holland); Bill Jordan; Dorothy Koreshoff; Mike Limb;
Mike Lorimer; John Naka; Geoff Owen; Roy Payne; Marcel Sallin; Roy Stenson; Hotsumi Terakawa; Christine
Tomlinson; Corin Tomlinson; Harry Tomlinson (Snr); Paul Tomlinson; William Valavanis.

Typesetting: Servis Filmsetting Ltd, Manchester; The Brightside Partnership, London